Ammonius

*Interpretation of Porphyry's
Introduction to Aristotle's Five Terms*

Ancient Commentators on Aristotle

GENERAL EDITORS: Richard Sorabji, Honorary Fellow, Wolfson College, University of Oxford, and Emeritus Professor, King's College London, UK; and Michael Griffin, Assistant Professor, Departments of Philosophy and Classics, University of British Columbia, Canada.

This prestigious series translates the extant ancient Greek philosophical commentaries on Aristotle. Written mostly between 200 and 600 AD, the works represent the classroom teaching of the Aristotelian and Neoplatonic schools in a crucial period during which pagan and Christian thought were reacting to each other. The translation in each volume is accompanied by an introduction, comprehensive commentary notes, bibliography, glossary of translated terms and a subject index. Making these key philosophical works accessible to the modern scholar, this series fills an important gap in the history of European thought.

A webpage for the Ancient Commentators Project is maintained at ancientcommentators.org.uk and readers are encouraged to consult the site for details about the series as well as for addenda and corrigenda to published volumes.

Ammonius

*Interpretation of Porphyry's
Introduction to Aristotle's Five Terms*

Translated by Michael Chase

BLOOMSBURY ACADEMIC
LONDON • NEW YORK • OXFORD • NEW DELHI • SYDNEY

BLOOMSBURY ACADEMIC
Bloomsbury Publishing Plc
50 Bedford Square, London, WC1B 3DP, UK
1385 Broadway, New York, NY 10018, USA
29 Earlsfort Terrace, Dublin 2, Ireland

BLOOMSBURY, BLOOMSBURY ACADEMIC and the Diana logo are trademarks of Bloomsbury Publishing Plc

First published in Great Britain 2020
This paperback edition published in 2021

Copyright © Michael Chase, 2020

Michael Chase has asserted his right under the Copyright, Designs and Patents Act, 1988, to be identified as Author of this work.

For legal purposes the Acknowledgements below constitute an extension of this copyright page.

All rights reserved. No part of this publication may be reproduced or transmitted in any form or by any means, electronic or mechanical, including photocopying, recording, or any information storage or retrieval system, without prior permission in writing from the publishers.

Bloomsbury Publishing Plc does not have any control over, or responsibility for, any third-party websites referred to or in this book. All internet addresses given in this book were correct at the time of going to press. The author and publisher regret any inconvenience caused if addresses have changed or sites have ceased to exist, but can accept no responsibility for any such changes.

A catalogue record for this book is available from the British Library.

Library of Congress Cataloging-in-Publication Data
Names: Ammonius, Hermiae, author. | Chase, Michael, 1959– translator.
Title: Interpretation of Porphyry's introduction to Aristotle's five terms / Ammonius ; translated by Michael Chase.
Other titles: Commentarius in Isagoge Porphirii. English
Description: London : Bloomsbury Academic, 2019. | Includes bibliographical references and index.
Identifiers: LCCN 2019009570| ISBN 9781350089228 (hb) | ISBN 9781350089242 (epub)
Subjects: LCSH: Porphyry, approximately 234-approximately 305. Isagoge—Early works to 1800. | Aristotle. Categoriae—Commentaries—Early works to 1800.
Classification: LCC B697.I83 A4613 2019 | DDC 186/.4--dc23 LC record available at https://lccn.loc.gov/2019009570

ISBN: HB: 978-1-3500-8922-8
PB: 978-1-3501-9132-7
ePDF: 978-1-3500-8923-5
eBook: 978-1-3500-8924-2

Series: Ancient Commentators on Aristotle

Typeset by RefineCatch Limited, Bungay, Suffolk

To find out more about our authors and books visit www.bloomsbury.com and sign up for our newsletters.

Acknowledgements

The present translations have been made possible by generous and imaginative funding from the following sources: the National Endowment for the Humanities, Divison of Research Programs, an independent federal agency of the USA; the Leverhulme Trust; the British Academy; the Jowett Copyright Trustees; the Royal Society (UK); Centro Internazionale A. Beltrame di Storia dello Spazio e del Tempo (Padua); Mario Mignucci; Liverpool University; the Leventis Foundation; the Arts and Humanities Research Council; Gresham College; the Esmée Fairbairn Charitable Trust; the Henry Brown Trust; Mr and Mrs N. Egon; the Netherlands Organisation for Scientific Research (NOW/GW); the Ashdown Trust; the Lorne Thyssen Research Fund for Ancient World Topics at Wolfson College, Oxford; Dr Victoria Solomonides, the Cultural Attaché of the Greek Embassy in London; and the Social Sciences and Humanities Research Council of Canada. The editors wish to thank David Blank, Marije Martijn, Mossman Roueché, and Donald Russell for their comments; David Robertson for preparing the volume for press; and Alice Wright, Publisher at Bloomsbury Academic, for her diligence in seeing each volume of the series to press.

Contents

Conventions	vi
Abbreviations	vii
Introduction	1
Textual Emendations	13
Translation	15
Notes	127
Appendix of Variant Readings	141
Bibliography	147
English–Greek Glossary	151
Greek–English Index	167
Subject Index	193

Conventions

[...]   Square brackets enclose words or phrases that have been added to the translation for purposes of clarity, as well as those portions of the *Isagôgê* which are not quoted by Ammonius.

(...)   Round brackets, besides being used for ordinary parentheses, contain transliterated Greek words.

<...>   Angle brackets enclose conjectures relating to the Greek text, i.e. additions to the transmitted text deriving from parallel sources and editorial conjecture, and transposition of words or phrases. Accompanying notes provide further details.

{...}   Braces or curly brackets are used to contain words that are not included in some of the major manuscripts.

Abbreviations

An. Post.	*Analytica Posteriora*
An. Pr.	*Analytica Priora*
Anth. Gr.	*Anthologia Graeca*
CAG	Commentaria in Aristotelem Graeca, 23 vols (Berlin: Reimer, 1882–1909)
Cat.	*Categoriae*
DA	*de Anima*
GC	*de Generatione et Corruptione*
Int.	*de Interpretatione*
Isag.	*Isagôgê*
LCL	Loeb Classical Library (Cambridge, MA: Harvard University Press)
LSJ	H.G. Liddell, R. Scott, and H. Jones, *A Greek-English Lexicon* (Oxford: Clarendon Press, 1996)
Metaph.	*Metaphysica*
MS	manuscript
MSS	manuscripts
Phys.	*Physica*
Rhet.	*Rhetorica*
SVF	H. von Arnim, *Stoicorum Veterum Fragmenta*, 4 vols (Leipzig: Teubner, 1903–24)
Top.	*Topica*
Vat. gr.	Greek manuscript of the Vatican Library

Introduction

Ammonius Hermeiou

The life and times of the Neoplatonist Ammonius Hermeiou (c. 445–517/526) have been well studied, and several of his works have already been translated in the Ancient Commentators on Aristotle series.[1] Head of the Neoplatonic School at Alexandria, he is thought to have been the teacher of most of the last generation of Neoplatonist professors of philosophy in late antiquity: Philoponus, Simplicius, Damascius, Olympiodorus, David, and Elias. Son of Hermias, a Neoplatonic philosopher who, like Proclus, had studied under the Athenian Syrianus, and of the pious pagan Aidesia, who took him to Athens to study under Proclus, Ammonius taught Plato, Aristotle, mathematics, and astronomy[2] at Alexandria. He seems to have preferred Aristotle over Plato;[3] yet, as was to be the case for all his students, he viewed the study of Aristotle as a mere preliminary for the study of Plato.[4]

The Alexandrian school, probably one of several private institutions in the city in which the professors made their living from honoraria paid by their students,[5] was the scene of lively, and sometimes violent, interactions between pagans and Christians.[6] The revolt of Illus (484-8), which was supported by some pagans,[7] and the ensuing clashes between students in the school of Horapollo ushered in a period of persecution by the ruling Christians against the pagans. After the beating of a Christian-inclined student by pagan students, several pagan professors, including Horapollo, were arrested and tortured, and in this dangerous atmosphere Ammonius seems to have entered into some kind of agreement with the Christian authorities. For this agreement, Damascius sharply criticized him, accusing Ammonius, who may have been in financial difficulties,[8] of unlimited greed.[9] Financial considerations aside, the concessions which Ammonius made to the Christian Patriarch Peter Mongus[10] may have included a promise to refrain from mentioning theurgy – although he would probably not have discussed this topic anyway in the context of a commentary addressed to beginning philosophy students[11] – and the worship of the pagan gods.[12] Yet there clearly were Christians present in Ammonius' classroom, and there are indications that Ammonius – if indeed he can be considered the 'author' of our commentary (see below) – may have adjusted his teaching accordingly. There are, for instance, numerous references to angels in our commentary,[13] and while angels did play a role in Neoplatonism as well, it was hardly prominent enough to justify the inclusion of angels alongside human beings, dogs, and horses as examples of substances. Even more tellingly, perhaps, the author of our commentary leaves open the question of whether or not the universe had a beginning,[14] perhaps the single issue which most divided pagans and Christians at the end of antiquity. Similarly, he expresses uncertainty as to whether the celestial bodies are animate and rational or not,[15] another key point of pagan-Christian controversies. Whether out of deference to his Christian students, fear of the Christian authorities, personal inclination, or a combination of all three, Ammonius(?) seems to be anxious to avoid sectarianism and to render his teaching acceptable to a multiconfessional audience.

It is hard to determine, however, to what extent Ammonius' alleged agreement and the generally precarious nature of Ammonius' position may contribute to explaining other differences between the philosophical 'system' one finds in his surviving works and those of other contemporary Neoplatonists, especially those of the Athenian school. Some of these differences – Ammonius' apparently simplified philosophical system and the fact that the highest principle he mentions is the Demiurge,[16] rather than the One – may be due to the more or less accidental fact that all we have from Ammonius are his commentaries on Aristotle, which were directed to students at a less advanced stage in their philosophical career. Ilsetraut Hadot has pointed out,[17] for instance, that one major doctrine often taken to be an innovation by Ammonius – the idea that Aristotle's Prime Mover is both a final and an efficient cause – is already to be found in the writings of Themistius (317–c. 390), and may even pre-date the latter.[18] Yet several recent studies tend to show, largely on the basis of the extant commentary on Aristotle's *Metaphysics* by Ammonius' student Asclepius, that Ammonius' basic metaphysical scheme was not very different from that of such Athenian Neoplatonists as Syrianus and Proclus.[19]

Another important feature of Neoplatonic teaching that may have been initiated as early as Porphyry, but was canonized by Iamblichus, is that of the *skopos* and the correct order in which the works of Aristotle and Plato are to be read. The doctrine of the *skopos* asserts that each philosophical work by the Ancients has a single goal (*skopos*, literally 'target'), to which all other features of the work are subordinate. Closely related to it is the doctrine of the reading order (*taxis tês anagôseôs*), which Ammonius(?) also discusses in the context of the preliminary questions to the study of the *Isagôgê*; it states that neither Plato nor Aristotle is to be read and studied in just any old way. In post-Iamblichean Neoplatonism, after preliminary ethical purification, provided by the study of the Pythagorean *Golden Verses*, the speeches of Isocrates and Demosthenes, or the *Manual* of Epictetus, the novice student was to begin with Porphyry's *Isagôgê*, then proceed to study Aristotle's *Organon*, in the order *Categories*, *De Interpretatione*, *Prior* and *Posterior Analytics*, *Topics*, and *Sophistical Refutations*. He then moved on to Aristotle's works on ethics, politics, and psychology, before completing the study of Aristotle, sometimes referred to as the 'Lesser Mysteries', by the study of the *Physics* and the *Metaphysics*. The student then concluded his studies with the 'Greater Mysteries', a selection of twelve Platonic dialogues, codified by Iamblichus, which began with the *First Alcibiades* and ended with the *Timaeus* and, finally, as the ultimate revelation of the highest philosophy, the *Parmenides*.[20]

Porphyry, *Isagôgê*

Porphyry's *Isagôgê*[21] thus occupied a key position as the first philosophical work read and studied, under the guidance of a teacher, by aspiring students of Neoplatonism at the end of Greco-Roman antiquity. This explains the presence in all the commentaries on the *Isagôgê* of a prologue discussing the nature of philosophy, a tradition which seems to have been initiated by Ammonius.[22]

Brief and concise, the *Isagôgê* consists primarily in a discussion of the so-called 'five words' (*quinque voces*) or technical terms – genus, species, difference, property, and accident[23] – which were considered necessary for understanding Aristotelian logic. At the same time, the work's very brevity and conciseness left plenty of work for subsequent commentators. Famously, Porphyry had refused to go into the question of whether genera and species are self-subsistent or exist only in the mind, providing the ultimate source for the medieval quarrel between Nominalists and Realists. Ammonius(?) shows no such reticence, providing a long and interesting account of the positions of each of the parties involved. Perhaps the most famous passage in the commentary is the discussion of the triple universal[24] (11,24 ff., and especially 39,14 ff.), with its analogy of (i) a signet ring that imprints an images of Achilles into (ii) a piece of wax, from which (iii) an observer forms an image of Achilles in his thought. Stage (i) corresponds to what the medievals would call the universal *ante rem*, or the intelligible form present in the mind of God or the Demiurge,[25] the study of which is reserved for (Platonizing) metaphysics or theology; stage (ii) to the universal *in re*, the form present in matter as studied in (Aristotelian) physics; and stage (iii) to the universal *post rem*, which we form in our minds by abstraction and which is the object of the study of logic. Ammonius(?)' clear exposition of this topic displays, beyond a shadow of a doubt, the fundamentally Neoplatonic structure of his metaphysics and ontology, and also develops what was probably Porphyry's original intent: a means to harmonize Plato and Aristotle. Whereas Aristotle appears to contradict Plato and deny the existence of separate intelligible forms, in fact, it is claimed, he is merely talking about class (ii) of the universals, whereas Plato was talking about (i). On Ammonius(?)' interpretation, the *Isagôgê* as a whole discusses philosophy only 'in a manner appropriate to the subject-matter of logic',[26] so that one should not expect to find in it discussions of Platonic forms, or even, for that matter, of the nature of physical reality.

Posterity of the *Isagôgê*

As the first work studied in the philosophical curriculum, the *Isagôgê* was, for many centuries, a massively popular work, as is shown by the number of surviving Greek manuscripts that preserve it today (over 170), and by its large number of translations: into Latin (twice, by Marius Victorinus and Boethius), Syriac (also twice), Arabic, Armenian, and Georgian. This popularity extended to its commentaries. In the Greek tradition, the commentary by Ammonius(?) is the earliest to have survived; it was followed by those of Elias, David, and several anonymous Byzantine works. Its influence on the medieval Latin West was immense,[27] and its impact on the medieval Arabo-Islamic tradition, although less thoroughly studied, was just as important.[28] The influence of the *Isagôgê* on medieval Jewish thought seems to have been mediated by the commentaries by al-Fārābī, which were translated into Hebrew at least four times in thirteenth–fourteenth century Spain and Provence.[29]

Ammonius(?)' commentary on the *Isagôgê*

It has sometimes been maintained that Ammonius was the first to comment on the *Isagôgê*, but this seems wrong. He clearly is responding to an established series of objections to the treatise.[30] The commentary attributed to Ammonius is, in many ways, a standard representative of the Neoplatonic commentary tradition of late antiquity. After a general introduction on the nature and divisions of philosophy, it proceeds (21,5–24,1) to discuss the traditional *kephalaia* or preliminary questions discussed before the study of every philosophical work: goal, usefulness, authenticity, order of reading, reason for the title, division into chapters, and to which part of philosophy it belongs. It then goes on to discuss the text of the *Isagôgê* lemma by lemma. The commentary does not, however, exhibit the later division into *lexis* and *theôria*, at least not in its fully explicit and systematized form. Yet some elements of the commentary seem to assume relatively advanced knowledge on the part of its audience: thus, Ammonius(?) assumes that his students are familiar with Euclid's *Elements* and with elementary geometry,[31] and, rather surprisingly, expects them to be able to understand a discussion on whether or not Porphyry has used a circular proof (74,5 ff.), which seems to presuppose some knowledge of logic. Similarly, our author presupposes (84,9 ff.) that his audience will understand him when he expounds upon the difference between homonyms and synonyms, although this doctrine is not studied until the introductory part of the *Categories*. When adducing the Aristotelian doctrine that there is no definition nor knowledge of individuals, the author adds (85,9) 'as has been shown (*dedeiktai*) in the <science of> demonstration', which might be taken to imply that his audience is familiar with the *Posterior Analytics*. Likewise, he takes it for granted that they are aware of the rule that predicates must have an extension greater than or equal to that of their subjects (88,20 ff.). Although it is true that many of these doctrines are latent in the *Isagôgê* itself, the fact that they seem to be considered self-evident in the commentary on the *Isagôgê* might be interpreted as additional evidence of the composite, heterogeneous nature of the commentary, at least in its later parts.

The reader may well judge that the most interesting part of our commentary is to be found in its earlier sections, which are also the most coherent, and, in my view, the parts most likely to go back more or less directly to Ammonius himself. The introductory section, with its five definitions of philosophy (1,5–9,24) and its divisions (10,10–16,10), provides precious insight into how philosophy was conceived in late antiquity.[32] Also interesting from the viewpoint of the history of philosophy are the account of the cognitive ascent from the sensible to the intelligible and the formation of the categories (17,1–20,10); the arguments in favour of the thesis that being is not a genus (29,14 ff.) and in particular not the genus of the categories (81,15 ff.); and the differences between Aristotelian and Platonic dialectic (34,16 ff.), with its division of Platonic dialectic into division, definition, demonstration, and analysis, the beginnings of which can be found in Middle Platonism. Also worthy of mention are the amplification of the Aristotelian idea that what is prior by nature is posterior to us, and vice versa (52,1 ff.); the excursus on the difference between definition and description (54,6 ff.); and the excursus on constitutive and divisive differences (58,1 ff.). Noteworthy from the point of view of Greek humanism and the history of racism is Ammonius(?)' remark, made in passing (96,8–9), that 'although someone is hook-nosed or black, he is no less of a human being', for (97,9–10) 'a human being is not more human than a<nother> human being, or more rational'.

Is the commentary really by Ammonius?

To what extent are we even entitled to speak of a commentary by Ammonius on the *Isagôgê*? The question is legitimate, and it can be raised with regard to most of Ammonius' surviving work, which – with the notable exception of the commentary on the *De Interpretatione*, a polished literary production written by Ammonius himself, evincing a very high degree of philosophical sophistication – all consist of notes taken by students in his classes. Often these class notes were taken, and later published, by John Philoponus, who was of course a highly gifted, albeit sometimes recalcitrant, student.[33] Other students in Ammonius' classes will, of course, have been less gifted or less attentive. If there were any doubt that this is the case with the present work, it is dispelled by the following passage (105,13–14):

> We have already stated everything in advance, and the rest of the text is clear. Let us read it, then, and if anything should come up, we will clarify it.

Clearly, the student scribe has dutifully and ingenuously transcribed here, word for word, the oral comments of his teacher, who, when he reached the first definition of the difference, announced how he intended to proceed from then on.[34] Was this teacher Ammonius, rather than any other representative of the centuries-long tradition of Neoplatonic teachers? There seems to be no overwhelmingly decisive reason to believe so. As the text proceeds, we find, with increasing frequency, instances where various sets of comments are given on the same text from the *Isagôgê*;[35] some of these comments are stupefyingly banal, and therefore hard to reconcile with Damascius' assertion that Ammonius was 'the greatest commentator who had ever lived',[36] while other key passages are left without comment at all. Elsewhere (97,16), a series of differing interpretations are offered of the same Porphyrian text, each alternative introduced by *kai allôs* 'and otherwise': this is a procedure typical of scholia, where various opinions and explanations are merely juxtaposed, without the author expressing any preference for one of them.

At least with regard to this last part of the work, therefore, it seems unwarranted to speak of a commentary on the *Isagôgê* by Ammonius. Clearly, the latter played a key role, if not in initiating, then at least in consolidating and disseminating the traditions of commentaries on the *Isagôgê*. But it would be a mistake to regard every word contained in the text as we have it today as Ammonius' *ipsissima verba*. The latter part of our commentary seems instead to consist of a collection of scholia of indeterminate date and authorship.

The text

This state of affairs is, moreover, reflected in the textual state of the work, which is highly complex, not to say inextricable. The editor Busse has made the best he could of a difficult situation, but a new critical edition is a desideratum.[37] Busse athetized large portions of the text which he read in his principal manuscripts. Sometimes he was clearly right to do so, since the text in question reappears, and is more at home, in the commentaries of Elias or David. At other times it is not clear why Busse has omitted a given text. I have in general followed him, but sometimes modified his choices, partly by consultation of the MS Vaticanus graecus 207 (fourteenth century), which Busse[38] consigned (without explanation) to his *codices deterrimi*, but which sometimes presents valuable readings. In any case, I include in an appendix a selection of some passages that Busse relegated to his apparatus.

Our commentary was translated into Latin by Pomponius Gauricus and published in Venice in 1539.[39] I know of only one complete translation into a modern language, contained in a Paris doctoral dissertation, defended in 2013, by Min-Jun Huh, 'Le premier commentaire de Boèce à l'Isagogè de Porphyre: introduction, traduction et commentaire'. I warmly thank Dr Huh for sharing his excellent work with me.

I have also provided what amounts to a complete translation of the *Isagôgê*. On the occasion of each lemma in the commentary, text from the *Isagôgê* which Ammonius(?) has omitted is supplied between square brackets [...].

Notes

1. G. Matthews and M. Cohen, *Ammonius. On Aristotle Categories* (London: Duckworth, 1991); D. Blank, *Ammonius. On Aristotle On Interpretation 1–8* (London: Duckworth, 1996); D. Blank and N. Kretzmann, *Ammonius. On Aristotle On Interpretation 9 with Boethius On Aristotle On Interpretation 9* (London: Duckworth, 1998). For a survey of the translations of Ammonius in the Ancient Commentators on Aristotle series, and on his life and thought in general, see R. Sorabji, *Aristotle Re-Interpreted: New Findings on Seven Hundred Years of the Ancient Commentators* (London: Bloomsbury, 2016), especially pp. 46 ff.
2. Damascius, *Philosophical History*, test. iii, p. 340, in P. Athanassiadi, *Damascius. The Philosophical History* (Athens: Apamea Cultural Association, 1999). See Sorabji, *Aristotle Re-Interpreted*, pp. 55–6. On Ammonius as the greatest geometer and astronomer of his time, see Damascius, *Philosophical History* fr. 57C.
3. We know, however, that Ammonius also wrote or lectured on Plato's *Gorgias*, *Phaedo*, and *Theaetetus*; see Sorabji, *Aristotle Re-Interpreted*, p. 46.

4 I. Hadot, *Athenian and Alexandrian Neoplatonism and the Harmonization of Aristotle and Plato* trans. M. Chase (Leiden: Brill, 2015), p. 16.
5 Hadot, *Athenian and Alexandrian Neoplatonism*, p. 23.
6 E.J. Watts, *Riot in Alexandria: Tradition and Group Dynamics in Late Antique Pagan and Christian Communities* (Berkeley, CA: University of California Press, 2010).
7 Watts, *Riot in Alexandria*, pp. 72 ff.
8 Hadot, *Athenian and Alexandrian Neoplatonism*, p. 19.
9 Damascius, *Philosophical History* fr. 118B. On this incident and the issue of Ammonius' compromises, see E.J. Watts, *City and School in Late Antique Athens and Alexandria* (Berkeley, CA: University of California Press, 2006), pp. 222–5; Watts, *Riot in Alexandria*, pp. 76 ff.; R. Sorabji, 'Divine Names and Sordid Deals in Ammonius' Alexandria', in A. Smith (ed.), *The Philosopher and Society in Late Antiquity: Essays in Honour of Peter Brown* (Swansea: Classical Press of Wales, 2005), pp. 203–13.
10 Whether the Patriarch in question was Peter Mongus or Athanasius II is open to debate; see M. Tardieu, *Les paysages reliques* (Louvain and Paris: Peeters, 1990), p. 20, n. 4. I thank Álvaro Fernández Fernández for pointing this out to me.
11 Sorabji, *Aristotle Re-Interpreted*, p. 47.
12 Hadot, *Athenian and Alexandrian Neoplatonism*, p. 19. Modern commentators debate whether Ammonius' concessions represent a more or less disgraceful caving in to outside pressure (Watts, *Riot in Alexandria*, p. 71), or instead did not go against his principles (Sorabji, *Aristotle Re-Interpreted*, p. 47). David Blank, 'Ammonius Hermeiou and His School', in L. Gerson (ed.), *The Cambridge History of Philosophy in Late Antiquity* (Cambridge: Cambridge University Press, 2010), pp. 654–66, at p. 660 even doubts the historical reality of Ammonius' agreement with the Christian authorities.
13 Ammonius(?), *in Isag.* 18,20; 19,1; 32,14.19; 40,15; 62,15; 70,17; 97,14; 100,14; 103,18; 114,7.
14 Ammonius(?), *in Isag.* 87,9 and note ad loc.
15 Ammonius(?), *in Isag.* 97,15.
16 In the context of the present commentary, however, the principle responsible for creating individual living things (40,4) and even genera and species, is not so much God or the Demiurge, but a hypostasized Nature, which creates rationally, even if it does not know what it makes (44,5 ff.). Similarly, for Ammonius(?) it is Nature, not Plato's name-giver or Porphyry's Council of Sages, who imposes names on things (50,17 ff.). Three pages later, however, he is happy to talk about 'the first imposers of names' (53,12). On the contrast between the doctrine of Ammonius and his teacher

Proclus on the question of names and the name-giver(s), see Sorabji, *Aristotle Re-Interpreted*, p. 55.

17 Hadot, *Athenian and Alexandrian Neoplatonism*, p. 28, pp. 93 ff.

18 Likewise, Hadot remarks that the tendency to harmonize Plato and Aristotle dates from well before him: it is, in particular, an important feature of the teachings of Porphyry (*c.* 234–*c.* 305).

19 Hadot, *Athenian and Alexandrian Neoplatonism*, p. 39, citing the studies of R. Loredana Cardullo.

20 This reading order has been thoroughly studied in a number of publications by Hadot; see, for instance, I. Hadot et al., *Simplicius. Commentaire sur les Catégories. Fascicule I: Introduction, première partie* (Leiden: Brill, 1990), especially pp. 12–35 on the *Isagôgê*; J. Mansfeld, *Prolegomena. Questions To Be Settled before the Study of an Author, or a Text* (Leiden: Brill, 1994).

21 For a study with complete bibliography, see R. Chiaradonna, 'Porphyre de Tyr, Isagogè', in R. Goulet (ed.), *Dictionnaire des Philosophes Antiques*, vol. Vb (Paris: Presses du CNRS, 2012), pp. 1335–43.

22 Sorabji, *Aristotle Re-Interpreted*, p. 48. For translations of the introductions to philosophy by Elias, David, and Olympiodorus see S. Gertz, *Elias and David. Introductions to Philosophy, with Olympiodorus. Introduction to Logic* (London: Bloomsbury, 2018).

23 cf. Aristotle, *Top.* 1.4, 107b17–26.

24 A doctrine which goes back at least to Proclus; see Proclus, *in Eucl. I*, 50,16–51,9, translated in R. Sorabji, *The Philosophy of the Commentators 200–600 AD. A Sourcebook. Volume 3. Logic and Metaphysics* (London: Duckworth, 2004), pp. 136–7.

25 See Sorabji, *Aristotle Re-Interpreted*, pp. 53–4, who emphasizes the innovative nature of Ammonius' claim that the highest Forms are not transcendent.

26 Ammonius(?), *in Isag.* 53,2; 69,1 ff.

27 See C. Erismann, 'Isagogè: la tradition latine médiévale', in R. Goulet (ed.), *Dictionnaire des Philosophes Antiques*, vol. Vb (Paris: Presses du CNRS, 2012), pp. 1344–9.

28 Some fifty authors of Arabic commentaries are known from the period 850–1550. See H. Hugonnard-Roche, 'Porphyre de Tyr: Tradition arabe', in R. Goulet (ed.), *Dictionnaire des Philosophes Antiques*, vol. Vb (Paris: Presses du CNRS, 2012), pp. 1453–60.

29 Hugonnard-Roche, 'Porphyre de Tyr', p. 1456, with reference to scholarship by the late Mauro Zonta.

30 Ammonius(?), *in Isag.* 26,17 ff.; 31,5 ff.; 71,25 ff. Also, see especially 72,14 ff.: 'All of the exegetes were at a loss for a defence against this <argument>, and they

say ...'; 111,7: 'Some problems are customarily (*eiôthe* (...) *aporeisthai*) raised against the present definition'; 113,25: 'They also raise problems (*aporousi de kai*) about baldness ...'. Many other topics addressed by Ammonius(?) were also no doubt traditional by his time. Asclepius (*in Metaph.* 142,34–7) reports a comment by Ammonius on Proclus' great admiration for a point made in the *Isagôgê* (Porphyry, *Isag.* 13,20–1), but this need not imply that he produced a written commentary on the work.

31 cf. the excursus on whether or not a square is made up of triangles, Ammonius(?), *in Isag.* 72,13 ff.
32 Such Alexandrian definitions of philosophy were influential on Arabic philosophical and theological thought as well, both Christian and Arabic; see E. Wakelnig, 'What Does Aristotle Have To Do with the Christian Arabic Trinity? The Triad "Generosity-Wisdom-Power" in the Alexandrian Prolegomena and Yaḥyā ibn 'Adī', *Le Muséon* 130.3–4 (2017), 445–77.
33 On the early date at which Philoponus begins to express disagreement with Ammonius, and more generally on the thorny issue of Philoponus' intellectual development, see Sorabji, *Aristotle Re-Interpreted*, pp. 70 ff.
34 Porphyry, *Isag.* 11,2. This example leaves one dubious about the student's level of discernment and overall intelligence, to say the least.
35 Ammonius(?), *in Isag.* 51,5 and note ad loc.; 59,4 ff.; 61,2ff. and note ad loc.; 71,12ff. and note ad loc.
36 Damascius, *Life of Isidore* fr. 57C.
37 At least 96 manuscripts (partial or complete) of the work exist today, more than twenty in the Vatican Library alone. Busse whittled these down to five, relying primarily on D, the MS Laurentianus Plut. 10.25, which he dated to the thirteenth century.
38 A. Busse (ed.), *Ammonii in Porphyrii Isagogen sive quinque voces*, CAG 4.3 (Berlin: Reimer, 1891), p. xxxv.
39 It has recently been republished with a useful Introduction by R. Thiel and C. Lohr (eds), *Ammonius Hermeae. Commentaria in quinque voces Porphyrii* (Stuttgart: Frommann-Holzboog, 2002).

Textual Emendations

The following list notes departures from the Greek text printed in A. Busse, *Ammonius in Porphyrii Isagogen sive V voces*, CAG 4.3 (Berlin: Reimer, 1891).

9,18   Reading *aidion* with the MSS, instead of Busse's *aidiôn*.
9,22   Deleting *philosophian* at 9,22 (Busse *in apparatu*).
10,18 Reading *eilêkhe* with MS Vat. gr. 207, instead of *eilêphe*, indicated by Busse as the reading of the other MSS.
11,23 Deleting *gar*, following a suggestion by Jonathan Barnes.
16,15 Reading *diorthoutai* with MS E.
23,1   Reading *eikotôs oun pro autôn tattetai* with MS M; *pro autou* with MSS DE.
24,20 Reading *hôs* instead of *kai* (Busse *in apparatu*).
25,12 Reading *ouk êgnounto ho ti dêlousi hai tôn <philosophôn> pragmateiai*, instead of Busse's *enoounto dêlon hoti hai tôn philosophôn pragmateiai*.
33,14 Reading *tou anthrôpou*, instead of Busse's *tou hupokeimenou*.
35,9   Reading *horistikou* instead of Busse's *horistikês*.
33,15 Reading *to zôion kai to logikon kai to thnêton* instead of Busse's *to zôion to logikon kai to thnêton*.
36,22 Reading *analuei* instead of Busse's *poiei*.
36,24 Reading *ho diaieretikos* instead of Busse's *hê diairetikê*.
36,27 Reading *ekeinos de dialutikos* instead of Busse's *ekeinê de dialutikê*.
37,6   Reading *kaitoi tautês* instead of Busse's *kai tauta*.
37,15 Reading *pleionôn haplôn* instead of Busse's *pleionôn*.
37,17 Reading *Oukoun ho analuôn ean eis ta pleiona analuêi, pseudos men ara to ton analutên eis haploun analuein to suntheton*.
37,18 Reading *to de eskhaton eis hen*, with most MSS, instead of Busse's *to de eskhaton ou*.
37,23 Reading *en huphêi logou* with most MSS, instead of Busse's *en hupokeimenôi*.

41,1	Reading *ti de esti ta huphestôta*, instead of Busse's *ti de esti 'peri ta huphestôta'*.
42,1	Reading *ou gar hê phusis alogôi dunamei <phusin> poiei* instead of Busse's *ou gar hôs hê phusis alogôi dunamei poiei*.
42,25	Reading *kataginesthai* instead of Busse's *kekhrêsthai*.
44,11	Reading *pan hoti entheôreitai en tois kath' hekasta*, instead of Busse's conjecture *pan hoti an theôrêtai*.
46,4	Reading *genos*, with most MSS, instead of *meros*.
46,18	Reading *parekhein*, with MS Vat. gr. 207, instead of Busse's *ekhein*.
49,1	Perhaps, instead of the reading of the MSS *diakrinei/diakrinetai tous karpous*, read *diaphtheirei tous karpous*.
55,15	Reading *tou panti genei epharmosai dumanenou*, instead of Busse's *ton panti genei epharmosai dumanenon*.
58,1	Omitting *all' eidê*.
59,20	Omitting *hoti* with Busse *in apparatu*.
60,22	Omitting *hôs ta eidê tôn atomôn*.
62,20	Reading *en tôi pôs ekhei*, instead of Busse's *pôs ekhon esti*.
71,24	Omitting *to eidos*, following Busse (*in apparatu*).
72,18	Omitting *legôn*, following Busse (*in apparatu*).
73,4	Restoring the reference to Euclid, omitted by Busse.
73,6	Reading *oude touto ex anagkês*.
79,9	Reading *diakheontai* (Busse, *in apparatu*) for *hêdontai* of the MSS.
87,4	Reading *autôi* instead of Busse's *autêi*.
87,10	Reading *êdunanto* instead of Busse's *edunato*.
89,20	Reading *to gar leukon katholou estin*, instead of Busse's *to gar katholou esti leukon*.
100,10	Omitting the following words that translate the Greek printed by Busse: 'because they have something prior to them, situated higher'.
100,11	Omitting the Greek words included by Busse that may be translated as, 'for animal is divided into these'.
109,29	Reading *dia tôn grapsantôn*, instead of Busse's *dia tôn hupogrammatôn*.
111,9	Reading *to ginesthai legô*.
122,7	Deleting *kai hippou*.

Ammonius

*Interpretation of Porphyry's
Introduction to Aristotle's Five Words*

Translation

Ammonius Son of Hermeias
Interpretation of the Five Words

Since we are about to embark upon the philosophical doctrines, it is necessary to learn what philosophy is. For the person who is beginning something must first learn what it happens to be, for in this way he will have a better grasp of the subject.

We learn things from definitions, and how could it be possible to learn a thing through definition if one is ignorant of what a definition is? Now a definition is a concise statement that shows the nature of a thing. It is called 'definition' (*horismos*) metaphorically from the boundaries (*horoi*) of properties. For as the latter encompass a piece of property and separate it off from those belonging to others, so definitions encompass a thing and separate it off from everything else.

One must then state the definition of philosophy, just as when we were beginning [the study of] grammar we learned its definition: that grammar is acquaintance with the things usually said by poets and prose writers.[1] Likewise, when beginning [the study of] rhetoric we learned its definition: rhetoric is the technical faculty of persuasive speech in public matters, the end of which is speaking well.[2] It is necessary, therefore, to learn the definition of philosophy as well, for it is philosophy that provides definitions for the other sciences and arts.

Every science and every art thus has some subject and end. The subject is what it is concerned with, and the end is what it aims at and what it wishes to set in order. For instance, a doctor has human bodies as subjects, for that is what he is concerned with, while his end is to heal them (for that is what he aims at). Likewise, a carpenter has wood as his substrate, and his end is to make a counting-board. Thus, definitions are taken either from the subject, or from the end, or from both. From the subject, as when we say 'medicine is an art that concerns itself with human bodies'; from the end, as when we say 'producing health'; and from both, 'an art concerning itself with human bodies that produces health'.[3] Likewise, astronomy, which is a science, has the heavenly bodies as its substrate,[4] and its end is the knowledge of their motions.

So let us learn what underlies philosophy and what is its end; in this way we will be able to give its definition. It should be known, then, that the other sciences and arts concern themselves with particular things: for instance, carpentry [concerns itself] with wood alone, astronomy with celestial things alone, but only philosophy concerns itself with all beings, and its end is not to make them but to know them.

Well then, many definitions of philosophy are accepted, for many of the more ancient authors have defined it in many ways. But lest we provide the censorious with grounds for a charge of inappropriate ostentation in this context by going through each of the definitions, it is enough to go through five or slightly more. Two of them are from the substrate, two from the end, and another from the superiority it has over the other arts.

The first one, then, is this: 'philosophy is the knowledge of beings qua beings.' 'Qua' stands for 'insofar as they are beings'. For the philosopher does not propose to know all the human beings in the world numerically, but what is the nature of the human being. For the philosopher investigates the substance of each thing and its being. Some define it as follows: 'philosophy is the knowledge of divine and human things.' It is clearly the same as the preceding one, and differs only in terms of clarity and lack of clarity. For it divided beings into divine and human, calling the perpetual ones 'divine', and those that are in generation and corruption 'human'. This definition, then, and the first one are given from the substrate, but they differ from one another, as was said, by clarity and lack of clarity. There is also this kind of definition from the end, which says, 'philosophy is assimilation to God, insofar as is possible for mankind'; for this is how Plato defined it.[5] For God has two kinds of activities: some are cognitive, by which he knows all things, as the poets also signify, when they say:

'But the gods know everything',[6]

and others that are providential of more inferior things, by which he exercises providence over the whole world, as the poets also say,

'The gods are givers of good things'.[7]

The philosopher wishes to assimilate himself to God in both respects. For he wishes both to be a contemplator of all things (for he investigates everything), and yet he also exercises providence over more inferior things (for the political philosopher judges and promulgates laws). Thus, philosophy is rightly assimilation

to God. 'Insofar as is possible for mankind' has rightly been added, for neither is   20
the knowledge similar nor is the providence the same,

> 'seeing in no wise of like sort is the race of immortal gods and that of men who walk upon the earth.'[8]

For those things whose substances are different have different perfections as well.   25

This can be seen in the case of other animals as well. Since human being and horse have a different substance, they have a different perfection as well. For the perfection of the human being is to live with reason and intelligence, while that of a horse is to run fast and be suitable in war. Even among irrational animals, there is a great difference in perfections, since there also is [a great difference] in their substances. A dog's perfection is one thing, but that of a   4,1
horse is another. If, then, the perfections are different in the case of these [animals] because of the different substance, how much more is this so in the case of mankind and God. Since they differ greatly in substance, it is reasonable for them to have differing perfections as well. It is right, then, that 'insofar as is   5
possible to mankind' has been added to the definition.

Philosophy, then, is assimilation to God insofar as is possible for mankind. It should be stated, however, what caused him [i.e. Plato] to begin to define philosophy in this way. Since, as I have said, the powers of God are twofold, cognitive and practical, and likewise twofold are those of our soul, the theoretical and the practical, and the philosopher wishes to set in order each   10
of the parts of the soul by imitating God, on the one hand investigating how the nature of beings is, and on the other setting in order the passive powers of the soul and taking care of others, Plato was right to define philosophy as assimilation to God insofar as is possible for mankind.   15

There is also another definition from the end, which says 'philosophy is a training for death.' Since the present definition defines philosophy as a training for death, it should be said how 'training for death' should be understood. For a man by the name of Cleombrotos, having studied Plato's *Phaedo* and learned that the philosopher must train for death, but not having learned in what way,   20
went up and hurled himself down from a wall. A witness to this is the poet who offered an epigram to this same Ambracian youth.

> You, Cleombrotos the Ambracian, said 'Hail, sun',
> And leapt from a lofty wall to Hades,

> You saw the evil of death as worth nothing, but read through
> one work of Plato's, the one on the soul.[9]

Because of this reasoning that occurred to the young man out of ignorance, one ought to investigate what the aforementioned training for death means. After all, Plato too exhorts us not to kill[10] ourselves, for he says as follows: 'now the doctrine that is taught in secret about this matter, that we human beings are in a kind of prison and must not release[11] ourselves or run away, seems to me to be weighty and not easy to understand.'[12] One must not, then, kill oneself. For as one who is in prison and in chains for some offence, if he were to wish to run away, would overturn the laws insofar as he was able, so he who hastens to loosen the bond of the body, which was tied by providence, overturns the demiurgic laws. Thus, one must not wish to die. If this is so, however, in what sense do we say that philosophy is a training for death? Pay attention to what is said, and the problem will be solved. It should be known that since the human being is a compound of soul and body, both the binding is twofold and the soul's release is twofold. For there is the so-called natural bond, by which the body is bound to the soul and is animated by it, and there is the voluntary bond, by which the soul is bound to the body, serving it and being dominated by it. Release, then, is also twofold: one is of the body from the soul, the other of the soul from the body. Death, too, is twofold:[13] one is natural, the one by which all human beings die, that is, the one by which the body is separated from the soul; and the other voluntary, with regard to which philosophers train to separate their soul from their body. It is in this sense that they are said to train for death, that is, the separation of the soul from the body. It should be known that it is not necessarily the case that when the body is separated from the soul, the soul is also separated from the body; for body-loving souls cultivate the love of bodies even after death, and they say that the shadowy apparitions around graves belong to these. But neither is the body wholly separated from the soul when the soul is separated from the body, for those who live philosophically, when they are still alive, separate themselves from the body. Thus, philosophy is a training for death, that is, a training for the separation of the soul from the body.

It is worth investigating next, why, if philosophy has the knowledge of beings as its end, we say that the definition that says that it is 'the knowledge

of beings qua beings', and again 'the knowledge of divine and human things', 30,6,1
is from the substrate and not from the end. For as we say that medical science,
when it is concerned with human bodies, is defined from the substrate, but
when it produces health, [is defined] from the end, since that is what it aims at,
so in the case of philosophy: if it has the knowledge of beings as its end, then 5
one must say that the definitions given are from the end.

Yet one must first consider how philosophy, which has one part theoretical
and the other practical, has a twofold end as well. For when we say that
philosophy is a training for death, we define it from its practical end, but when
[we say that] it is the knowledge of beings qua beings [we define it] from its
cognitive [end], and when [it is defined as] assimilation to God insofar as is 10
possible for mankind, from both. Medicine, therefore, which is mixed, when it is
defined solely with regard to its theoretical element, is said to be a science that
concerns itself with human bodies, and we rightly say that this definition is
from its substrate, whereas when it is considered with regard to the final cause,
[it is said] to be productive of health, and we say that this definition is from the 15
end. Philosophy, for its part, which has a purely theoretical form (for it exists
only for knowing realities), could not receive one definition from the substrate
and another from the end. For knowledge is knowledge of some things:
simultaneously, therefore, [the definition] will encompass both the fact that it is
knowledge and of what things it is knowledge. And I think that whether one 20
said such a definition came from the substrate or from the end, one would not
be wrong, but rather it would be from both. But perhaps it was with a view to
distinguishing it from the other definitions – from the one that says 'assimilation
to God insofar as is possible for mankind' without giving an additional definition
of what the assimilation consists in, and from the one that says 'training for
death' – that we called the aforementioned definitions 'from a substrate'.

There is also another definition by Aristotle of philosophy, from its 25
superiority over the other sciences and arts, which says that 'philosophy is the
art of arts and the science of sciences'; and he proceeds as follows towards this
account. Of [kinds of] knowledge, some are appropriate for the arts, others for
the sciences. Yet these arts and sciences do not differ at all from each other with 7,1
regard to their formulae, for the formulae of each one are infallible per se, but
they differ in their matter. For sciences concern themselves with things that are
always the same, such as astronomy, geometry, and arithmetic; whereas the arts

[concern themselves with] what is for the most part and in process of change. Hence, the formulae of geometry remain infallible, like this one: 'of every circle, the distances from the centre to the periphery are equal to one another' – for this remains the same, whereas those of medicine are fallible, such as the one that says, 'contraries are cures for contraries',[14] since they do not concern themselves with what is always the same. In the first place, there are not even cures for all illnesses, for what if the illness is fatal? There are times, moreover, when they do not apply contraries, but similar things, as in the case of [cures] that happen accidentally. For, often, cold water when poured out restores attenuated heat.[15] Now philosophy gives their principles to all sciences and arts: [it gives] universal formulas to geometry (for it pertains to philosophers to search for the universal). Moreover, the geometer takes the point to be partless, and divides magnitude to infinity, and uses these principles without demonstration, whereas the philosopher proves them, for he says that everything that limits is less than what is limited by one dimension. For the body, which has three dimensions, is limited by the surface, which has two dimensions, length and width, for it has no depth, by which it is less than the body. The surface, for its part, which has two dimensions, is limited by the line, which has only one dimension, length, while the line is limited by the point, which clearly will not have even one dimension, but will be partless, since, as has been said, every limit is less than what is limited by one dimension. That every magnitude is divisible to infinity, he shows by assuming that the cuts take place at points, which are not compound, nor do they make up a body. Thus, a body has three dimensions when it is divided at points, for division eliminates nothing from a body except the quantity of magnitude, but the fact of having three dimensions is not eliminated. Therefore, the formula of body allows cutting to infinity. But if it is impossible for us to accomplish because of our innate weakness, it is not thereby eliminated.

To medicine, [philosophy gives] the four elements. For since philosophers demonstrate that there are four elements of bodies in generation – these are the well-known ones, and there are neither more nor less – they take this as agreed upon and say that out of these, as proximate elements, the four humours are generated, assuming them to be analogous to those more distant elements. In addition, philosophy gives its principles to rhetoric as well, for the rhetor takes examples and enthymemes as analogous to induction and to syllogism.

For as a syllogism is true since it possesses necessity, so the enthymeme wishes to be true, but falls short of the syllogism by one premise, whence it is called an imperfect syllogism. But a syllogism is an argument in which, certain things being posited, something other than what is present occurs necessarily because they hold true.[16] In the same way, examples are analogous to induction. For as the latter has the character of 'for the most part' and 'likely', but not necessarily that of truth, so does the example.[17] They too differ from one another, however, in that induction is an argument that confirms universals from particulars, while examples confirm individuals from particulars. He [i.e. the rhetor] also takes his arguments from there, for Aristotle discussed topics in logic, and in general he dealt with rhetorical arts. Thus, rhetoric too has taken its principles from philosophy, especially because the rhetor makes use of the beautiful, the just, and the expedient, without knowing where the just is observed, nor whether it is the same as what is expedient.[18] For there are times when they introduce it as identical to the just, and others when they divide it and posit it as contrary; yet they are shown to be identical and convertible. Likewise for grammar, for it concerns itself with pitch and times,[19] which pertain to music, while music is a part of philosophy.[20]

Yet it is not only the rational arts and sciences that require philosophy, but also the so-called mechanical arts. For a house-builder uses a plumb line for discerning whether a wall is straight or not, but what a plumb line is, he no longer knows. The philosopher, in contrast, knows the cause right away, for he will say that all heavy objects tend spontaneously towards the centre, whence heavy objects descend from everywhere at right angles, but right angles are undeviating. Carpenters also make use of a line for making wood straight, yet they no longer know what is the nature of a straight line. Geometry, in contrast, which is also some part of philosophy, will say: a straight line is that which lies at an equal distance to the points upon it.[21] Likewise, one can discover that all the other sciences and arts have their principles from philosophy. Thus, philosophy is the art of arts and the science of sciences.

Pythagoras, however, says that 'philosophy is the love of wisdom', and he was the first to notice the error of the ancients. For since they called 'wise' whoever practised any kind of art – one of these was Archilochus, who said:

'Noble the three-pronged spear, and a wise pilot'.[22]

and the poet:

'Since wise carpenter fitted it,'[23]

and

'well-skilled in all wisdom (*sophiês*) by the promptings of Athena,'[24]

he [Pythagoras] shifts this appellation to god, for only he is called wise – God, I mean – in that he has wisdom and the perpetual knowledge of beings.[25] However, seeing that some rush towards rhetoric, others towards grammar, others towards the consideration of natural things, and again, others to other things, he calls those who practise the consideration of natural things 'philosophers', as if loving the wise one, whom he thought fit to call God, and the knowledge of these things, analogously,[26] the love of wisdom; for, as has already been said, he named the knowledge of God 'wisdom'. Thus Pythagoras. There are also other definitions of philosophy, but these suffice.

Since every reality is either divisible or indivisible, we must also say whether philosophy is divisible or not. Before this, however, it is just to say what division is in general, and what a further division is, and what is a subdivision. Indeed, he who is discussing division must previously state what each of these is. Division, then, is the cutting of a reality in a first approach; a further division is the cutting of the same reality in a second approach. For instance, in a first approach I section 'animal' into rational and irrational – this is a division – and in a second approach [I divide] the same thing into mortal and immortal – this is a further division. They differ from one another only in order.

A subdivision is the cutting of a part or species of a thing that has already been divided – by species I now mean the subordinate species – for instance, of the celestial, one part is fixed and the other wandering.[27] For 'celestial' was a species of 'animal', and we divided this into fixed and wandering.[28]

Now that we have taught what a division is, what a further division is, and what is a subdivision, it is also fitting to speak of division in philosophy. For it is divided,[29] as one can divide from the top, according to some into two, and according to others into three. For some divide philosophy into three: theoretical, practical, and logical. Let us examine whether or not this is so.

It should be known that of the division, the theological [part] is truly first, for the divine things are the principles of all things. Hence, it was not inappropriate for the ancients to place this [part] first. The [part] dealing with the science of nature is first with regard to us (for we could not know intelligible substance before the sensible one), but last with regard to what is true. For enmattered substance is last; hence it has obtained[30] the last position. Intermediary between these two is the mathematical [part], since it has a middle position by nature as well. Some of the ancients placed this [part] before the [part] dealing with the philosophy of nature, some of them following Plato, so that, they say, we may recognize or recollect the ideas that are already stored in the soul as we observe what is in individuals, using mathematics as a kind of path or ladder. Others, following Aristotle, wish to habituate us, [starting] from enmattered substance, to know intelligible substance, which is invisible, but has a greater and clearer mode of existence than the one associated with matter. After all, here we learn the line that is in matter, not so that we may know matter or the wax or the bronze, but so that we may strip it off and store it in the intellect, where we see its mode of existence as more steadfast. It is immediately clear that the figure, such as a line or a triangle, does not share in the wax in its substance.[31] For instance, when the figure of a triangle is changed when one of its sides is eliminated, the wax does not change along with it, although if it had shared in substance, it should have changed along with it.[32]

Thus, as has already been said, philosophy is divided into the theoretical and the practical. It is worthwhile inquiring for what reason [it is divided] into two, and why it is divided into these [two], and not into more or into less. The division could not have been made into fewer elements, for one could not be divided into one.

Why, then, [was it divided] into two and not more? There are two reasons for this. For since we said that philosophy is assimilation to God, and God has twofold activities, some that are cognitive of all beings, and others that are providential of us inferior beings, philosophy is rightly divided into theoretical and practical. For through the theoretical we know beings, while through the practical we exercise providence for the inferior, and thus we assimilate ourselves to God. Again, the activities of our soul are twofold: some are cognitive, such as intellect, discursive reason, opinion, imagination, and sense-perception, others vital and appetitive, such as will, ardour, and desire. The philosopher, then, wishes to set all the parts of the soul in order and bring them to perfection: thus, it is through the theoretical [part of philosophy] that the cognitive [part] within us is perfected, and through the practical [part of philosophy] that the vital [part is perfected]. Philosophy is thus rightly divided into two, the theoretical and the practical. Again, the theoretical is divided into the theological [part], the mathematical [part], and the [part] concerned with the study of nature. This too is right, since[33] the philosopher wishes to consider all beings, and there are three orders of all beings.

For some realities are entirely separable from matter, both in their mode of existence and in the concept concerning them, as are divine things. Others are completely inseparable from matter, both in their mode of existence and in the concept about them, as are natural and enmattered forms, wood, bone, flesh, and in short all bodies (we call them 'natural' qua having been created proximately by nature). Others, which are between these two [kinds], are separable in one respect and inseparable in another, as are mathematical things. For a circle and a triangle and such things cannot subsist by themselves without some matter, and in this sense are inseparable from matter. However, when, having observed a wooden circle and a bronze one and a stone one, we receive an impression of the form of the circle itself in our discursive thought and possess it within ourselves without its matter, as if wax were to take on [the] figure in relief of a ring without receiving any of its matter. In addition, in this respect they are separable from matter, insofar as they are separated in thought. Of beings, then, some are completely separable, some completely inseparable, and some separable in one respect and inseparable in another. Thus, the theoretical is divided into the theological [part], the mathematical [part], and the [part] concerning the study of nature. They attribute things that are completely separable to the theological part; those that are completely inseparable to the [part] concerning the study of nature; and those that are separable in one respect and inseparable in another to the mathematical [part].

That enmattered forms are completely inseparable from matter, while mathematical things are separable, is clear from the definitions. For when we define a circle, we do not include any matter, saying: 'a circle is a plane figure contained by one line, such that all the straight lines drawn to meet the circumference of the circle from one of the points lying within the figure are equal to one another.'[34] When we define a house, by contrast, we are unable to define it without matter, so we say: 'a house is a shelter that prevents rain and heat, made of stone and wood.'[35] For if we do not add the matter, one could understand a tent or some other such shelter. The mathematical [part] is rightly intermediate, for since we cannot ascend immediately from natural to divine things, and from those that are completely inseparable from matter to those that are completely separable, we journey by way of mathematics, which are separable in one respect, but inseparable in another. For this is why they are called mathematics (*mathêmata*): because it is necessary to have learned them (*mathonta*) and accustomed oneself to thinking incorporeally, that one may ascend to the divine things. Indeed, the divine Plotinus says: 'mathematics must be imparted to the young, so that they may become accustomed to incorporeal nature.'[36] For if we wished to raise ourselves up immediately from matters concerning the study of nature to theology, we would go blind, like those who come straight out of the darkest house into an illuminated one. For one must first spend time in a moderately lit house, and then go into the brightest one. Thus, after natural things, one must ascend to theology after spending time with mathematics: for mathematics are a kind of ladder and bridge, sharing with natural things insofar as they are inseparable, and with divine things insofar as they are separable.

Both the [part] concerning the study of nature and the theological [part] are susceptible of subdivisions, but we shall keep silent about their subdivisions, since they are unsuited to the ears of beginners. The mathematical [part] is divided into four: geometry, astronomy, music, and arithmetic. Arithmetic investigates numbers (arithmetical theorems are divine, for arithmetic does not consider the number that is so called by laymen, by which they count, but what kind of relation the forms of number have to one another. For instance, six has the double ratio to three, and nine has the [ratio] of one and a half to six. Moreover, it investigates the comings-into-being of numbers: even, odd, and odd-times-even,[37] and many other such things), whereas geometry [considers] magnitudes and figures, and music the harmonies of strings. It also practises certain songs that calm the soul's passions and awaken it to virtue. That this is so is shown by the traces that are still preserved and [are] as it were the depositions of music. For when we hear a trumpet we become more disposed to anger (which is why the trumpet is used in wars), while when we listen to theatrical songs we become more unbridled in our souls. A story circulates that Pythagoras, having seen a youth following a female flautist who was playing an unbridled song, ordered her to turn the flute around and play, and when this happened the young man's desire ceased.[38] Thus, one must not disbelieve what is said about divine music. This is why the divine Plato exhorts young people to go through music and gymnastics, so that they may adorn their soul through music, and their bodies through the gymnasium. Astronomy concerns itself with the positions of the stars.

Let us now say why mathematics is divided into four, and neither more nor less. It should be known that the mathematical [part] concerns itself with quantity, and of quantity one [part] is continuous, another discrete.[39] Each of these is divided into two: the continuous into the mobile and the immobile (and again, of the mobile, one [part] is moved eternally, another is not moved eternally), while discrete quantity [is divided] into the per se and the relative. The earth (*gê*) is a continuous quantum, immobile in position, with which geometry concerns itself.[40] Thus, geometry is the knowledge of the continuous quantum, immobile in position. The sky is an eternally moved quantum with which astronomy concerns itself, and astronomy is the knowledge of a continuous, eternally moved quantum. Astronomy and geometry concern themselves with continuous quantity, where continuous is that whose parts are in contact at some common border.[41] We also said that of the discrete quantitative, one [part] is per se and the other is relative. Number is a discrete quantum per se, when we consider it by itself, such as the even-times-even or the odd-times-even number,[42] and not its relation to something else by accident (this pertains to music, which concerns itself with this). Thus, number is a discrete quantum per se when considered by itself. Arithmetic, then, is the knowledge of the quantitative that is per se discrete. The mutual relation of tones, with which harmonics concerns itself, and which we know by number, is a discrete quantum with regard to something else, and music concerns itself with it. Music is the knowledge of a discrete quantum that has a relation of one thing to another. It has been shown, then, that music and arithmetic concern themselves with discrete quantity. Discrete is that whose parts are observed per se, so that they do not entail one another. Into how many [parts] the theoretical [part] is divided, and which ones, and what is its limit, is clear from what has been said.

But since we also spoke of the practical part of philosophy, we must divide it as well. Now, the practical [part] is divided into the ethical, the economical, and the political [parts], for he who does something good either does it to himself, setting in order his character (*êthê*) and life, and he is called 'ethical' (*êthikos*), or to his household (*oikos*), and he is called 'economic' (*oikonomikos*), or else he sets in order the entire city (*polis*), and is called 'political' (*politikos*). Some say that the political [person] is also ethical and economical; for he who can set the entire city in order can a fortiori do so for himself and his household, and they identify the political [part] with the practical. We reply to them that many people, overcome by vanity, set the city in order but neglect themselves. This is why the aforementioned three species of the practical [part] have been divided from one another. Each of these is divided into the legislative and the judicial: for the political philosopher either promulgates laws, according to which people in the city must live, or he judges them and considers some of them to be worthy of rewards, while he punishes those who have infringed something of the laws in force. It should be known that legislating and judging are also observed in the economic [part]. After all, in the household we lay down laws and pass judgement on those of our slaves and children who transgress. Yet these things are observed not only in the economical [part], but also in the ethical one. After all, the ethical person lays down laws for himself, when he says:[43]

> Accustom yourself to master these things
> the belly, first of all, and sleep and sex,

and again, when Isocrates[44] says 'fear the gods, honour your parents, be modest before your friends', for these are ethical statements and laws. And [such a person] judges himself when he says:

> Do not admit sleep upon your tender eyes
> Before you have gone over each of the day's deeds thrice.
> Where did I transgress? What did I do? What duty did I leave undone?
> Beginning with the first, go through them in detail; if
> you've performed foul deeds, rebuke yourself, but if they are good ones, rejoice.[45]

The economic and political [parts] will also be discussed at the proper moment.

Now, however, we must speak to the division of the ethical [part], and first of all of what character is. Character is the order of a human being, and order is the perfection of each thing, which is achieved by the privation or observation of the extreme terms, both excess and lack. For both superabundance and deficiency are [instances of] disorder: after all, one would call a person lacking a part, such as a hand or some other part, 'disorderly'; and again, one would also call 'disorderly' a person who had more parts than the complete number, such as a six-fingered or a six-handed man, like the giants according to the poet Apollonius.[46] Therefore, both excess and deficiency are disorders, and disorders are imperfect, since order is contrary to them. Hence, perfection comes from the observation of superabundance and lack, which are imperfections; for perfection is contrary to imperfection, and contraries are corrected[47] by the observation of contraries.

We have learned, then, what philosophy is and which are its parts. It is divine and desirable, and it has been well said about it that 'such a good has never come to mankind, nor shall it ever come'.[48] Let this much be said in general about philosophy.[49] In particular, we say the following about the present book.[50]

It has been said that philosophy is the knowledge of beings qua beings. The philosophers have therefore inquired in what way they might become knowers of beings. And since they saw that particulars are generated and perishable, and infinite as well, whereas science is the knowledge of perpetual and limited things (for the object of knowledge tends to be comprehended by knowledge, while what is infinite cannot be comprehended), they raised themselves up from particulars to universals, which are perpetual and limited. For as the divine Plato says,[51] 'science (*epistêmê*) has been so called from the fact that it leads us to a standstill (*epi stasin*) and definition of realities.' We obtain this through the ascent to the universal. Thus, they ascended from particular human beings to the universal human being; for philosophers do not propose to know how many human being there are in the world, but what is the nature of the human being: i.e. that he is a rational mortal animal. For he who has come to know this will also know all the human beings in the world, both those that have already come into being and those that will come into being in turn. Thus, from the particular human being, they raised themselves up to a certain commonality, that of human being, and again, from particular horses to a certain commonality, that of horse, which contains all the particular ones, having said that a horse is a four-footed animal capable of neighing. For the philosopher does not wish to know particular horses – for instance, what Xanthus is and what Balias is[52] – but what the universal horse is. For universals are always in the same state, not one way now and another way later, as particular things are. For the nature of the horse Balias is one thing, and that of Xanthus is another, just as the nature of Plato is one thing and the nature of Alcibiades is another, whereas the universal human being and the universal horse are always in the same state. For every horse is a four-footed animal capable of neighing, and again, every human being is a rational mortal animal. The same holds true for a dog and for the other species of animal. Thus, having observed these species, which, although limited, at any event cannot be comprehended by human discursive thought (for it is not surprising that there are many animals unknown to us), they raised themselves up to a certain commonality that contains all the particulars of [the universal] animal. After all, the human being is an animal, and horse, dog, and the others do not differ at all qua animals, for they are all animate substance capable of sensation. Thus, he who has come to know what [the universal] animal is, will have known all animals. Again, from this fig tree or this vine and this plane tree and this olive tree, they raised themselves up to the universal fig tree and vine and olive tree and plane tree. Again, they reduced[53] these things – the universal fig tree, and the vine, and the olive tree, and the others – to a certain common genus, [that of] plant, containing the particular plants. They thus obtained two commonalities: that of animal and that of plant. Again, they reduced animal and plant to living being; after all, a plant is a living being, for it grows, and nourishes itself, and engenders something similar to itself. But since inanimate is opposite to animate, and inanimate is that which does not participate in a soul, such as stone, wood, and whatever is similar to these (there are many of these among particulars, [in fact] an infinite number), for this reason they again raised themselves up from particular stones to the universal stone, and from particular pieces of wood to the universal wood, and likewise from the rest, and from universal stone and universal wood to a certain common genus, [that of] inanimate, which contains all these things. They thus obtained the two commonalities of animate and inanimate. Again, they reduced these to a certain common genus, body, which is three-dimensional: indeed, rocks, wood, human beings, and in general all that is body has the three dimensions. Again, from soul, angel[54] and such things, they raised themselves up to a certain commonality, that of the incorporeal, which is opposed to the body: for what is three-dimensional is also divisible in every direction, whereas [the incorporeal] is completely partless and unextended. Thus, they inquired what is common in both, and found that both are substance. After all, the body is a substance, as is the incorporeal, such as soul, angel, or god. They were thus able to raise themselves up to a certain common genus: substance, where the name 'substance' denotes a self-subsistent reality. We could learn what is said from the contrary: there are some realities that cannot subsist by themselves but have their being in others; they are called 'accidents', such as whiteness, blackness, sweetness, and so on. For these things cannot subsist by themselves, but whiteness necessarily subsists either in white lead or in milk, which are bodies, and similarly with the rest. Thus, whatever can subsist by itself and does not require anything else for its subsistence is called a substance, such as human beings, souls, stones, and so on. They rose, then, as has been said, to a certain commonality, i.e. substance.

Does substance include all beings, then, since the philosopher professes to be a knower of all beings? Not at all. For again, they found two things, and ten, and twenty, which they reduced to a certain common genus, i.e. number. Again, they found something large and small, and called these things 'continuous'. Since, then, number and the continuous have something in common, insofar as they are quanta (for each is a quantum), they reduced these things to the universal quantum. They thus obtained two commonalities, containing many realities: substance and the quantified.

Again, there is something white, and many particular instances of white, for white is either in white lead, or in snow, or in a swan. They thus subsumed all these things beneath the same 'simply white'. The same holds true for black and grey; and they subsumed such things beneath colour. Again, there is sweet, bitter, hot, and cold. Thus, they subsumed all these things that have been enumerated – colour, sweet, hot, and such like – beneath a certain common genus, i.e. the qualified. A qualified is that after which the participant is named paronymously,[55] for a white person (*leukos*) is so called from whiteness (*leukotês*), and the grammarian (*grammatikos*) is so called from grammar (*grammatikê*). Again, there is something on the right, something on the left, [something] double, and [something] half, and they subsumed all these things beneath a certain common genus, the relative, which is the relation of one thing to another. Again, there is something that is being in the Lyceum, or in the market, and all such things, which they subsumed beneath 'where', which signifies place. Again, there is something that is yesterday, last year, tomorrow, and so on, which they subsumed beneath 'when', which signifies time. Again, to lie down, to stand, and to sit are something, which they subsumed beneath 'being-in-a-position'; and 'being-in-a-position' is such-and-such a position of the body. Again, to be shod, to be armed, to wear a ring: they subsumed such things beneath 'having', for 'having' is placing a substance around [another] substance. Again, striking, heating, and cooling are something: they subsumed them beneath 'acting' (*to poiein*). Acting is doing something with regard to something else. Again, having observed some things being whitened and struck, they subsumed these things beneath 'being affected', which is to be altered by something else.

They thus obtained these ten commonalities: substance, the quantified, the qualified, the relative, where, when, being-in-a-position, having, doing, being-affected. Thus, each and every being ends up beneath one of these commonalities. They called them 'categories', since they are addressed (*agoreumenas*) and said of (*kata*) of some things, i.e. some of the things that end up beneath them.

Aristotle, then, wrote a book about these ten categories, and in his teaching he made mention of five words that are unknown to us in customary usage: genus, difference, species, property, and accident. Indeed, the philosopher Porphyry, acting out of love for both mankind and philosophy, wrote this book, teaching us what each word means, so that once we have learned them, we might be able to more easily follow what is said by Aristotle about the categories. This, then, is Porphyry's goal. He entitled his book 'Introduction' (*Isagôgê*), since it is a path towards all of philosophy. For the *Categories* precedes all the philosophical writings, and this [i.e. the *Categories*] [is preceded by] the *Isagôgê*.

What the philosophers did[56] in the case of all beings (for they subsumed all beings beneath the ten commonalities, and there is none of the beings that is not necessarily found to be subsumed beneath one of such commonalities), the grammarians did for words. For since they wished to go over the infinity of words, but were unable [to do so], they brought together words of one kind to a certain commonality, that of 'noun', and of another kind to a certain commonality, that of 'verb', and thus they made their eight parts of speech, beneath which all particular meaningful words are subsumed.

It has been stated, then, into how many [elements] each part of philosophy is divided, and what they are, and what is their result. But we must also state what the philosophers call 'the prolegomena or things given technical treatment in advance' in the case of every book.[57] These [preliminary questions] are as follows: goal, usefulness, authenticity, order of reading, reason for the title, division into chapters, and under what part [of philosophy] the current work is subsumed. The philosophers thought to say these things beforehand, not because they were devising something superfluous in addition to them as compared to the other arts, but because they wanted to make their readers more eager. For if one is reading and does not know the goal of the book, one hesitates and gives up halfway through, having the same experience as those walking towards a destination they do not know.

This, then, is why they state the goal. But even he who has come to know the goal does not undertake his task eagerly before he learns what usefulness derives from it; thus, they rightly state the usefulness as well. Once we have learned this, moreover, we doubt that it is useful before we know whether the book is the authentic work of an ancient [author] whom we know to be held in esteem, such as Aristotle or Plato, for we assume that everything they said is useful. This, then, is why we state the authenticity. Out of the knowledge of these things emerges the question concerning the order, whether [the book] should be ranged first or later; and this is why they state the order as well. [They state] the title, since it contains an abbreviated version of the goal. In addition, [they state] under which part of philosophy it is subsumed, for the sake of knowing where it contributes the most. Since it has been shown for what reason the philosophers state these things in advance, it is now time for us, too, to state the prolegomena of the book.

The goal for Porphyry here is to speak about five things, which all beings are, or else which are observed in all beings. They are as follows: genus, species, difference, property, and accident. The book is useful for all of philosophy, for it teaches us the per se attributes of species, which are the causes of their constitution. But we take demonstrations from the causes of [a thing's] constitution. Thus, it teaches demonstration, and is useful for all philosophy, for it is through demonstration that we come to know its ends. Its authenticity is indicated by the phraseology, which is clear, and by the fact that he mentioned the theories in this book in other books of his. In addition, [it is indicated by] the fact that he addresses it to Chrysaorius. For having addressed other books to him, he addressed this one [to him] as well, for the following reason. He was the teacher of Chrysaorius, and was explaining lessons[58] to him. He needed to investigate the fire of Etna, and went abroad. During this time, Chrysaorius discovered Aristotle's *Categories*, and he could not understand it at all when he studied it. He therefore wrote to Porphyry while he was there, indicating what had happened, and [telling him that] if he [had finished] investigating the fire, he should come, but if not, he should write an introduction for him, by means of which he could understand the book. Since Porphyry could not return at that time, he wrote this book for him, almost collecting it from what was said by Plato and Taurus,[59] and going through their words. From these considerations, it is clear that the book is authentically by the ancient one.

It is first in order, for if it introduces to Aristotle's *Categories*, which is about simple expressions, and these are the starting points of logic, it is clear that it is first in the order of logic. Rightly, then, it has been ranged before it.[60] So much for the order.

It has been entitled 'Isagoge' ('Introduction'). Some raise the problem[61] of why he entitled it indefinitely 'Isagoge', for it is unclear whether it is rhetorical, logical, or grammatical. We say to them that we are accustomed to signify outstanding realities indefinitely, as when we wish to signify Homer, we say 'the poet' par excellence. What, then, prevented the person who wished to signify philosophy from speaking indefinitely par excellence? Then, we also say that an introduction to an art or science is indisputably an introduction, while philosophy is the art of arts and the science of sciences. How, then, intending to introduce us to it,[62] and by means of it to all the arts, if the definition is true, was he going to entitle the book an introduction to one art? So much, then, about the title.

It should be known that this work has been divided into three, and in the first part he teaches about the five aforementioned words, [while] in the second he combines them two by two and teaches what is common to them and what is proper, such as what is common to genus and species and what is proper, and to genus and difference, and so in the case of them all. In the third, he teaches what things are common to all at the same time. Before these, in the prologue, he introduces the goal of the book by way of a prelude, and teaches its usefulness and the manner of its teaching, i.e. that it will be rather simple and introductory.

The present book is subsumed beneath the logical instrument of philosophy, for it teaches the things that contribute to the principles of demonstration, which is a syllogism in genus; the latter is a species of the compound statement, which again is a statement in genus.[63] Then, it also introduces to Aristotle's *Categories*, which pertain to logic. But logic is not a part of philosophy, but its instrument, as we shall show elsewhere.

1,3 It being necessary, Chrysaorius, [for the teaching of the *Categories* in Aristotle as well, to know what a genus is, and what is a difference, and what is a species, and what is an accident . . .]

All beings spontaneously desire the good, since there is one principle of all being, the good. All things, then, reach upwards toward the good as their own good, and each being is perfected by participating in it according to its own measures. No one, therefore, desires evil, but those who desire it yearn for it as the good, following irrational opinion. Whenever someone wishes to urge someone [else] to do something, he shows forth the good deriving from it, so as to attract him by this means. This, then, is what the philosopher Porphyry does. For wishing to urge beginning students to read the book, he announces at the outset the good that will derive from it. But since the good is twofold, one as an end, and the other as a means to the end – the one as an end, as when we say that health is good, and the other as a means to an end, as when we say that bloodletting is good, not by itself but because of health – what is necessary is said to be good not in the proper sense, but as referred to the greater good. For we say, 'if he is going to be healthy, it is necessary that he be bled.' Therefore, he said 'necessary' in this way, since the book is referred to some other end, that is, the categories, and it is not good as an end, but is taken as with regard to something else. In short, here he calls the book 'necessary' in the sense of referring it to a greater good, and either as useful, or as necessary per se, since[64] without it the other works of the philosophers cannot be read. For it should be known that the philosophers speak of the necessary in two senses, for they call 'necessary' either what is useful or what is distinguished as opposite to the contingent. They call 'useful' that which contributes to something, such as being shod, and being clothed, for these contribute towards bodies receiving less damage, and therefore enduring for a longer time. Also called 'necessary', as I said, is that which is distinguished as opposite to the contingent, without which it is impossible to exist. For instance, it is absolutely necessary for animals that have lungs to breathe, in order for them to live. Therefore, breathing is a necessary thing, for without it, it is impossible for animals that have lungs to live. Thus, this book is said to be necessary, either according to the first meaning or according to the second, and we say it is not according to the second, but according to the first. After all, before Porphyry came into being, they were not unaware of what the treatises of the philosophers show.[65] Clearly, then, it is called 'necessary' in the sense of making their comprehension useful and easy. Perhaps, however, 'necessary' can be said according to the second meaning as well, without which it is impossible for those things to be thought: not that we are thinking of the necessary in the case of the work itself, but in the case of the consideration of the aforementioned five words themselves; for without the knowledge of them it is impossible to know the rest accurately. Hence, Porphyry did not say 'this work being necessary', but 'the consideration of these things being necessary'. After all, before Porphyry wrote about these things, the consideration of them was necessary for the comprehension of the philosophers' theories, and without it, it is impossible for them to be understood. Such, then, is the usefulness that came about from the present book, that it collected the sayings of the ancients, scattered here and there, and made the consideration of them rather easy for us and concise. Hence, neither did Porphyry claim for himself the discovery of their theory, but 'I will try', he says, 'to go over the things [found] among the ancients'.[66]

It should be known that right from the prologue, he discusses these three things: he says what is the purpose of this work – it is to discuss those five words – and what its usefulness is – it is useful not only for Aristotle's categories, but also, generally speaking, for every method of discovery in philosophy, and what is the mode of teaching he has used: it is clear and suitable for the ears of beginners. For he does not teach theorems that exceed [the capacities of] beginners, nor does he draw out the work in length, nor does he make use of unclear terminology, so that by these means he may encourage young people to choose the book. The conjunction 'also' indicates to us that the book not only contributes to the teaching of the categories, but also to all of philosophy. Besides, he said 'and to the [teaching] of those [categories] in Aristotle',[67] since it contributes not only to Aristotle's book of the *Categories*, but also to the categories of others. For it should be known that many of Aristotle's companions wrote *Categories*[68] and *On Interpretation* and *Analytics*, in emulation of their teacher. Thus, this book contributes not only to Aristotle's *Categories*, but also to those of Archytas,[69] and to all the treatises of the philosophers.

Some raise right at the outset a problem – an irrational and inconsequent one – about [the phrase] 'being necessary', but which it is well to state because of the consideration of its solutions, which are rather subtle and useful. They raise the difficulty, then, as follows. Of being, they say, one part is necessary, another contingent, and another that which obtains.[70] Necessary is that which is always in an identical state and is extant by necessity, such as the fact that it is day when the sun is over the earth. Contingent is that which potentially has the subsistence of the two contraries, such as that of reading and of not reading, but is not yet either one, but is considered as being only in potentiality. What obtains is the contingent that has been brought to actuality and is present. However, the being of these things is not equal, for they do not reciprocate according to implication of existence,[71] as do the property and the definition, when predicated of one another or acting as subjects for each other. For these two things, the property and the definition, are coextensive, predicated of their subjects and acting as subjects to the predicates.

But which is the predicate, and which is the subject? The subject is that to which the article is attached; the predicate is that with which 'is' is coupled, either potentially or in act. For since predicates are either nouns or verbs, the word 'is' is coupled with nouns in act, and with verbs potentially. For instance, if I say 'the man', I have stated a subject; but if I add 'is an animal', I have stated a predicate. Being, then, whether subject or predicate, is not equal to the necessary or to the contingent or to what obtains, but has greater extension, since they do not reciprocate according to the implication of existence. For everything, if it is something necessary, or contingent, or obtaining, is also existent, but it is no longer the case that if something is existent, then it is at any rate necessary, or contingent, or obtaining, but whatever is one of these, is not the others. For instance, if it is contingent, it is neither necessary nor obtaining. If, however, being does not reciprocate according to the implication of existence, then it is of wider extension than the necessary, the contingent, and what obtains. Why, then, since every predication tends to be either of extension wider than or equal to the subject, but never lesser, did he [Porphyry] himself predicate the necessary, which has lesser extension, of what is of wider extension, I mean being, by saying 'it being necessary'?[72]

We say, then, that it is true that things of lesser extension are not predicated of things with wider extension, but being does not have wider extension than the necessary. For in the proper sense of the term, those nouns have wider extension which, being predicated of many things and having their existence in many things, are also one reality having its own existence and considered by itself, such as 'animal'. For it is predicated of a dog, a human being, and a horse, and it has existence in them, and again, it has its own substance when considered and thought of by itself. Thus, we define 'animal' by saying that it is an animate, sensitive substance, since all things that do not have their own existence, but are homonymous expressions, such as 'dog', 'Ajax',[73] and such like, do not have wider extension, for they are mere words, not realities. But that which has wider extension than something must first be something by itself, then have wider extension than others. Since being does not exist on its own, but there is only a commonality of a word in these things, i.e. the necessary, the contingent, and what obtains, does not have a wider extension than any of them, for it is a mere word. Then, if they say that being has wider extension, it is at any rate as a genus that they consider it to have wider extension. But a genus, when it is sectioned, makes the species subsist at the same time, with none being necessarily either prior or posterior. They must agree, then, that the necessary, the contingent, and what obtains, come about at the same time, which is absurd, for the necessary has the [property of existing] always, while the contingent and what obtains have the [property of existing] sometimes. Being is therefore not the genus of the aforementioned things, and therefore it is not necessarily of wider extension, for being is a homonymous word, not a genus, nor is it a determinate nature belonging to each of the particulars, as genera are. Moreover, we state all realities either indefinitely or with quantification. There are four quantifications: all, some, not all, and none,[74] and they say that they have been called quantifications (*prosdiorismous*) because it is from them that the person discussing determines (*horizein*) whether he is discussing some universal or some particular:[75] for if he says 'all', he signifies a universal, and if he says 'some', [he signifies] a particular.

These things being so, since it has been shown by all the philosophers that saying something indefinitely is equivalent to [saying something] with a particular quantification, such as 'some' (for 'man went' is the same as 'some man went'), if these things are so, then Porphyry, having said 'being' indefinitely and having attached [to it] 'necessary', took being to be particular, as if he said 'some being is necessary'.[76] Yet since it is particular, it is equal to the necessary, as they too agree. Thus, even if being were not a mere word, but a reality having its own existence like 'animal', he was not wrong to predicate 'necessary' of being, predicating it indefinitely. In addition, when we wish to signify realities, the whole of each of them, we signify them in the nominative case: [for instance], 'human being', 'horse', 'ox'; but when we want [to signify] a part of realities or something that exists around realities, we signify it by the genitive case. For instance, if we say 'of Socrates', we either signify one of his parts, such as his hand or his head, or one of the things that are around him, such as a house or a book. Thus, if Porphyry had said 'being is necessary' by means of the nominative, he would have intended to signify the reality itself, and in this way perhaps he might have seemed to predicate the part of the whole. But since he said 'it being necessary', by means of the genitive, he must have indicated either a part of the reality or something around the reality. But 'necessary' is equivalent to 'some part of the things around being', as 'human being' is equivalent to 'some animal', and 'hand' is equivalent to 'some one of the things of a human being'. On this account as well, therefore, even if someone says being has its own existence, Porphyry was not wrong to predicate 'necessary' of being, since we have granted this, for he predicated the equal of the equal.

However, on another account as well, it is shown that being is not a genus, either of the aforementioned three,[77] or of substance, accident, and the rest of the categories. For in those things in which something is first and [something else] second, what is predicated of them in common is not a genus. For a genus is a genus of species, but species subsist at the same time, and each has its being in itself, not in other things. But if the accident is second to substance and has its being therein, and what obtains is second to the contingent and has its being therein, then being will be predicated of them homonymously, not synonymously. It is not a genus, since first and second things appear in them. Whence is it clear that the accident has its being in substance, and what obtains [has its being] in the contingent, but not in themselves? Because when substance and the contingent are eliminated, the accident and what obtains are eliminated along with them. Yet if they[78] were species deriving from being, divided off in opposition to them,[79] and the former did not have their being in the latter, then when these species, such as substance and the contingent, are eliminated, the other one would not be eliminated along with them. For if some one species of animal perished, such as dog or horse, it would not co-eliminate the other species, such as human being, ox, camel, or any other of the remaining species.

These then, are the ways in which the irrationality of the difficulty and the subtlety of the solutions have been shown.[80]

1,3 It being necessary, Chrysaorius, also for the teaching of the *Categories* in Aristotle, to know what a genus is and what a difference ...

Aristotle, in his *Categories*, discusses the most generic words, and separates them by differences and properties. If, then, Aristotle there discusses genera, differences, and properties, then knowing what a genus is, and what a species is, and what a property, is rightly useful for an easier understanding of them. He used the copulative conjunction 'also', since it is not only useful for Aristotle's *Categories*, but also for the things he mentions further below. Some claim that he said 'and to Aristotle's categories' in the sense that the knowledge of these five words is also useful for [the categories] of Archytas; after all, he too wrote *Categories*. But it is absurd to say this, when Porphyry himself has clearly shown the rest of the things for which the knowledge of the genus, the difference, and the rest is useful. He ranged the difference before the species, since it naturally precedes the species; we shall show this when we proceed to it in its appropriate place. Now, the instruction deals with that about which Porphyry proposes to carry out his instruction, and that is genus, difference, species, property, and accident.

It is worth inquiring here why the philosopher set forth the words in order in this way, for he had no need to do this in vain. But if we wish to know this, let us begin from slightly above. It should be known that among realities there are some that are particular, [and others that are] universal. Since the particulars were going to perish and as it were cease to exist, nature contrived something more generic than them, which included all [the particulars] and preserved the shape of each one, and this is called genus or species. But in order that we should not be without a conception of them, and might learn the reason for the order, let us state what each one is, by way of example. The philosophers call Socrates, then, and Plato and Alcibiades and particular persons 'particular' and 'individual'; likewise Xanthus and Balias and this particular horse. Those things that immediately contain the particulars they call species, such as the universal human being – for the universal contains the particulars – and similarly for the others. Again, they call what contains these 'genera', such as animal, for it contains horse and mankind. In between these two are the differences, for as Porphyry himself will say as he proceeds,[81] a difference is that by which one thing differs from another. For it is by it that the difference between realities shows itself, since no difference is made manifest by the genus. For instance, animal is a genus, according to which nothing differs from anything else, for all are called 'animals': horse, dog, ox, and mankind. But if I say that of animal, one part is rational and another irrational, by subdividing I have made the difference, by which it has become apparent that mankind differs from horse, ox, and the rest of the irrational [animals]. For what is called rational is that which spends its life with reason and some kind of judgement, such as mankind or angel, whereas irrational is that which is without reason and judgement, such as horse, ox, and the other irrational animals. Thus, this [difference] is more particular than the genera, but more universal than the species, such as rational and mortal. For rational is more particular than animal – since this animal contains both rational and irrational – but it is more universal than the species, for rational contains many species, such as angel and mankind.

Moreover, the difference is more particular than the genus, in that it falls beneath the genus, but more universal than the species, in that [the difference] contains two things, rational and irrational, beneath which all animals fall. The species, in contrast, contains only one thing, such as mankind, horse, or something else. The property, for its part, belongs to one species alone; for instance, the property of mankind is said to be 'capable of laughing', for it belongs to [mankind] alone, and to all its members.

An accident is that which can be taken away from that in which it is present without any damage, such as white, black, sitting, standing.

Of these [five words], some are completive of substance or existence: genus, species, and the difference which is between them; they are called substantial, for these things are completive of every animal.

For each one participates in all three of them: Socrates, for instance, insofar as he is an animal, has the genus; insofar as he is rational and mortal, he has the difference; and insofar as he is a man, [he has] the species. Similarly for Plato and Alcibiades. The other two are called adventitious, I mean the property and the accident, because neither contributes to the account of the substance of the substrate. Of these, the property is closer to the substantial ones, since it always belongs to something, while the accident is distant, since in one sense it belongs, and in another sense it does not. The same things are also called separable, since when they are separated conceptually they do not damage the substance of human being:[82] for if they did, there would be no black human beings – which is absurd – and if we lose the power of laughing, we are none the less human beings, performing all the activities of human beings. These things being so, see how Porphyry proceeded in order, for he placed the substantial and completive things first, and the adventitious ones later. Again, of the substantial things, he placed the genus first, as more universal, then the difference, as more particular than it, and then the species, as more particular than the latter. Of the adventitious things, since the property is closer to substance, he placed it first, since it is more akin to the aforementioned things, while the accident received the last position, since it does not have anything in common with the aforementioned things, and it alone comes into being and departs without corruption of the substrate.

It is worthwhile inquiring why the accident has been distinguished as opposite to the genus and the species, although the accident itself is sectioned into species and genera. I say, then, that it is one thing to investigate each of the ten categories, insofar as it has its being without relation, and another qua having assumed a relation to something else. For whenever we investigate what each one is in and for itself, we say that one thing is substance, another quantified, another qualified, and the rest. But when we look to the categories after substance, as not subsisting by themselves but requiring [substance] for existence, we say they supervene upon substance. Again, in each of the categories, when we attend to them and see one thing more universal, another more specific, and another by which the more specific are sectioned from the more generic, then we call one of these things 'genus', another 'difference', and another 'species'. So that the same thing, considered in one way, is called genus, or species, or difference (insofar as they do not differ by categories), but in another way, one thing is substance, and another accident.

1,5 The consideration of these things being useful for giving definitions and, in general, for matters concerning division and demonstration.

It should be known, first, that dialectic according to Aristotle differs from that according to Plato. Dialectic according to Aristotle follows opinions in five ways, as he established in the *Topics*,[83] whereas [dialectic] according to Plato takes place in four ways, according to division, definition, demonstration, and analysis. That which is 'useful for giving definitions and for matters concerning division and demonstration' will clearly be useful for dialectic according to Plato as well. But if this is true, then it is clearly also [useful] for all philosophy. They are, as has been said, divisional, definitional, demonstrative, and analytical. The meaning of the passage should be thus understood as if Porphyry had said that this work not only contributes to the works of the philosophers, but that even if there were no writings, it contributes to the very methods of the philosophers, by which philosophers are capable of discovering each reality. Let us state in order what the function of each of these is.

The function of the divisive [method] is to divide the proposed genus in good order into its proper differences: for instance, animal into rational and irrational, [or] into mortal and immortal, and not to say that of animal, one [part] is human being, another horse, and another something else again. For these people, as the divine Plato says,[84] resemble butchers who section food badly, and not according to the joints; that is, like laymen and unsystematic persons.

It pertains to the definer[85] to give the definition of each reality appropriately. He follows the divider, who is first, since the former requires the latter; for definitions derive from the genus and the constitutive differences. It is from the already-divided genus, then, that the definer selects what is useful for the definition. For instance, once animate has been divided into animal and plant, and animal into rational and irrational, [and the former] into mortal and immortal, the definer, wishing to define the human being, selects animal, rational, and mortal.[86]

The function of demonstration is to carry out the demonstration of things from the very substance that is proper to them. For demonstration is not such a thing as [when] the rhetoricians adduce proofs from generally admitted and persuasive premises, but as when Plato,[87] wishing to demonstrate the argument about the soul's immortality, made use of the account of its substance, saying that the soul is self-moved, what is self-moved is eternally moved, what is eternally moved is immortal, therefore the soul is immortal. This is what he who wishes to demonstrate must do. Genuine demonstrations take place from definitions, for definitions indicate the nature of a reality, and demonstrations must come about from the very nature of realities, not from external concomitants, in a non-necessary way. Thus, demonstration occupies the third rank, since it makes use of the definer, while the definer makes use of the divider.

The function of analytics is to analyse compound things into the simple ones of which they consist: for instance, a phrase into nouns and verbs, and these into syllables, and these into letters. These things [are what is done by] grammarians. Philosophers, by contrast, [do this] in the case of realities, for instance [they analyse] the human being into head, hands, and feet; these into bones, flesh, and sinews; these into the four elements; and these into matter and form. We also make use of analytics in the case of syllogisms, analysing them into premises, and these into terms, as he teaches us in the *Analytics*. First of all, then, is division, second definition, third demonstration, fourth analytics. He mentioned only three, since the book is useful for them, in that it teaches about genera and differences. Division, then, divides genera into species in good order, through the proper differences; definition defines from genus and differences; and demonstration carries out demonstrations from definitions; while definitions, as has been said, are from the genus and the constitutive differences.

[The fact that Porphyry mentioned only three can be explained] in another way,[88] because the three of them need one another. For definition requires division, demonstration [requires] both, since he who demonstrates takes the definitions of things in order to know the substance of the reality, while the definition requires division. Analytics, by contrast, does not require any, for it is contrary to division, in that the latter takes one thing and makes it many, while analytics ends up in one thing. For it takes a human being, and analysing him, it analyses him[89] into parts, and these into humours, and humours into elements, and these into matter and form, for the elements are composed of matter and form.

In another way, because the divider[90] proceeds from simple to compound things, while the analyser [proceeds] from compound to simpler things. [The analyser is opposed][91] to the definer, in that the latter is a uniter of substance, while the former[92] is a dissolver. Again, if he is opposed to the divider, without whom the definer cannot define, he is clearly [opposed] to the definer as well. But also to the demonstrator, for if demonstration requires definition and division, but analytics is opposed to these, then analytics is opposed to demonstration as well.

And why did he mention definition first, and not division, although[93] the latter is first? Because the matter at hand was to give definitions of the things proposed. Synthesis does not differ from analysis at all in substrate, for as uphill is necessarily downhill as well,[94] so analysis is necessarily synthesis.

But they differ in relation, for when it proceeds from above and from the first principles to the last things, it is synthesis, whereas when it rises from last things to the first principles, it is analysis; and synthesis ends with what is compound, while analysis [ends] with what is simple. For clearly, he who analyses, analyses something compound, unless he were to toil and labour at impossible things by striving to analyse what is simple. But what is compound is made up of several simple[95] things; thus, if the analyser analyses into several things, it is therefore false that the analyst analyses what is compound into [what is] simple.[96] This is nearly true, except that one may say that he analyses into several proximate things, but what is last into one thing.[97] It should have been known, to speak clearly, that the simple is combined into many, but is not analysed into anything; while the last compound thing is analysed into several things, but is no longer combined into what is highest.

Some raise the problem of why he placed the definition, which is posterior, before division. And we say that in the first place, in the web of speech it is indifferent to place things together in whatever way,[98] then that the compound things known through definition are also first with regard to us, so that even if he did not place them together at random, he was right to place the definition first. As for analysis, he perhaps omitted to mention it because it is the same as synthesis in substrate, differing only in relation, as has been said.

1,6 This consideration (*theôria*) being useful [for giving definitions and, in general, for matters concerning division and demonstration . . .]

[He says this] instead of 'the knowledge (*gnôsis*) of these things', for the philosophers call knowledge 'consideration'.

1,7 [I will make a concise teaching for you, trying to] go over, as in the manner of an introduction, what is found among the more ancient [philosophers].

Since there is another concise treatment, summary, and for purposes of reminding, which is extremely concise and takes place in very few words, this is why he said: 'concise as in the manner of an introduction'.

1,8 I will abstain from deeper questions, [and aim at the more simple ones, in a moderate way.]

There are three things that make young people rather reluctant to read the writings of the ancients: the length of what is said, as in Galen's works;[99] the obscurity of the terminology, as in the *On Interpretation*; and the profundity of the notions, as in the *Demonstration*.[100] Encouraging the student, therefore, Porphyry promises that the book is free of these [defects], and is neither lengthy nor obscure in terminology – as is indicated by 'in the manner of an introduction' – nor [does it contain] deeper questions. But by saying 'abstaining from deeper questions', he indicated that it is free from depth of ideas, while by saying 'but the more simple ones', he indicated that it is free of obscure terminology. By saying 'aiming in a moderate way', he showed that it is free of length consisting in many lines. But he said 'aiming at the simple ones in a moderate way' not with regard to realities – for it is not aiming that pertains to philosophers, but proving everything scientifically; while aiming pertains to rhetoricians[101] – but with regard to his student Chrysaorius; that is, 'aiming at your thought'. For whatever the philosopher proposes to teach, he imparts scientifically.

1,10 For instance, concerning genera and species, [whether they exist or reside in mere conceptions alone, or, if they exist, whether they are bodies or incorporeals, and whether they are separable, or subsist in and around sensible things, I will decline to say, since such a subject is too deep, and requires another, more extensive inquiry.]

Porphyry had promised that he would make his instruction concise, his terminology clear, and that he would abstain from deeper questions. Lest someone should say that there was no deep question about these things, this is precisely what the philosopher wishes to present to us for this reason, that there was a rather deep question about them, but he omitted it deliberately. In order that what is said may become clear, let us say the following.[102]

Of beings, some exist, while others are in mere concepts, such as the centaur and goat-stag,[103] which, when conceived, exist, but when they are not conceived they do not exist, but when the concept ceases they cease along with it. For the centaur does not have extra-mental existence,[104] but once we have observed a horse and a human being, we fashion something composite in our conception, i.e. the centaur. Similarly, Nature created the goat and the stag, but by fashioning by ourselves in our conception we produce something composite, the goat-stag, and it has its being thereby. Now, Antisthenes used to say that genera and species were in mere conceptions, saying that 'I can see a horse, but I cannot see horseness,' and again, 'I can see a human being, but I cannot see humanness.'[105] He said these things because he lived by sense-perception alone, and was not able to raise himself up by reason to a greater discovery.

Of subsistent things, then, some are bodies, others incorporeals. In general, of the ancients, some said the latter exist, others that they do not. Of those who said they exist, some said they are bodies, others incorporeals, and those who said they are bodies all maintained the same opinion, while of those who said they are incorporeals – since of incorporeals, as the division has been made, some subsist by themselves, such as angel and god, others in other things, such as whiteness and figures – some, therefore, said these [genera and species] subsist by themselves, others within sensible things. Again, since the incorporeals subsisting in sensibles are either present throughout, like the whiteness in white lead, or at the surface, like a spherical figure, of those who said they subsist within sensibles, some said they are present throughout, others at the surface. Again, others said they subsist around subsistent things. What are subsistent things?[106] For instance, such as place – for it contains sensible things – and time.

Such, then, being the schools of thought about whether these [genera and species] exist or do not exist, he says it was possible to investigate, with regard to genera and species, whether they exist or whether they reside in mere conception; for this is what Antisthenes thought. Having found them to be subsistent, he was once again able to inquire whether they are bodies or incorporeals; for there have been champions of each section of the division. Again, having found them to be incorporeals, for instance, he was able to inquire whether they are inseparable from matter and in the many, or prior to them, and have become separate.

In order that what is said may be clear, let us go through the argument by means of an example. For it is not thus in an absolute sense and as chance would have it that some say that they are bodies, and some that they are incorporeals, but [they did so] with some rational argumentation. Nor are they contrary to one another, for each group says reasonable things. Let one consider, then,[107] a ring with a figure in relief of Achilles, for instance, and several pieces of wax alongside it, and let the ring stamp all the pieces of wax. Later, someone comes in, and, having observed the pieces of wax, having noticed that all of them are from one relief figure, let him have in himself the impression, which is the relief figure, in his thought. The seal in the little ring is said to be before the many, the one in the pieces of wax is in the many, and the one in the thought of the person who has received the impression[108] is over the many and last-born. Let one consider this, then, in the case of genera and species as well, for the Demiurge has within himself all the models of all things:[109] for instance, when he makes human beings, he has within himself the form of human beings, and he makes them all while gazing at it. If someone were to object, saying that the forms are not in the Demiurge, let him listen to this: either the Demiurge creates while knowing what is created by him, or not knowing. But if it were while not knowing, he would not create, for who would make something while being unaware of what he is going to make? For nature does not make [things] by an irrational power;[110] hence nature makes things without attending cognitively to what comes into being. But if he [i.e. the Demiurge] makes something according to a rational disposition, he necessarily knows what comes into being somehow. If, then, God does not make things in a worse way than human beings do, he knows what has come into being by his agency. But if he knows what he creates, it is immediately clear that the forms are in the Demiurge. The form is in the Demiurge as the impression in the ring, and this form is said to be prior to the many and separable from matter. But the form of human being is also in singular human beings, like the impressions in the wax tablets, and such things are said to be in the many and to be inseparable from matter. Having observed that particular human beings all have the same form of the human being, as in the case of the person who came along later and observed the wax tablets, we received its impression in our thought, and this [form] is called 'over the many' or 'after the many', and 'last-born'. Such things are separable from bodies – for they do not subsist in a body, but in a soul – but not simply separable. For they cannot be known in and by themselves, as Plato supposes [is true] of the forms before the many. For he will not have it that they are simply the Demiurge's thoughts, but at any rate intelligible substances, looking at which, as at archetypes, the Demiurge makes the things in this world as images. This, then, is what he [i.e. Porphyry] says it is possible to inquire: whether, being incorporeals, they are separable like what is with the Demiurge, or inseparable like what is in the many, or after the sensibles, that is, what is over the many. But he declines to say all these things.

It should be known that Aristotle and Plato seem to disagree about these things, for Aristotle says they are inseparable from matter, but Plato [that] they are separable. But now is not the time at present to examine whether the philosophers disagree with one another or not, for Aristotle seems to concern himself[111] with them [i.e. these things] qua physical.

1,14 However, I will now try to show [how the ancients, and among them primarily those from the Peripatos, dealt with them and the matters at hand in a more logical way.]

The philosopher's promise was to make the book useful, inter alia, for Aristotle's categories, which are the paths and preludes to the philosophers' entire logical theory. There are many parts of the phrase:[112] declaratory, optative, vocative, imperative, interrogative, and there are others, if we look into the matter in detail. In the *Categories*, however, he does not discuss all of them, but merely the declaratory phrase, for it is the messenger of the cognitive soul, while the others are [messengers of] the appetitive soul. For he who prays for something does so while desiring something, and he who addresses someone does so while desiring something, as does he who calls someone by name. Only the declaratory phrase, however, contains truth and falsehood,[113] for the others are neither true nor false. For if one calls someone, he speaks neither truth nor falsehood, and likewise if he prays or addresses. But the declaratory phrase is either true or false. For instance, it declares with regard to the soul that it is mortal or immortal, and necessarily this is either true or false, for a declaratory statement is that which declares one thing as belonging, or not belonging, to another. It contains two things within it, the predicate and the subject. So that our discourse may be clear, let us say as follows: it should be known that what is called 'subject' is what a statement is about, while 'predicate' is what is said about it. For instance, 'the human being is an animal': human being is the subject, while animal is predicated. Likewise with regard to the fact that the soul is immortal. What am I talking about now? Clearly, about the soul: the soul is the subject, while 'immortal' is predicated of it. Thus, it has been well said that the declarative statement has a subject and a predicate.

It is possible, then, to discuss genera and species theologically, when we inquire whether God has within him the imprints of genera and species, or not, [and] whether Plato's opinion is true, that the ideas are intelligible and self-subsistent, which he also calls truly substances and primary substances, or not, as is Aristotle's view. [It is also possible to discuss them] from the viewpoint of physics, as when we examine whether nature has within it the rational formulas of genera and species, or not. For it is not as snow cools irrationally or as fire burns that nature makes things, but clearly [it makes] everything by means of some rational formula, even if it does not know what it makes.

In another way, one can also inquire about them from the viewpoint of physics, whether these things are in the many, animal in the absolute sense in all the singulars and man in the absolute sense, or not, and some common substance observed in all the singulars, but everything that is observed[114] within singulars is individual.

One can also inquire into them logically, that is, in a way that is declaratory and appropriate for logical theory. For it is suitable for the latter to inquire which of these serve as substrate for the [others], and which are predicated of [others, i.e.] that genera are predicated of differences and species, but not vice versa. For we have said that genus, difference, and species maintain some order with regard to one another, and that the genus comes first, the species has second rank, and the difference the middle rank, and that the higher things must be predicated of the lower, for it is not the lower [that are predicated] of the higher. For instance, if we say 'every human being is an animal', we speak the truth, but if we convert and say 'every animal is a human being', we lie. Again, if we say 'every horse is irrational', we speak the truth, but if we convert and say 'every irrational [animal] is a horse', we lie. One cannot make just anything a subject, for one cannot say 'animal is a human being', as has been said. It is therefore necessary to say what kind of things must be made subjects, and what kind of things predicates, which the Philosopher [i.e. Porphyry] will also teach. And this is why he said 'more logical', instead of 'in a manner appropriate to the study of logic'.

1,14 However, I will now try to show how the ancients [and of these primarily the Peripatetics] dealt with them and the matters at hand in a more logical way.

In the proper sense, what is called 'to deal with in a more logical way' is to inquire into the accidents of realities; in a physical way, to inquire into substances, [and] in a theological way, to investigate whence all things have proceeded, and the principle of the constitution of each thing. Since, then, it is possible to deal from a physical viewpoint, as we have just said, with genera, species, and the rest – as when we inquire into the ones that are among the sensibles, as Aristotle dealt with them – and from a theological one, as when we will inquire into those that are in the Demiurge, as Plato dealt with them in the *Parmenides*[115] – it is possible to deal with them in a more logical way, since in the study of logic we require declaratory statements, but in declaratory statements some things are subjects, others are predicated, and the subject and the predicate are either genus, or species, or difference, or property, or accident.

'How ... he [dealt with] them' [is said] instead of 'with genera and species'; after all, they were the topic of his recent discussion. By adding 'about the matters at hand', he signified the remaining three, I mean the difference, property, and accident. Or one must say the reverse: that by saying 'How ... he [dealt with] them' he indicated the genus, difference, and species, while by saying 'and the matters at hand' he indicated what concerns the other two, the property and the accident.

1,15 and among them primarily those from the Peripatos.

The philosopher Porphyry does not attribute the discovery and teaching to himself, but says that of those who long ago dealt with them from a logical viewpoint, it was above all the Peripatetics who worked out this kind[116] in detail. The name 'Peripatetics' came about from the following cause. They say that the divine Plato carried out his conversations with his companions while walking in the Academy in order to make the body suitable, through exercises, for the soul's illumination. For as is the condition of the instrument, so the activity of the craftsman shows itself. This is why they were called Peripatetics. Now, after Plato's death, Aristotle and Xenocrates succeeded to the leadership of his school, Aristotle in the Lyceum and Xenocrates in the Academy, so those of Aristotle were called Peripatetics from the Lyceum, and those of Xenocrates,

Peripatetics from the Academy. Later on, Aristotle's [Peripatetics] received the nickname deriving from the activity, having lost the one deriving from the place, and they were called Peripatetics, while those of Xenocrates, receiving the [nickname] that derives from the place and having lost the one that derives from the activity, were called Academics. Since, then, the Philosopher intended to provide[117] some notion in his teaching of the things imparted by Plato, since he too was a Platonist, since he wrote the book because it is useful for Aristotle's *Categories*, he said: 'I will teach about them, as the ancients dealt with [them], and of these the Aristotelians', by saying 'and above all the Peripatetics'.

1,18 But it seems that neither the genus nor the species [is said in a simple sense. For what is called 'genus' is the collection of persons who are disposed in a certain way towards something that is one, and to each other. It is according to this meaning that the genus of the Heraclids is so called, from the relation deriving from one thing – I mean, from Heracles. And the multitude of the persons who somehow have with regard to one another the kinship deriving from that thing is [so] called to distinguish it from all the other genera.]

Having stated the goal and the usefulness, as well as what the introductory mode is – i.e. that it means abstaining from deeper questions and aiming at the simpler ones – and which are the deeper ones and which the simpler, he accordingly began the particular teaching.[118] He first deals with the genus, because the genus has the first rank in the things listed, and because it contains several species. The genus is causally prior to the species, although genus and species belong among the relatives. Yet there are some relatives in which we say some things take precedence over others and are their causes. For instance, we say that a father, qua human being, is cause of and prior to his son, although relatives are known simultaneously and are constitutive of one another, insofar as they are relatives; for relatives must be substances first. When considering the pre-existent substance of the relatives, whichever one we find to be pre-subsistent either in time or by nature, we say it takes precedence causally. For between the father and the son, the father takes precedence in time, insofar as he is a human being, which is his substance, a substance which becomes constitutive of the substance of the son. This, then, is why we say the father takes precedence over the son, although they are said relative to one another. The ruler takes precedence over the ruled, and the teacher over the student, by cause alone and not by time. For they might sometimes also be posterior in time, qua human beings, I mean the ruler to the ruled and the teacher to the student. The same holds true, then, of the genus and the species, for genus and species belong to the relatives, and relatives must first be substances. In substance, the genus pre-subsists by nature, not by time, and becomes constitutive of the substance of the species, for the genus is sectioned into species, and all that is sectioned is prior in nature to the section, and constitutive. Therefore, if the genus is prior in substance to the species, but those relatives that are prior in substance are prior causally, then the genus takes precedence over the species, and it is rightly placed before the rest, for this is the order that nature has used in the process of generation. For having taken up a seed, she first vivifies and animates it; then, as she proceeds, she provides it with sensation and makes it an animal; then, [providing it with] ardour and desire, she makes it an irrational animal; then, at the end, [providing it with] reason, she makes it a human being.[119] Thus, qua substances genera exist prior to species, whereas qua genera and species they subsist concomitantly with one another and are co-eliminated, for 'genus' and 'species' are the names of their mutual relation to one another.

It is worth inquiring why, when teaching about the genus, he also made mention of species, and not of the difference and the others. We say, then, that the genus and the species are relatives, as we said – after all, the species is the species of a genus, and the genus is genus of a species – and for this reason he rightly mentioned the species at the same time as the genus. For in teaching about the relatives, it is altogether necessary that he who is teaching about one of them, insofar as they are relatives, also mention the remaining one.

Here, Porphyry has made use of an Aristotelian rule.[120] The rule is as follows: he who is about to carry out teaching about some homonym – that is, whether many things are signified by the same name – must first divide the many things signified by the name, then state about which of the things signified he is carrying out his teaching. For homonymy tends to generate obscurity and error, with the teacher assuming this name applies to one meaning, and the student that it applies to another. For instance, if someone wishing to teach about the astral dog[121] says, 'the dog creates burning heat or separates fruits,'[122] without previously stating which dog he is talking about, he instils error in the student. One must therefore first, after enumerating the meanings of 'dog', i.e. that one is astral, another terrestrial, another marine, and another philosophical, say that 'I am talking about the astral one.'[123] Porphyry, then, doing this philosophically, lists the meanings of 'genus', and indicates which one he is talking about.

1,18 It seems that neither genus nor species is said in a simple way.

He said 'it seems', not because he is in doubt, but instead of 'it is apparent'. 'In a simple way' is said in four senses: it signifies what is general, as the rhetoricians say 'and simply speaking' instead of 'generally speaking'; what is in the proper sense, as when Aristotle says 'generation simply',[124] that is, the one properly so called; and [it signifies] the one that is in vain and without any reason, as when we say 'he strikes him simply' instead of 'in vain'. It also means 'in one way', as when it is said in Euripides,[125]

'the word of truth is simple.'

Here, though, it stands for 'in one way', for he says that it is apparent that neither the genus, nor the species, nor the rest, are said in one way.

1,18 For what is called 'genus' is [the collection of] persons who are somehow disposed towards something that is one, [and to each other].

He states the first meaning of the genus, according to which it assumes two relations: of a plurality to a plurality, and of a plurality to one person, for instance of the Heraclids to Heracles, insofar as they are said to have their genus from him, and of themselves to one another, insofar as they are called 'uncles' or 'cousins' by one another, or in whatever other way.

He did well to add 'somehow', for different persons of those who are beneath the same genus will have different relations: for they are either uncles to one another, or children, or siblings, or some other one of things that are completive of such a genus.

1,20 It is according to this meaning that the genus of the Heraclids is so called.

For by saying 'of the Heraclids', he separates them from the other genera, such as the Tantalids and the others.

1,20 From the relation deriving from one thing – I mean, from Heracles.

Again, insofar as two relations are taken of one person to another, of cause and effect, as for instance of Heracles to one of the Heraclids – Heracles being the cause and the person deriving from him being the effect – or of the fatherland and the person brought up in it, as we say that Plato is Athenian in genus, while Pindar is Theban. It should be known that relation is said either by art, as of a teacher to a student; or by chance, as of a master to a slave; or by choice, as of a friend to a friend; or by nature, as of father to son. The relation of the things mentioned, then, is by nature.

1,22 [And the multitude of persons who somehow have with regard to one another the kinship deriving from that thing is [so] called] to distinguish it from all the other genera.

For it should be known that meaningful words and names usually separate realities from one another. Indeed, nature contrived[126] that this thing here should be called 'human being' or 'dog' or something else, so that she might separate each thing from the others. And each of the arts, since it intends to teach something more novel and extraordinary as compared to the other arts, imposes names on its own instruments so that it can somehow clarify them. For it is in this way that the geometers, having discovered many differences of triangles, such as that one has its three sides equal, another only two, and another all three unequal, made use of their own names and called the one having the three sides equal 'equilateral', the one having only two of them equal 'isosceles', and the one having all three unequal 'scalene', wishing to indicate each one by these names. This, then, is the way names signify realities.

2,5 [Again, also called 'genus', in another sense, is the principle of generation for each person, either from the progenitor or from the place in which one came into being. Thus, for instance, we say Orestes has his genus from Tantalus, and Hyllos from Heracles. Again, [we say] Pindar is Theban in genus, and Plato Athenian: after all, the fatherland is a kind of principle of the genus of each person, as is the father]. This appears to be the meaning close to hand, [for those who are descended from the genus of Heracles are called Heraclids, and Cecropids those [who are descended] from Cecrops and their next of kin. Indeed, it was the principle of the generation of each person that was first named 'genus', and after that the multitude of those who [derive] from one principle, such as Heracles. Delimiting and separating it from the others, we called the entire collection 'the genus of the Heraclids'.]

The philosopher has created a certain obscurity by immediately proceeding to the first meaning of 'genus', without pointing this out; for he should have distinguished which meaning of 'genus' is being discussed. For that he is talking about the first one, not about the one we just stated, is shown by the examples he sets forth; for he says that this meaning of 'genus' seems to us to be 'at hand' from customary usage, and more familiar. He says that the meaning at hand in customary usage is the relation from one person to many and from many to a plurality.

It is worth raising the problem of why he said this [meaning] was 'at hand', and not the relation of one person to another, for nature knows this one first, for she first makes one person from one, and then many from many. We shall say in response to this that the second meaning of 'genus', which is second with regard to us, is first by nature – for from Heracles, one person comes into being first, and then, in this way, the plurality – but the first meaning is second by nature, and that which is second by nature is first to us. In general, the things that are first by nature are posterior for us, while the things that are second by nature are first for us. For instance, matter and form are prior by nature, then the four elements, then flesh and bones and the remaining homoeomeries,[127] then the human being. Nature thus moves from higher things to secondary ones, while we, as if walking with our head down and looking up from below, and wishing to go from more proximate things to distant ones, and from more enmattered to immaterial ones, we first know human beings, then [we know] that they consist of bones and flesh, then that the latter consist of the four elements, then that these [consist] of matter and form. Thus, the things that are prior by nature become posterior to our knowledge, and those that are posterior by nature are prior to our knowledge; so what is first is more clear, and what is second is more obscure. This is why Porphyry undertook to teach about them in this way – for teaching must be carried out from the things that are more clear to us – and because the genus among the philosophers, which is what is under discussion, resembles the aforementioned genera and has a certain similarity to them.

It is worth wondering for what reason, when there are other meanings of 'genus', he enumerated only these. That there are other meanings is clear from these considerations. Plato called substance, identity, otherness, motion, and [the] rest 'genera of being'.[128] But he[129] did not enumerate them, since his task, as he indicated beforehand, was to write about Aristotle's views. Aristotle himself also seems to call the matter underlying every art 'genus' in the *Physics*,[130] as wood in carpentry, human bodies in medicine, and prime matter in all natural things. But it was not Porphyry's task to discuss these things from a physical viewpoint, but in a manner appropriate to the subject-matter of logic.

> **2,10** Again, in another sense that to which the species is subordinated is called 'genus'; perhaps [it is] so called from its similarity with these.

He enumerates the third meaning of 'genus', which is also the one the philosophers talk about; yet it has a certain similarity to what is before it. For as the first meaning of 'genus' has two relations, that of many to one person and that of them to them,[131] so species have a relation both to the genus and to one another. Again, as the second meaning has a relation of one person to one person, and that of cause to effect,[132] so this one also has a relation of one to one, such as of animal to man, of effect to cause. Indeed, perhaps the first imposers of names,[133] wishing to distinguish the various generations of men, called one the genus of the Heraclids, another of the Aeacids, and another of the Pelopids. Then, in imitation of them, the philosophers later named the genera current among them. For as the genus of the Heraclids is [made up of] those who have come into being out of Heracles, so animal is also said to be a genus, for animal in the absolute sense is said to be the genus of particular animals – human being, dog, horse, and the others. Often, however, the philosophers first discovered the genera current among them, and then, in imitation of them, the name-imposers came along later and named the genera that are current in human usage; for one can conceive of either possibility. Since this is ambiguous – whether the philosophers or the name-imposers discovered the principle of such nomenclature – this was why he said 'perhaps', since he too was hesitant.

> **2,14** Thus, since 'genus' is said in three ways, discussion among philosophers is about the third sense, and they gave the following descriptive account of it.

Having enumerated the meanings of 'genus', Porphyry says that discussion among the philosophers is about the third one.

2,15 and they gave the following descriptive account of it.[134]

We must, therefore, first state what a description is and what a definition is, and in what respect a definition differs from a description; then, following that, seek the reason why he teaches it[135] by means of a description and not by a definition, although definitions usually signify the substance of the underlying reality, and enclose what is proper to it, while not laying claim to anything extraneous. It should be said, then, that every reality is both one and many, and this is why each is signified both by a name and by an account (*logos*): by a name, when it is considered as something [that is] one, and by an account when [it is considered] as something with many parts. For instance, we signify a human being both by the name 'human being' and by the account which says: 'rational mortal animal receptive of intellect and knowledge'.[136] This account, signifying the underlying realities, is taken either from what belongs by substance to realities, or from what happens to them accidentally. If it is taken from what belongs to them substantially, it is called a definition, such as 'rational mortal animal' – for these complete the substance of a human being – while if it is taken from what happens to them accidentally, it is called a description, such as 'a human being is an animal who walks upright, has flat nails,[137] and uses his hands', for these supervene upon the substance of 'human being': they do not complete the substance of 'human being', but supervene upon it. This, then, is how definition differs from description: i.e. by the fact that the definition indicates realities on the basis of substance, but the description [does so] on the basis of accidents. It is called a description (*hupographê*) as if it were a kind of sketch (*skiagraphia*), for as among painters the sketch indicates an imitation of the image, but not in an articulated way, so a description also somehow indicates the reality, but not in an articulated way. The definition, by contrast, clearly presents to us the reality itself. Thus, the definition is analogous to the complete painting (*graphê*), and the description to a sketch; this is why it is called a description.[138]

Since, then, definitions are taken from the genus and the constitutive differences, but there is no genus of the most universal genus, so that from it and the differences he might give the definition of the genus, but the topic of his discussion is now the most universal genus: for this reason, since he could not give a definition of the genus, Porphyry signified it by a description. For in the case of those realities of which we cannot give definitions, we content ourselves with signifying them by a description. We lack definitions in the case of the genus, first, as we have already said, because the discourse we are carrying out is about the genus in the absolute sense, which[139] is able to fit every genus, but it is not possible to discover a genus of the most universal genus, for in that case it would not be the most universal. But where there is no genus, there can be no definition, for every definition consists of a genus and the differences that are constitutive of the *definiendum*, but if there is no genus, there cannot be constitutive differences, for the constitutive differences of species are the same ones that are divisive of genera, as we shall learn later on. That which does not have a genus, therefore, cannot have constitutive differences, either. Since, then, there is neither a genus nor constitutive differences of the most universal genus, there cannot be a definition of it, either. First, then, it is for this reason that one cannot give a definition of the genus.

Then, also because 'genus' is homonymous, for it is said in ten ways, as one can learn in the *Categories*. Yet one cannot give definitions of homonyms, for they are mere names that differ in the realities signified by them. But the definition signifies substance.

Those things whose definitions are the same also have the same realities. Therefore, it is not possible to give a single common definition of homonyms; hence we signify them by a description. For the same accidents may belong even to things that differ in substance, so that here too, there occurs to genera, which are many and different in substance, one and the same relation to the species that are subjected to them, and it is according to this relation that some are called 'genus', and others 'species'. This, then, is why Porphyry did not give a definition of the genus in the absolute sense, but a description, so that he could fit it to the ten genera.

In response to this, someone might raise the difficulty to us that if we do not define homonyms – for the definition signifies substance, but the former are mere names – then why do we give a description of them? After all, a description, through the concourse of accidents, signifies the substance that underlies them, for it brings us to a notion of the substance to which these things have occurred. Since, then, we give one description of homonyms, and through the description proceed to a notion of the underlying substance, it will be found that not only the names, but also the realities are the same, which is absurd. For the ten genera will be found to be the same, such as substance, quantity, quality, and the others, to which the genus is homonymous.

Such, then, is the puzzle. We have just solved it beforehand potentially, when we said that it is possible for the same things – according to which the description comes about – to happen accidentally to things that differ in substance, just as it happened to the ten categories that they received the same relation to what is beneath them. For as substance, which contains 'body' and 'incorporeal', is their genus,[140] while they are species, so the quantified, which includes two species, the continuous and the discrete, is their genus. Likewise, the qualified, which contains several species, is their genus; and similarly for the others. Thus, the same relation has happened to all the categories; and we should not be surprised if it is possible to give one description of things that differ in substance, without making the described realities identical. For instance, in the ten genera, the fact of being predicated of several things is similar, but it is not of the same things or the same number [of things] – one of them may, for instance, be predicated of four species, and another of some other number of them – and all are homonyms and are predicated of several things, but not either of the same things or similarly.

The description is thus taken either from etymology or from the concourse of accidents, which is called 'description' in the proper sense of the term. From etymology, as in 'a human being (*anthrôpos*) is what can gaze upwards (*anô athrein*) or look up at (*anathrein*) what he has seen',[141] or 'that which has its face (*ôpas*) on high (*anôthen*)'. From accidents, as we have already said previously. The definition is taken either from the matter, as when we define anger as 'boiling of the blood around the heart',[142] or from the form, as in 'desire for vengeance', or from both, as in 'boiling of the blood around the heart from a desire for vengeance'.[143] And when it is taken from matter alone, or from form alone, it is imperfect, but when [it is taken] from both, then it is a perfect definition, since it signifies both. The perfect definition is the one that is from genus and constitutive differences. The genus occupies the rank of the matter, and the differences that of the form. It is intermediate realities that are susceptible of this definition, neither the very first nor the last ones; for the last things have neither genera nor constitutive differences,[144] like individuals. Hence, we give descriptions of them, not definitions, such as 'Socrates is the son of Sophroniscus, Athenian, philosopher, pot-bellied, bald, hook-nosed,' and whatever other accidents he may have. Those who say that the most generic things have constitutive differences are not correct, for they have not constitutive differences but divisive ones, since all that is constitutive takes precedence over what is constituted. For as I said shortly before, the differences that are constitutive of certain things are, far earlier, divisive of the more generic things. For rational and mortal, which are constitutive of human being, and mortal and irrational, [which are constitutive] of horse, are divisive of the genus, I mean of animal, for this is what is divided into rational and irrational, mortal and immortal. Thus, it was well said that the differences that are constitutive of some things tend to take precedence over them, but nothing takes precedence over what is most generic. These things being so, he rightly carries out the teaching of the universal genus by means of a description, since he cannot give a definition of it.

In order that we might learn what the description that has been given might be, and whence it was taken, one should say the following – at the same time, we will learn that Porphyry did not take up the five words at random, but that it is necessary, in a way, for every word to be subsumed under one of these words. Of words, some are meaningless, such as *knax*, *blituri*,[145] *skindapsos*, and others meaningful. The latter are either said of one thing, such as when we say 'Plato', 'Socrates', or of some singular; or of many. The latter are predicated either of substantial things or of adventitious things,[146] {either of things that differ in species, such as genera and differences (and these are predicated essentially, like the genus, or qualitatively, like the difference); or of things that differ in number, such as the species. Either they are predicated of one species, like the property, or of many, like the accident.} It is apparent from this division that it is entirely necessary to make use of the aforementioned five words, and neither more nor less. For we have said that of words, some are meaningless, others meaningful, and of the meaningful ones some are predicated of one thing, others of several, and those [that are predicated] of several include the genus, the species, the difference, the property, and the accident. Thus, since there are seven words: the meaningless ones, those said of one thing, and those said of several things – I mean the genus, the difference, the species, the property, and the accident – once two [types of] words are removed, five are left remaining. For the meaningless ones are removed, since they do not contribute anything, either to grammarians or to rhetoricians, and much less to philosophers. The [words predicated] of one thing are also rejected, since they are particular, but particular things are infinite and cannot be comprehended, while philosophers profess to know everything scientifically. Yet as Plato says in the *Cratylus*[147] 'knowledge (*epistêmê*) has been said from the fact that it leads us to a kind of rest and term of realities and questions.'[148] Since, then, particular things are many and infinite, they do not produce knowledge. Those that are predicated of one thing are predicated of particular things. They are rightly rejected, and what henceforth remains are the five words, genus, species, and the difference, which is intermediate between them, [in addition to] the property and the accident, and you will find everything else ending up beneath these words, and every other word, whether you say 'motion' or 'infinite'. These things have now been said in summary form in the division, but we will examine their detailed explanation later.

Of words, some are meaningless, such as *knax*, *blituri*, and *skindapsos*, and others significant; and the meaningless ones are of no account to us. The insignificant ones are thus called non-categorical, since they not addressed (*agoreumenai*) or said of (*kata*) anything.

Of meaningful [words], some are said of one thing, such as Socrates and Plato, others of many, such as genera, species, differences, properties, and accidents. It has been said, however, that particulars are of no account to philosophers. Of those that are said of many things, some are predicated essentially, such as genera, differences, and species (for they are completive of substance); some not essentially, such as properties and accidents, for these do not complete the substance of their substrates. Of those that are predicated essentially, some are said of things that differ in species, such as genera and differences; others of things that differ in number,[149] which differ from one another not by form (*eidei*)[150] but by matter, I mean such as Xanthus the horse and Balias, for these do not differ from one another in form, but in matter.

Again,[151] the number ten is made up of ten monads that are not confounded, but are separated from one another, for if the monads were confounded, we could not say that the number ten is made up of monads. Thus far, from this we have the difference between species, genus, and difference: for they differ from one another by the fact that the species is predicated of what differs in number, while genus and difference [are predicated] of what differs in species. Of those that are predicated of what differs in species, some are predicated essentially[152] – we say that something is predicated essentially, when being asked 'what is a human being?', for instance, we say that he is an animal, which is a genus; thus, the genus is said to be predicated essentially – others qualitatively,[153] as when, having been asked 'what kind of an animal is a human being?', we answer 'rational', which is a difference. Thus, the difference is predicated qualitatively. In these remarks, the difference between the genus and the difference has become apparent to us. They differ from one another in this, insofar as the genus is predicated essentially, while the difference [is predicated] qualitatively.

Of things said non-substantially, some belong to some single species, such as properties, and others to several, such as accidents. From this division, then, the difference between property and accident has become apparent to us, for they differ at least insofar as the property belongs to one species, and the accident to several. It is clear from the division, moreover, that it is necessary for every word to end up under one of these five words. At the same time, it is clear that from the present division we may give the definition or description of each thing by selecting what is useful for giving the account of each thing, just as he has done. For he says: 'the genus is that which is predicated essentially of several things that differ in species.'[154] 'Of several' distinguishes it from individuals (since they are said of one thing), while 'that differ in species' distinguishes it from species and property. 'Predicated essentially', for its part, distinguishes it from difference and accident. We have given a more detailed division in this way because we wish to teach the difference between the words, and that it is altogether necessary for Aristotle to use these five words alone, neither more nor fewer. For since the words are seven in all, and two are eliminated, five alone are left. The philosopher Porphyry, since he did not wish to demonstrate here why Aristotle made use of the five words alone, but only the difference between the five significant words, narrows down the division, and says as follows:[155] of meaningful words, some are said of one thing, others of several (for he omits the upper part of the division[156]). [Some such words are] predicated of one thing, as individuals, such as Socrates, Plato, and Alcibiades. Of [those that are predicated] of several, some are [predicated] of what differs in species, such as the genus, the difference, and the accident. After all, the genus, such as animal, is predicated of many species, such as human being, horse, and dog, while the difference, such as rational, is predicated both of men and of angels, and mortal of horse, human beings, and the other animals; and the accident is predicated of many species: of whiteness and of blackness, and of standing and of sitting. Among those that [are predicated] of what differs in number are the species and the property.

Of those that are predicated of what differs in species, some are predicated essentially, others qualitatively and relatively.[157] Essentially, is the genus; qualitatively, the difference; and relatively, is the accident. For if we are asked how Plato is disposed (*pôs ekhei*), we say that he is in good health, or ill, or sitting, or standing, and such like.

It is worth raising the problem: if the aforementioned five words are reduced under 'word' as a genus, but the genus is subsumed beneath these, then there will be a genus of the most generic genera, which is absurd. We say that it is not qua realities that genera are subsumed beneath this division, but qua words; qua realities, however, the most generic things are no longer reduced to something more common.

2,17 For of predicates, some are said of one thing alone, such as individuals [for instance Socrates].

By these [remarks], he indicates how the description given of the genus separates it from all the others.

2,18 And 'this person' and 'that thing' [others of several things, such as genera, species, differences, properties].

For these are particular, since they are said of one thing alone. We say 'this one' and 'that one' and 'other one' while pointing [to something]. The philosophers did well to refer this account to particulars, for they are what fall under demonstrative reference and sensation. For the universal human being and the universal animal, since they are in the Demiurge, do not fall under demonstrative reference or sensation. They thus did well to subsume singulars beneath demonstrative reference, but not universals. These are called 'individuals' (*atoma*), since they cannot be sectioned either into things of the same kind or into things of a different kind, like genera and species, but perish together with the sectioning. For the animal in me is not common, but has been circumscribed in me, and likewise rational; and the compound formed out of them, i.e. 'human being' has all been circumscribed.

> **2,19** and accidents [are said] in common, but not properly to anything.

Such as whiteness and blackness. For particulars are not said of several things, such as the whiteness in this body here or the scar in Odysseus, from which the nurse recognized him,[158] for it belonged to him alone. For if it did not belong to him alone, how was she able to recognize him from it? This, then, is why he said: 'the accidents that belong in common, but not properly to anything', instead of 'the universals, not the particulars'.

> **2,20** The genus is for instance animal, the species, for instance, human being, [difference, such as rational, property, such as capable of laughing, accident, such as white, black, sitting].

He provides instruction about them in outline form, as it were, teaching us each of the five [words] through an example.

> **2,22** Genera differ from what is predicated of one thing alone by the fact that the latter have been accounted for as being predicated of several things.

By these [remarks], he shows how the definition or description given of the genus separates it from all the others. For the genus is predicated of several things that differ, not in number alone, but also in species, while the species [is predicated] of things that differ in number alone. Thus, one must carry out the definition or description of each word as follows: that genus is a meaningful word predicated essentially of several things that differ in species; difference is a meaningful word predicated qualitatively of several things that differ in species; species is a meaningful word predicated essentially of several things that differ in number; property is a meaningful word, non-substantial, predicated of one species; while accident is by nature a meaningful word, adventitious, predicated relatively of several things that differ in species.

> **2,27** [Of things that [are predicated] of several things, they differ from the species in that the species, although predicated of several things, these things do not differ in species but in number. For human being, which is a species, is predicated of Socrates and Plato, who do not differ from each other in species, but in number.] Animal, which is a genus, is predicated of human being, ox, and horse, which differ in species, not merely in number.

It should be known that things that differ in species from one another also differ in number, while those that differ in number do not differ in species as well. The account is not reciprocal. It ought to be known that 'identical' is threefold: for something is identical either in genus, in species, or in number. Identical in genus, is like human being, horse, [and] ox, for these are identical in genus, since they are all animals. Identical in species is like Theon, Plato, and Alcibiades, for these are the same and one in species. Identical in number is like human being and mortal, sword, and dagger.[159] Now, if being identical is threefold, then being other is necessarily threefold as well: for things differ and are other than one another either in genus, in species, or in number. Things that differ from one another in genus necessarily differ in species and in number as well. For instance, they differ from one another in genus like human being and white – for human being is an animal, but white is a qualified – but also in species, for the species of human being is other than that of white. Human being is a species of animal, which is a genus, while white is a species of quality and of colour. But [they also differ] in number, for the perceptible man, such as Socrates, is other than Plato. Thus, we have done well to say that the things that differ from one another in genus also differ in species and in number, whereas those that differ in species differ of necessity in number, but not of necessity in genus as well, such as human being and horse. These differ from one another in species – for the species of human being is one thing, and that of horse is another – but also in number, for the matter of human being is one thing, and the matter of horse is another. But they do not differ in genus, since both are animals. Things that differ in number, in contrast, do not differ of necessity either in species or in genus. This, then, is why he said: 'which differ from each other in species as well, not only in number',[160] since it is clear that things that differ from one another in species of necessity differ in number as well.

3,5 [Again, the genus differs from the property in that the property is predicated of only one species, of which it is the property, and is predicated of the individuals beneath the species, as capable of laughing [is predicated] only of human being and of particular human beings, whereas the genus is not predicated of one species, but of several different ones.] Again, the genus differs from the difference and the common accidents [in that although the differences and the common accidents are predicated of several things that differ in species, they are not predicated essentially.][161]

He says that the genus differs from differences and universal accidents in that the latter can be predicated qualitatively or relatively, while the genus [is predicated] essentially.[162]

> **3,14** [For if we are asked what it is that these things are predicated of, we do not say that it is predicated essentially, but rather qualitatively. For in asking what kind of thing a human being is, we say that he is rational, and [in asking] what kind of thing a crow is, we say that it is black: for rational is a difference, but black is an accident. However, when we are asked what human being is, we answer 'animal', for the genus of human being, [as we saw], is animal.] Thus, the fact that the genus is said of several things distinguishes it from those that are predicated of only one of the individuals.

He shows succinctly how each of the things taken up has been taken appropriately with regard to the description of the genus.[163]

> **3,18** [while [saying] 'things that differ in species' differentiates [it] from the things predicated as species or properties, and 'being predicated essentially' separates it from differences and common accidents] which are predicated of what they are predicated of not essentially but qualitatively or relatively.

Difference and accidents are not only predicated qualitatively, but also relatively. For when we are asked, 'How is Socrates disposed?', we answer either that he is healthy, or that he is ill. For the other differences are near to the accidents, such as snub-nosed, hook-nosed, and bald.

> **3,17** The fact of being predicated essentially separates it from the differences and the common accidents, which are predicated of each thing of which they are predicated not essentially, but qualitatively or relatively.[164]

The difference is predicated qualitatively, but the common accidents relatively. Some say that by saying 'or relatively' he also included the accidents that occur to something properly. We say, then, that even if they too are predicated relatively, they nevertheless belong to what is predicated of one thing. But he separated the genus from these above, by saying,[165] 'the fact that the genus is said of several things distinguishes it from those things that are predicated of only one of the individuals.'

> **3,19** The stated description of the concept thus contains nothing superfluous or deficient.

Definitions tend to fit with one reality alone, and to encompass it in its totality. This is why they are called definitions (*horismoi*), because they encompass the *definiendum*, taken in the sense of boundaries (*horôn*) in real estate. Definitions are ruined in two ways, either by being superfluous or by being deficient. For it has been well said by the philosophers that every due proportion is flanked by two disproportions: thus, justice is one virtue, but it is flanked by excessive humility and by greed. The excessively humble person is he who claims for himself less than his due, while the greedy person [claims] more than his due. Again, temperance is a virtue, but it is flanked by insensitivity[166] and licentiousness. The insensitive person is he who is moved less, while the licentious person is he who is moved more, and in a disorderly way. Thus, as in the case of these things, so it is with the definition, for that definition is best which circumscribes its own object and leaves nothing outside of it, while laying claim to nothing of what flanks it. What flanks it, as for the other virtues, are excess and deficiency, as has already been said. When they[167] are excessive, they make things deficient, but when they are deficient, they make things excessive. For instance, the definition of human being is 'rational mortal animal', and this definition separates human being from all the others, and encompasses all human beings. When it is deficient, it makes the thing be excessive, such as 'mortal animal'; for not only the human being is a mortal animal, but also the horse, dog, and many others. Again, when it is excessive, it makes the thing deficient, such as 'rational mortal literate animal', for it no longer includes all human beings, but only those who are literate. And rightly so, for as things become more compound, they contract.

When they are simpler, they extend further and are applied to more things, inasmuch as they are closer to the first, common principle of all things. For this reason, animal, in and of itself, is applied to more things, but when combined with rational [it applies] to fewer. When rational animal is coupled with mortal, it contains still fewer things, while if literate is added as well, it becomes still more particular. Thus, when definitions are deficient, they make things excessive, and when they are excessive they make [things] deficient. Having pointed out these things, then, Porphyry says that the given definition or description of the genus is free from the two [factors] that ruin definitions: for it is neither excessive nor deficient.

69,1 It has been said[168] that genera are threefold: some before the many, some in the many, and some after the many, which are also called last-born and conceptual, since they are in our thought. Porphyry's task, then, is to teach about genera, neither about those that are before the many, nor about those that are in the many, but about those that are after the many, that is, about the
5 conceptual ones.[169] This is why he said 'description of the concept', that is, of the conceptual genus. The conceptual genus is when we define according to the concept by which we take things. For instance, we take human being in our own thought, and calculating with regard to it, we say that human being is a
10 rational, mortal animal. Porphyry says, then, that the description of the genus has nothing excessive or deficient with regard to that concept.

On Species

3,22 Species is also said of the shape of each thing.

The discussion of the genus is complete. The differences occupy the second
15 rank among these things. But since genus and species are relatives, and exist and are thought simultaneously, for this reason he placed the species before the difference, not in accordance with natural order but in accordance with pedagogical implication, and because he had made mention of the species in the teaching about the genus, and it was necessary that the student not remain
20 without a conception of this for long. Here, too, using the usual rule, he first enumerates the meanings of species, then adds the additional specification of which one he is discussing. For there are other meanings of species, about which it is not his task to speak, but he lists those meanings of species that fit
25 with the discipline of logic. He says, then, that the meaning of species is twofold: species is said to be the shape of each thing, and it is according to this meaning
70,1 that we speak of 'shapely' or 'misshapen' people. Also called species is that which falls beneath the genus, or that whose genus is predicated essentially, but this definition is of the most specific species and of that which is not most specific. Also called species, in another sense, is that which is predicated essentially of
5 many things that differ in number. Since the meanings of these names, I mean of the species that is not most specific and the most specific one, are unclear to common usage, as the discussion proceeds he clarifies them, examining the

finest of the categories, I mean substance, which is a self-subsistent reality and the most generic genus, for the other categories are accidents of it. For if all the others are in substance, and are observed in it, and cannot exist without it, it is clear that substance is self-subsistent, while the other nine categories occur to it accidentally. He therefore takes substance and weaves out of it a series such that of substance, one part is body, the other incorporeal; and of body one part is animate, the other inanimate; and of animate one part is animal, the other plant, and another zoophyte; and of animal one part is rational, the other irrational; and of rational one part is angel, another human being, and another demon. Among these, then, the most generic genus is substance, and the most specific species is human being. The same intermediate genera are also called species, species of what is before them, and genera of what is after them. The preceding description, then, which says that species is that which falls beneath the genus or that of which the genus is predicated essentially, contains all the species in common, both the most specific and the subordinate ones. For of these descriptions, each is the same as the other in substrate, and they differ from one another in relation alone. There are also many other things which are the same in substrate but different in relation, such as ascent and descent.[170] For the same thing – the ladder – underlies these things, but the ascent differs from the descent by relation alone, in that the ascent is the way up from below to above, while the descent is the way down from above to below. Seed and fruit, too, are the same in substrate, but are different only in account and in relation.[171] As matters are with these things, then, so they are with the twofold nature of the description of the species: for they differ from one another by the fact that one of them begins from the genus and stops at the species, [while] the other one begins from the species and stops at the genus. Thus, these things too differ from another by relation alone, but are the same in substrate. Again, he begins from the more familiar meaning of species, since it has a similarity to [the one] used by the philosophers: for as the species in the case of shape[172] contains all the parts, so the one in use among the philosophers [contains] the particulars.

3,22 Species is said of the shape of each thing,[173] [as has been said: 'first of all, an appearance (*eidos*) worthy of a tyranny'.][174]

As in the case of the genus, before teaching what the genus is, or what it is like, he disambiguated its homonymy and first began to teach about the meanings of genus that were not under discussion, then about the one that was under discussion; in the same way here he first disambiguates the homonymy, then states what the species is, and what its meaning is.

> **4,2** Also called species is what is ranged beneath the given genus. In this sense, we are accustomed to say that human being is a species of animal, where animal is a genus; white is a species of colour, and the triangle is a species of figure.

Having stated the meanings of species, and what it is his task to talk about, he now teaches by an example how the meaning of species that is under discussion is subsumed beneath the genus;[175] for he takes the triangle and the figure, the figure as genus and the triangle as species. Some object to him that it was improper for him to say that figure is the genus of triangle, or triangle is the species of figure, for they say that among things in which there is [something] first and second, that which is predicated of them in common is not a genus.[176] But the triangle is first [as compared] to the square, for one derives from three lines and the other from four, but three is first [as compared] to four. In another way: every square is divided into two right-angled triangles, for joining the square ABCD at the diagonal AC divides [it] into two right-angled triangles, ABC and ADC. Thus, when the square is eliminated the triangle is not eliminated, but if the triangle is eliminated it is impossible for there to be a square. Thus, the triangle is first by nature [with regard] to the square. In the same way, it will be shown to be first [with regard] to all the remaining rectilinear figures, I mean the pentagon, the hexagon, and the rest, for each of these can be divided into triangles. If, then, the triangle is first, and the square and the others are second, then that which is predicated of them in common, I mean the figure, is not their genus, so that they are not its species. It remains, therefore, that Porphyry did not properly say that the triangle is a species of figure.

All of the exegetes were at a loss for a defence against this [argument], and they say that for the sake of an example, he called figure the genus of the triangle in a rather loose sense. We, however, solve this difficulty by saying that if triangles were really elements of the square, such that it would not be possible for a square to come into being unless it were made up of triangles, as Plato teaches in the *Timaeus*,[177] analysing all rectilinear figures into triangles as to the most simple elements, then what is said would be true, and the triangle would be the first of the figures, and figure would not be their genus, if it is true that in those things in which there is something prior and posterior, what is predicated in common of them is not a genus. As things are, however, there is no necessity, in order for a square to come into being, for triangles to exist previously, and then for the square to come into being out of their composition. For even if there is no triangle, there is nothing to prevent us from joining four straight lines and making a square, as Euclid teaches, who in his forty-sixth theorem drew a square without triangles, by means of straight lines.[178] Thus, it is not true that if the triangle is eliminated, the square is also eliminated. If it is because by joining the diagonal we divide the square into two triangles that they say the triangle is primary and as it were an element or a part of the square, this is not necessary either;[179] since it is possible to divide the same square into two oblong rectangles, by dividing the opposite sides into two and joining, for instance, from A to B, and making two oblong areas, C and D,[180] it is said as though the oblong rectangles were first with regard to the square. Thus, the contrary [is also true]: a square is also first with regard to an oblong rectangle, if we divide into two squares an oblong rectangle that has one side double the length of the other. If, moreover, one were to draw the diameter on a circle, one will divide the circle into two semicircles, A and B, and clearly each of the semicircles is a figure composed of a semicircular line as its arc and of the diameter as its straight line. Thus, it will follow that the simple figure, the circle, will be made up of mixed semicircles,[181] and what is mixed will be first by nature with regard to what is simple, I mean the circle. Thus, just as in these cases our conception carries out such a division, but this does not make it necessary for the oblong rectangles to be first by nature with regard to the square, since oblong rectangles can also be divided into two squares if one of the sides is double the other – if, once again, mixed figures consisting of straight lines and arcs are not first with regard to the circle – so, neither is it necessary, because it is possible to divide the square by its diagonal into two triangles, for it to be made up *ipso facto* of triangles, and for triangles to be first by nature with regard to it. Thus, Porphyry was right to say that figure is the genus of triangle.

4,4 If, however, when giving an account of the genus, [we made mention of the species, saying 'that which is predicated essentially of several things differing in species', and we say that the species is what is beneath the given genus. It should be known that since the genus is the genus of something, and the species is the species of something, each one of each one, it is necessary to make use of both in the account of both.]

'If, however', he says, 'when giving an account of the genus, we made mention of the species, saying that it is that which is predicated essentially of several things that differ in species', and again, defining the species, we made mention of the genus, saying that 'the species is what is beneath the given genus', let no one blame us'. Indeed, by saying these things, Porphyry is considered to have used a circular proof. Circular proofs are disparaged among the philosophers, because they make the same things first and second, and exchange the order of premises and conclusions: for they make what is second first, and what is first second, and they make the same things clearer and more unclear than the same things. For instance, if someone says to me that the soul is immortal, I say, 'Yes'. Why? Because the soul is self-moving; what is self-moving is eternally moved, what is eternally moved is immortal; therefore the soul is immortal. If he says to me: 'Whence is it clear that the soul is self-moved?,' and then, wishing to prove this, I say that the soul is immortal; what is immortal is eternally moved; what is eternally moved is self-moved; therefore, the soul is self-moved. This is called a circular proof. For wishing to prove that the soul is immortal, it took what is self-moved first, and concluded to what is immortal, while again, wishing to prove that the soul is self-moved, it took as first what was said last, i.e. immortal, and concluded that it is self-moved, making what was first last. Thus, a circular proof is one that makes the premises conclusions, and again, the conclusions premises, whence it has been disparaged. For every demonstration takes clear and agreed-upon premises, while by means of the premises it clarifies and renders evident the conclusion, which is unclear. Rightly worthy of censure is the [demonstration] that inverts the order of these things, clarifying the conclusion, which was previously taken to be unclear, by taking it up in the rank of a premise, while now turning the premise, which we previously took to be agreed upon, into an unclear conclusion. Again, if we wish to prove that this woman has milk, let us say that this woman has given birth; she who has given birth has milk; therefore, this woman has milk. Again, wishing to prove this very fact, i.e. that she has given birth, let us say: this woman has milk; she who has milk has given birth; therefore, this woman has given birth. Here, once again, we took the same things to be prior and posterior to the same things, and more and less clear. For we previously took the fact of having given birth to be clear and prior, and the fact of having milk as unclear and posterior. Later, we took having milk to be clear and prior, and having given birth to be unclear and posterior. Thus, in such a proof the same things are taken to be both prior and posterior, more and less clear than the same things. For every proof either proves what is unclear from what is clear, or what is clear from what is unclear, or the unclear from the unclear, or what is clear from what is clear, and it is obvious that only the one that proves what is unclear from what is clear is a proof in the proper sense. The other three would therefore be blameworthy, and not proofs at all. For it is not possible to prove what is clear from what is unclear, nor what is clear from what is clear; for neither does what is clear require proof, so that it should be shown from something else that is clear. It is thus far more absurd to say that unclear things are proven from unclear things. Thus, there is one proof alone in the proper sense: the one that proves what is unclear from what is clear. The circular proof has therefore been rightly disparaged, which makes what is clear and primary unclear and posterior, and conversely makes what is unclear and posterior clear and primary.

Since, then, the philosopher Porphyry noticed that he was making use of a circular proof (for in the teaching of the genus he took up the species, and conversely the genus in the teaching of the species, which one might perhaps censure), he defended himself in advance, for he said that the genus is genus of a species, and the species is species of a genus. Therefore, he who is teaching about the genus must make mention of the species as well, and talking about the species, [he must] mention the genus as well. For relatives subsist simultaneously,[182] and are thought simultaneously, for the genus is the genus of something – i.e. of the species – and the species is species of something – i.e. of the genus – and it is impossible to know one of these without the other. Thus, it is altogether necessary for the person carrying out the teaching of one of these to mention the other as well, for he who is unaware of one of the relatives shall not know the other one either.

4,10 [They also gave the following account of the species:] Species is that which is ranged beneath the genus, and of which the genus is predicated essentially.

He gives two descriptions of the species, which are the same in substrate (for both are predicated of several things), but different in relation, as the ascent and descent,[183] which are one in substrate, are different in relation. For when we begin from above, we call it a descent, and [beginning] from below [we call it] an ascent. Likewise, there are two relations here: that of the species to the genus, according to which [the former] is beneath [the latter], and of the genus to the species, according to which [the former] contains [the latter]. The relation from the genus to the species resembles a descent, while the one from the species to the genus [resembles] an ascent. These are the more general descriptions. Next, after these, he gives the complete description, the one taken from the division of words; i.e. that 'species is that which is predicated essentially of several things that differ in number.'[184]

It is worth inquiring for what reason Porphyry made use of a description in the case of species as well; for there is no longer any place for the reason stated in the case of the genus, since the species does have a genus. Yet the most exact and common reason must be stated: because definitions are definitions of things, indicating their natures, while genera and the rest are not things (*pragmata*), nor do they have a determinate nature. Therefore, they are not subsumed under any one of the categories, but are observed in all of them. After all, there are genera, species, and differences in substance, in the quantified, in the qualified, and in the rest of the categories. Thus, they are not things, but relations that indicate things. Since, then, as has been said, definitions are definitions of things, but these words are not things, it is rightly not possible to give definitions of them, either.

4,11 [Also in this way:] Species is what is [predicated essentially] of several things that differ in number.

He gives another description of the species, similar to the aforementioned one given from the genus.

4,12 But this account would be of the most specific and that which is species alone, whereas the others would be of the ones that are not most specific as well. [What is said might become clear in this way: in every category, there are some things that are most generic, and again, others that are most specific, and others between the most generic and the most specific. Most generic is that above which there would not be another higher genus, and most specific, after which there would not be another inferior species, while between the most generic and the most specific there are others, which are both genera and species, albeit taken with regard to different things.]

This last-given description of the species, he says, does not fit with all [species], but only with the most specific ones. So that we may learn what the most specific species are, he makes use of a division such as this: of substance, one part is body, the other incorporeal; and of body, one part is animate, the other inanimate; and of animate, one part is animal, another plant, and another zoophyte – for the plant has only three faculties: of nutrition, growth, and generation, whereas animals have, in addition to these, the perceptive faculty and that of motion from place to place. The zoophyte is intermediate between both, for in addition to these three faculties it has the sense of touch, but it does not pass from place to place, as oysters and sponges do [i.e. not pass from place to place], for they grow upon rocks, but when something hostile is at hand they contract, when something agreeable [is at hand], they relax. Again, of animal, one part is rational, another irrational; and of rational, one part is god, and another human being. Again, of human being, one part is Socrates, another Plato, and the particulars, but these are of no concern to philosophers, as has often been said.

In this division, then, substance comes first, and human being is posterior, while the so-called subordinate ones are intermediary; they are both genera and species with regard to different things.[185] Substance is said to be the most generic genus, human being the most specific species, and the others both genera and species, when taken with regard to different things. For body is a species of substance, but genus of animate, and animate is a species of body, but genus of animal, and animal is a species of animate, but genus of human being, while human being is a species of animal, but is no longer a genus as well, for it is predicated of things that differ not in species but in number, such as of Socrates and Alcibiades. It is therefore not a genus, but neither is it an individual, for it contains particular individuals.

It remains, therefore, that human being is a most specific species. He says, then, that the last description given of the species does not fit with every species, for it does not do so with animal and animate, but only with the most specific species, such as human being, horse, and dog, which are species alone.

4,21 Let what is said become clear in the case of one category. [Substance is also a genus: beneath it is body, and beneath body is animate body, beneath which is animal; beneath animal is rational animal, beneath which is human being; beneath human being are Socrates, Plato, and particular human beings. Of these, substance is the most generic, and that which is genus alone; human being is what is most specific and that which is species alone; body is a species of substance, but the genus of animal. Again, animal is a species of animate body, but genus of rational animal, while rational animal is a species of animal, but the genus of human being. Human being is a species of rational animal, but it is no longer the genus of particular human beings, but a species alone.]

There are genera and species in the case of all the categories, but substance is the most generic genus. Beneath it is body, and beneath body is animate (for he took this part of the division, leaving out [the part] of the incorporeal,[186] since sensible things are more familiar to us). Beneath animate there is animal, and beneath the latter is rational, and beneath it is human being. But substance is the most generic, and that which is genus alone (for nothing is prior to substance), while human being is most specific and that which is species alone (for nothing comes after human being among the universals), while body is both genus and species, but species of substance, and genus of animate. Animate is a species of body, but the genus of animal, for what is called animal is that which is animate and participates in sensation, while animate is that which is nourished and grows and generates something similar to itself. Thus, plants, which participate in these faculties, are animate, but are not animals as well. Oysters and sponges are animate, and in addition participate in the faculty of sensation (for when something hostile approaches them, they contract, and when it goes away they relax[187]).

In one respect they are similar to plants, i.e. by being rooted and nourishing themselves, and in another [they resemble] animals, i.e. by having sensation. Again, animal is a species of animate, and is the genus of rational, and rational is the genus of mortal, but a species of animal, and mortal is a species of rational, but the genus of human being.

4,32 Everything that is proximately predicated before the individuals would be a species alone, but no longer a genus as well. [Thus, as substance, which is the highest, was the most generic genus owing to the fact that there is nothing before it, so human being, which is a species, after which there is no species, or any of the things that can be cut into species, but the individuals (for Socrates, Plato, and this instance of white, are individuals), would be species alone, and the last species, and, as we said, the most specific one. The intermediate ones would be species of the ones that are before them, but genera of those that are after them.]

[He says] 'proximately' instead of 'right away', 'immediately', for animal, too, is before the individuals, but not immediately, but through the intermediary of human being. Human being, then, is proximately before the individuals, and is a species alone. 20

5,7 Thus, these things have two relations, [one towards what is before them, according to which they are said to be their species, and the other towards what is after them, according to which they are said to be their genera. The extreme terms have one relation: the most generic one has the relation as towards the things that are beneath it, since it is the highest genus of them all, but it no longer has the one towards the things before it, since it is the highest, and like a first principle, and, as we said, above which here would not be another higher one.]

Substance has one relation, i.e. the one to the things that are after it: it no longer has the one to the things before it, for there is nothing higher than substance. 80,1 Again, the species has one relation, i.e. to what is before it: it does not have one to what comes after it, for there is no species after it. The intermediate ones have two relations: one to what is before them, according to which they are called species, and one to what is after them. According to the first relation 5 they are called species, according to the second one, [they are called] genera. The extreme terms – both the most generic and the most specific – have one relation.

5,14 [The most specific one also has one relation: the one towards what is before it, of which it is the species, but it does not have a different one towards what is after] but it is also said to be the species of individuals, [but it is said to be the species of the individuals as containing them, but, again, the species of the things before it as being contained by them].

For the most specific species also has a certain relation to the individuals themselves, but it does not also have the same relation to what is before it. For 10 human being is not said to be the genus of Socrates and Plato, but the species, insofar as it contains the individuals.

5,17 However, they define what is most generic as follows: [that which, being a genus, is not a species, and again, that above which there would not be another higher genus. What is most specific is that which, being a species, is not a genus; and which, being a genus, we could not divide further into species; and that which is predicated essentially of several things that differ in number. Those which are intermediate between the extremes are called subordinate genera and species, and they hold that each of them is a species and a genus, albeit taken with regard to something different each time. The things that are before the most specific ones, going up as far as the most generic one, are called genera, species, and subordinate genera, as Agamemnon is an Atreid, and a Pelopid, and a Tantalid, and, finally, of Zeus.]

Having stated the most generic genus, and the subordinate ones, and the most specific species, for the rest he now describes them and says: what is the most generic genus? It is 'that which, being a genus, is not a species, and that beyond which there could not be another higher genus.'[188] What is the most specific? 'That which, being a species, is not a genus, and which we could not divide into species.'[189] What are the subordinate ones? Those that happen to be 'both genera and species'.[190] This, then, is what he wishes to discuss, and for the sake of clarity he takes up the example of genealogy. For he says that as in the case of genealogies, Zeus is a kind of principle and father alone, and not, for instance, a son, while Orestes, for instance, is only a son, and Agamemnon is the father of Orestes, but the son of Atreus, while Atreus is the father of Agamemnon, but the son of Pelops; so it is the case of the genus and species said among philosophers: some are only genera, such as substance, others only species, such as human being.

6,3 But in the case of genealogies, they usually trace back the principle to a single being: Zeus, for instance, [but in the case of genera and species this is not so; for being (*to on*) is not one common genus of all things, nor are all things homogeneous in accordance with one highest genus, as Aristotle says.]

The example may have inspired a difficulty in us, which Porphyry solves in advance. For one might suppose that perhaps, as in the case of genealogies, series almost go back to one principle, let us say Zeus (for mythology calls

Zeus the father of all beings, of men and of gods[191]), here too, all the categories go back to some one principle, such as that of being (*on*). After all, substance (*ousia*) is extant (*on*), as is the quantified, and the other categories. And if this is so, then there will no longer be ten most generic genera, but being will be some one common genus of all. Having pointed this out, then, Porphyry says that being is not the genus of the categories.

That being is not the genus of the ten categories, we shall prove as follows. Everything that is divided is divided either (1) as genera into species – as when we say that of animals, one is horse, another dog, and another human being – or (2) as a whole into parts. The latter is twofold: for it is divided either into similar parts or into dissimilar parts: divided into similar parts are veins, arteries, and bones, for these things, when they are divided, have their parts similar to each other and to the whole. [Divided] into dissimilar parts are when we say that of the body, one part is the head, another the hand, another the foot. Or (3) as a homonymous word [is divided] into different meanings, as when we say, 'of dog, one kind is terrestrial, another marine, another astral'.[192] If, then, it were shown that being is not divided into the categories either as genus into species or as whole into parts, it remains that it is sectioned into various meanings like a homonymous word.

That it is not divided as genus into species is clear from this: when the genus is divided into species, it is equally present to all its species, and among the species nothing prior and posterior is observed with regard to participation in the genus, for a human being is not more of an animal than a horse. Again, if one species is eliminated, it is not necessary for the remaining species to be eliminated, for if human being is eliminated, animal is not eliminated, nor are the remaining species, such as horse, dog, and the others. If, then, being is divided into the ten categories like a genus into species, there should not have been first and second among them, nor should one of them participate more in being, and another less. As things are, however, the prior and the posterior do exist, for we say that substance is prior, and the remaining ones come after it, since once it is eliminated, the accidents are eliminated along with it. Hence, we say that it participates in being to a greater extent, since substance gives their being to accidents (for they subsist in it), and it does not need things that occur accidentally to it in order to exist. The accidents, however, would not exist if that to which they occur did not exist: for that which occurs to something as an accident presupposes that to which it occurs. Therefore, being is not divided into the ten categories as a genus into species, for if one species is eliminated, the genus would not be eliminated, as we have said. As things are, however, if substance is eliminated, the other categories are also eliminated, for they have their being in it. Therefore, being is not divided like a genus, so that being cannot be divided into the ten categories as a genus into species.

I say that it cannot [be divided] as a whole into parts either, for this is divided either as something consisting of similar parts, or as something consisting of dissimilar parts, as has been said. That which consists of similar parts is that which has its parts similar to the whole, so that the parts are named by the name of the whole and do not differ from one another at all. For the parts of wood are each called 'wood', and do not differ from one another at all.

Similarly, a part of a sinew is called by the word for the whole, and [so is the part of] flesh and a vein. It is therefore impossible for being, as something consisting of similar parts, to be divided into the ten categories, for the parts, that is, the categories, although they are called by the appellation of the whole – for all of them are called beings – nevertheless differ from one another in name and reality, and are not similar to one another.

For substance signifies one thing, and the quantified another. Again, that which is divided as consisting of dissimilar parts does not have its parts named by the appellation of the whole, which parts also differ from one another. For instance, the parts of a face are the nose and eyes, which are neither called by the name of the whole, nor are they similar to one another, for we would not say a nose is a face, nor is an eye. Thus, being cannot be divided as something consisting of dissimilar parts, either. For if the parts, too, are different from one another in name and in reality, and for this reason, being will appear to consist of dissimilar parts, nevertheless the parts are called by the name of the whole – for substance, and the quantified, and the qualified are extant (*on*). But things consisting of dissimilar parts are not called by the name of the whole. If, then, being cannot be divided into the ten categories either as something consisting of similar parts or as something consisting of dissimilar parts, but it has been shown that [it cannot be divided] as genus into species, either, it remains that it is divided as a homonymous word into various meanings.

6,6 But let it be assumed, as in the *Categories*, [that the ten primary genera are like ten primary principles].

Let it now be supposed, he says, that there are ten principles of things and, as it were, ten genera. For to demonstrate that there are only ten principles pertains to another more perfect discipline, for in the *Categories*, it is shown that there are ten of them. For the moment, however, let it be merely supposed, as if agreed upon.

> **6,8** Indeed, even if one called them all 'beings', he will do so homonymously, he says, not synonymously. [For if being were the one common genus of all, all would be called beings synonymously. But since the first ones are ten, the commonality is according to the name alone, but not also according to the account that is in accordance with the name. The generic things are thus ten, but the most specific ones are in some number, but not infinite.]

Homonyms are what shares in the same name, but does not also participate in the same reality that is signified by the name, such as the astral and the terrestrial dog. For sharing in the name, they differ in the realities signified by the names. Synonyms are those things whose name is common, as is the definition according to the name, as for instance human being and horse are each an animal. After all, they have a common name, that of animal, and the same definition, the one that corresponds to animal, which is 'animate, sensitive substance'. He says, then, that although we call them all beings, we are speaking homonymously, not synonymously. For as has been said, homonyms are that which share in the name alone, while synonyms are that [which share in] both the name and the definition. Being, then, provides only a commonality of name to what is beneath it – for the ten categories are said to be beings – but they do not also share with each other according to the definition of the name. For another category, insofar as it has being, has received another name and the definition corresponding to the name. Hence, being is divided as a homonymous word into the ten most generic categories: into substance, quantified, qualified, relative, where, when, acting, being-acted-upon, being-in-a-position, having.

> **6,15** Individuals, which come after the most specific things, are infinite. [Therefore, when we descend from the most generic things, Plato ordered us to stop at the level of the most specific things, but to descend through the things that are in the middle, dividing by the specific differences.]

He says they are infinite, not in being, but because they come into being again and again. [He says:] 'by the specific differences' instead of 'by the essential differences', such as animal into rational and irrational; for there are also non-essential differences.

6,16 He says to let the infinite things go, for there can be no knowledge of them.

Plato says this in the *Sophist*,[193] for science wishes to take the *definiendum*. Thus, what cannot be comprehended cannot be knowable. Indeed, as was shown in the *Demonstration*,[194] there is neither definition nor knowledge of singulars, but only of universals.

6,16 Descending towards the most specific things, [we must go through a multitude by dividing]

He said that being is not the genus of the most generic things, which are limited by nature and known to us. He wishes, then, to investigate with regard to the most specific species, whether the same holds true of them as of the most generic genera.

He says, then, that the most generic things have a number that is both limited and known to us – for there are ten most generic genera – whereas the most specific species – such as human being, horse, ox, dog, vine, olive tree, after which comes the division of individuals – while also limited in their nature, are unknown to us, since they occur in various places. That they are limited, however many they may be, we shall prove by making an evident assumption: that there is no greater multitude than the infinite. This having been assumed beforehand, let it be supposed that the most specific species are infinite. Since there are several individuals for each species – for the human species, although it is one, is divided into countless equal individuals, i.e. particular human beings, and similarly the equine species, although one, has a great many individuals beneath it, and the same holds true of each of the rest – it is clear to all that the sum total of individuals exceeds the entire total of species by many times. If the individuals beneath the species are many times as numerous as the species, but the number of most specific species is infinite, then the number of individuals is greater than the infinite number of species, and many times so. Since, then, it is impossible for anything to be many times as many as the infinite, or in general greater than it, it is impossible for the number of species to be infinite. For by the very fact of saying that one number is greater than another, we define and limit the lesser one, for that which is greater than something is greater by some excess, so that when the excess is removed, the remainder is defined and limited. It has thus been shown that the most specific species are not infinite.

Likewise, we will show that the individuals that are beneath the most specific things are not infinite either, although they are many times as numerous as the species. For if someone says that the individuals are infinite, either he will say that the individuals beneath each species are infinite – as, for instance, that those of the human species are infinite in and for themselves; likewise, that the individuals of the equine species are also infinite; and likewise those that are beneath each of the remaining species – or else he says that the individuals beneath each species are limited, but that the total of all the individuals together that are beneath all the species is infinite. If, then, he says that the individuals beneath each species are infinite, once again it will follow that something is greater than the infinite, and many times greater than it. For since particular human beings are infinite, and particular horses are infinite, the sum of both of them will be twice the infinite, and the sum of all of them will be many times as many, which is absurd. It is therefore impossible for the individuals beneath each species to be infinite. If, on the other hand, the individuals beneath each species are limited, then the multitude made up of all of them is also finite, for that which is made up of finite things is also finite. Thus, the number of individuals is finite, but they have their infinity by the fact that they continuously come into being into the All, which is perpetual, as number too is said to be infinite by the fact that it can always be increased and never be exhausted, whereas the one that is taken in actuality is always limited. Likewise, it is shown that sand is finite; hence the oracle:[195]

I know the number of the sand and the measures of the sea,

For if [the number of individuals] were infinite, since the number of human beings and the number of horses, when added to it,[196] makes the sum of both greater than either one, then there will be something greater than the infinite, which is impossible. Thus, the most specific things are determinate by nature, but are unknown to us; while individuals are indeterminate by nature, owing to the fact that they come into being again and again. To us, however, the things that come into being and are in actuality, and the things that have already come

into being, if coming-into-being had a beginning,[197] although it is not known
how many they are, still they could have been known[198] as far as their nature is
concerned, like the most specific species, since it has been shown that their
number is determinate.

> **6,18** But ascending to the most generic things, it is necessary to gather the multitude into one.

Here, Porphyry wants to say what happens to those who rise from the most specific things to the most generic, and what [happens to] those who descend from the most generic to the most specific.

> **6,19** [For the species,] And even more so the genus, [is a gatherer of the many into one nature, whereas the particulars and the individuals, on the contrary, always divide the one into multiplicity. For it is by participation in the form that the many men are one, while by the particulars the one and common [one] is many. For the individual is always divisive, whereas the common is comprehensive and unifying.]

For the species contains the particulars, while the genus [contains] the species as well. For to those who are ascending from the individuals below to the most generic things, things are contracted in multitude, but increased in power; because species are fewer than individuals in multitude, but exceed them in power and in increase. Likewise, genera are [fewer] than species, until we arrive at the most generic one. And rightly so: since the cause and principle of all things is one, for this reason, what comes near to it is contracted in multitude, but is increased in power; while conversely that which is farther from it is multiplied in number, but diminished in power.

> **6,24** Having given an account of what each of the genus and the species is, [and since the genus is one, and the species are many – for the genus is always sectioned into several species – the genus is always predicated of the species].

Porphyry has promised[199] to teach about the words under discussion in a more logical way, that is, in a way that is suitable to the discipline of logic. Now, after teaching what each of the genus and the species is, he wishes to add how the consideration of them is useful in the discipline of logic. For the discipline of logic is concerned with demonstration, but demonstration is a kind of syllogism, and in the syllogism we need premises, but the premise consists of two terms, one of which is subject and the other predicate, and the subject is that which the discourse is about, while the predicate is the one that is said about it. For instance, 'Socrates walks' – for Socrates is the subject which the discourse is about, while walking, which is said of him, is predicated. Again, if I say that the soul is self-moving, the soul acts as the subject, while self-moved is predicated, and the same holds true of every premise.

With regard to genera and species, he wishes to say which ones are predicated of which, and which act as subject for which. So that we may know how, when combined, they make premises, out of which the syllogism comes about, with which the discipline of logic is concerned, he says that the genus is always predicated of the species, such as animal of human being and substance of animal, but the species is never predicated of the genus. For it is not true to say that substance is an animal, or that animal is a human being. It is clear, then, that genera are always predicated of species, but species are never [predicated] of genera. In sum, predicates must either have greater extension than the subjects, as animal than human being, or be coextensive, as capable of laughing (*to gelastikon*) [is coextensive] with human being. Things that are coextensive are convertible: for as we say 'all human beings are capable of laughter', so all that is capable of laughter is a human being.

> 7,2 and all that is above of what is below, [but the species [is neither predicated] each of its proximate genus nor of what is above it; for they do not reciprocate. For either what is equal must be predicated of what is equal, as capable of neighing [is predicated] of horse, or what is greater of what is less, as animal of man, but what is less [is] not also [predicated] of what is greater, for you would not also say that animal is a human being.]

For instance, as substance [is predicated] of the body, and the body of what is animate, and the animate of animal, and animal of human being.

> 7,8 The genus of the species is necessarily predicated of whatever the species is predicated of, [as is the genus of the genus, until one reaches what is most generic. For if it is true to say that Socrates is a human being, and human being is an animal, and animal is a substance, then it is also true to say that Socrates is an animal and a substance. Since, then, the higher things are always predicated of the lower things, the species will be predicated of the individual, the genus of both the species and the individual, and what is

most generic both of the genus or genera, if the middle and subordinate ones are several, and of the species and of the individual.]

He imparts another theorem, which is also useful for the discipline of logic. It is as follows: if the species is predicated of something, then the genus of its species will be predicated of the same thing, and this takes place as far as the most generic [genus]. For instance, human being is predicated of Socrates, and animal is predicated of human being. Therefore, [animal] will be predicated of Socrates as well. Likewise, animated [is predicated] of animal; therefore, [animated is predicated] of human being and of Socrates as well. Again, body [is predicated] of the animate, and substance of body, and therefore substance and body will be predicated of animate, animal, human being, and Socrates.

7,16 For what is most generic is said of all the genera, species, and individuals beneath it [whereas the genus that is before the most specific one [is said] of all the most specific ones and the individuals; that which is a species alone [is said] of all the individuals; and the individual of only one of the particulars].

For if what is above is always predicated of what is below, it is clear that what is most generic will be predicated of all the genera, species, and individuals that are beneath it, while the species [will be predicated] of individuals alone.

7,19 What is called an individual is Socrates and this [instance of] white, [and this approaching son of Sophroniscus, if Socrates was his only son].

By adding 'this' he made what is designated particular, for white is a universal.[200]

7,22 [Such things are called individuals because each of them consists of properties] the aggregate of which could never be the same in the case of another.

He did not say 'each one of which', but 'the aggregate of which', for each one can belong to other things as well, but all of them together to none.

7,24 [For the properties of Socrates could never be the same in another of the particulars.] But the properties of human being, I mean the common one, could be the same [in the case of several, or rather in the case of all particular human beings, qua human beings].

The properties of Socrates could not be the same in the case of anything else, while those of human being belong to particular human beings as well, such as rational mortal animal, and in general, whatever you wish to mention, is such. It should be known, then, that the genus has certain properties, as does the species and the individual; yet those of the genus and the species can belong to several things, while those of the individual, when taken in the aggregate, [can belong] only to that individual and to nothing else. What do I mean by this? There are properties of the genus, such as [those] of animal: substance, animate, sensitive. Yet these belong to several things, for [they belong] to human being, and to horse, and to dog, and to particular animals.

Let us move on to the species, such as human being. Its properties are animal, rational, receptive of knowledge: all of these belong to all human beings.

Let us move on to the individual, such as Socrates. His properties are: philosopher, bald, being pot-bellied, son of Sophroniscus, Athenian, and so on. Taken by itself, then, each of these can belong to others as well – for there are other bald men and snub-nosed men and philosophers and Athenians, and perhaps even sons of Sophroniscus – but the aggregate of all of them – bald, philosopher, snub-nosed, being pot-bellied, and having come to be in such-and-such a time – belongs to Socrates alone, and to no one else.

> **7,27** [Thus, the individual is contained beneath the species,] the species beneath the genus. For the genus is a kind of whole,

For the genus is exclusively a whole, and the individual exclusively a part. The species is both whole and part: a whole with regard to the individual, and a part with regard to the genus.

> **8,2** [and the individual is a part, while the species is a whole and a part,] but a part of one thing, and a whole not of another thing, but in other things, [for a whole is in the parts.

Since whole and part belong to the relatives, and of relatives, we say some of them in the nominative case, some in some of the oblique cases. For instance, a father is the father of a son: here, the construction is in the genitive, but the construction is in the dative if I say 'the friend is a friend to a friend,' and it is in the accusative if I say, 'the striker strikes what is struck.' It is because of this is so that he said 'a part of one thing', while the 'whole' is 'in other things'; for we say that a part is a part of a whole, and of course we give the construction in the genitive, but we no longer say a whole is a whole of a part – for the whole is not made up of one part but of many – but we say that the whole is a whole to its parts, and the construction is given in the dative, for the whole is a whole to its parts. He was right, then, to say that 'the whole is not of another thing but in other things'. It should be known, however, that it is also possible to give the construction in the genitive – not the singular but the plural – and to say: 'the whole is a whole of parts', but Porphyry follows the common usage when he gives the construction in the dative.

8,5 [The genus and the species, and what is the most specific,] and which are both genera and species,

These are the subordinate ones, for these are both genera and species.

8,5 [and what are individuals,] and in how many ways the genus and the species [are said, have now been discussed].

The genus is said in three senses, and the species in two.

On the Difference

8,8 Let the difference be said in the common sense, in the proper sense, and in the most proper sense.[201]

That the difference is prior to the species, and for what reason he discussed the species first has already been said. Now, therefore, he discusses the difference, and using the aforementioned rule once again, he enumerates the meanings of 'difference'. So that we can understand what is to be said, however, let us say the following: a difference is the otherness of some things with regard to others. This otherness is therefore either separable and accidental, of such a nature as to be separated from those things whose otherness it is, or inseparable. For instance, some people differ from one another by the fact that one is standing and another sitting, and the one who is sitting can stand and the one who is standing can sit, and they differ from one another in this regard. This difference is said to be separable, and Porphyry calls it 'in the common sense', since it does not belong to one particular thing determinately, but in common to all.

This [difference] is separable and accidental. If the difference is inseparable, it is either per se, that is, completive of the substance of the substrate, or accidental, that is, contributing nothing to the being of the thing. This [difference] is inseparable and accidental, such as hookedness, snubness, greyness [of the eyes], for some people differ from each another by the fact that one is snub-nosed and the other hook-nosed. Yet these [differences] are accidental, since they are not completive of the substrates – for Socrates might not have been snub-nosed, and still be Socrates – but inseparable – for they are not by nature such as to be separated from the substrate. Porphyry calls these 'in the proper sense', since snub-nosed belongs determinately to this particular individual.

Inseparable and not accidental, but completive of substance, are for instance rational and mortal; for we differ from irrational animals in that we are rational, while they are irrational. He called this difference 'in the most proper sense'. Of difference, then, one is said in a common way, another in the proper sense, and another in the most proper sense. [Said] in a common way are those that are accidental and separable; [said] in a proper sense are those that are accidental and inseparable, while those that are inseparable and completive of the substance of the substrate, and are per se, are said to be in the most proper sense.

This, then, is the first division of the differences. Again, subdividing them, he says that 'of differences, some make the substrate of a different sort (*alloion*), others make it something else (*allo*)'.[202] The difference said in a common and proper sense makes it different in sort – for sitting and standing are different in sort, and snub-nosed and hook-nosed are different in sort, while the ones [said] in the most proper sense make it something else (*allo*); for the rational is one thing, and the irrational is something else. For what is different in sort causes a variation in something that belongs to the thing, while what is other (*allo*) makes [a thing] necessarily other (*heteron*), for a rational animal is other than an irrational one, but a sitting person is not something other (*allo*) than a standing person, but is something different in sort (*alloion*), and similarly with the hook-nosed and the snub-nosed person. Thus, since differences are said in three senses, some in the common sense, some in the proper sense, and some in the most proper sense, what philosophers talk about are the most proper ones, for the ones [said] in a proper and a common sense are not useful for the division of genera. For no one says that of animals, some are sitting and others are standing (for we do not include all of them[203]); nor [do we say] that some are snub-nosed and others hook-nosed, for the same reason. But if they are not useful for division, then neither are they [useful] for definitions. Thus, only the most proper ones are useful.

> **8,8** And let [the difference] be said in [a common sense, a proper sense, and] a most proper sense.

By adding 'let it be said' (*legesthô*), he signified that he himself coined this name. For the ancients were accustomed, when they used a current name, to say 'it is said' (*legetai*), but when they themselves coin names, they were accustomed to say 'let it be called' (*kaleisthô*) or 'let it be said' (*legesthô*).

> **8,10** [One thing is said to differ from another in the common sense which differs in some way by otherness, either with regard to itself or with regard to something else.] For Socrates differs from Plato by otherness.

For insofar as they are human beings, they do not differ at all, but insofar as one may be sitting, for instance, and the other walking, they differ.

> **8,12** [and himself from himself when he is a boy and a grown man, and performing some activity or ceasing [to do so],] and always in the othernesses of relative disposition.[204] [One thing is said to differ from another in the proper sense, when one differs from another by an inseparable difference. An inseparable accident is for instance having grey eyes, or being hook-nosed, or even a scar that has hardened from a wound.]

That is, these differences are observed accidentally. But instead of saying 'accidentally', he said 'in the diversities of relative disposition', since the accident is predicated in the [category of] what is in a certain state.

> **8,16** [One thing is said to differ from another in the most proper sense when it diverges by a specific difference,] as human being differs from horse by the specific difference that is the quality of being rational.

That is, the one that is completive of the species. For animal, when it takes on rational and mortal, produces human being, while mortal and irrational produce horse, dog, and the other animals. These differences, then, when combined with the genera, produce the species, and this is why they are called 'specific'.

8,19 [In general, then, every difference makes [a thing] diverse, when it attaches itself to something; but the common and proper ones make [a thing] of another sort, while the most proper ones make it other, for] of differences, some make a thing other, others make it of a different sort.[205]

He sets forth another division of the differences. Some, he says, make [a thing] other (*allo*), and others make it of a different sort (*alloion*). Those that make [a thing] something else are per se, while those [that make it] of a different sort are accidental and separable. They call 'separable' the one that [is said] in a common sense, and the one [that is said] in a proper sense. This one is also separable conceptually, for I can conceive of Socrates both as bald and with hair on his head. The one [that is said] in the most proper sense, in contrast, I cannot separate from him even conceptually, for it is not possible to conceive of human being outside of rational, since he would no longer be a human being, for all human beings are rational, and all are mortal. Thus, I can think of a snub-nosed person as hook-nosed, with the person remaining the same human being, but I cannot think of human being outside of rational or mortal, for he would no longer be a human being. Thus, the differences that are said in the proper and common sense are separable. For when a standing person sits down, he has not become other, but merely different in sort, as the poet indicates about Odysseus, who has been transformed by Athena with regard to the accidents that occur to him, when he says:[206]

'You seem different (*alloios*) to me now, stranger, than awhile ago.'

For he did not say 'other' (*allos*), but 'different in sort' (*alloios*). But in fact if a snub-nosed person were conceived as hook-nosed, he would not become other because of this, but of a different sort, for he can be the same [person]. Those [differences] that make [someone] other are specific, for rational does not make a human being of a different sort from a horse, but other: for we call 'other' the things that differ in substance, as we just said, such as human being and horse.

9,2 [Those that make [it] other are called specific, and those [that make it] of another sort [are called] simply differences. For when a difference, that of rational, is added to animal, it makes it other, while that of moving makes it only of a different sort with regard to what remains still, so that one makes [a thing] other, and another merely of a different sort.] It is according to the differences that make something other that the divisions of genera to species take place, [and that definitions are given, which derive from the genus and such differences. It is in accordance with the ones that merely make [a thing] of a different sort that the othernesses alone are constituted, and the changes of the relatively disposed.]

For we say that of animal, one part is rational and the other irrational, and one part is mortal and another part immortal. Again, we give definitions by means of these, for we say: what is a human being? A rational, mortal animal, receptive of intellect and knowledge.

9,7 [Again, beginning from above, it should be said that] of differences, some are separable, and others inseparable, [for moving and staying still, and being healthy and being ill, and whatever is similar to these are separable, while being hooked-nosed or snub-nosed or rational or irrational are inseparable].

Here, once again, he begins the more complete division, as if from some principle with a view to separating them from each other. Of differences, then, some are separable and others inseparable, and by this the differences commonly [so called] are distinguished from the ones [so called] in the proper and most proper sense. Again, of differences, some make [things] other, others [make them] of a different sort, and by this the differences [so called] in the most proper sense are distinguished from the ones [so called] in the proper and common sense. From these oppositions, then, by which the differences are distinguished from each other, there come about six combinations,[207] two of which, by common agreement, are non-existent, for separable and inseparable do not exist, or [difference that makes things] of different quality and other. Of the remaining four combinations, one is non-existent – the one that is separable and makes [things] other – while the remaining three do exist. Those that are separable and make [things] of a different sort are the ones [that are said] in the common sense; those that are inseparable and make [things] other are the ones [said] in the most proper sense; and those that are inseparable and [make things] of a different sort are the accidental ones and [are said] in the proper sense, such as hooked-nosedness. It might seem that there is something else different: [the class] of [differences] that are separable and make [things] other, but the truth is that this combination is also non-existent. For rational belongs to human being per se – for human being is rational per se, therefore all human beings are rational – while hook-nosed, or black, or standing, or anything similar, is not per se. For it is not insofar as one is a human being that he is hook-nosed, or black, or any of the rest, since if this were the case all human beings would have to be black or hook-nosed. Thus, although someone is hook-nosed or black, he is no less of a human being. Therefore, no such difference makes any thing other. It is therefore non-existent.

> **9,14** [Of the inseparable ones, some are per se, others accidental; for rational belongs to human being per se, as does mortal and being receptive of knowledge, while being hooked-nosed or snub-nosed is accidental, not per se. For those [differences] that belong per se] are taken up into the account of the substance [and make [the thing] other, while those that are accidental are not taken up into the account of the substance, nor do they make [a thing] other, but of a different sort].

[He says this] instead of 'in the account that indicates the nature of the thing', that is, in the definition. For definitions come from the genus and the constitutive differences, that is, the specific ones, which are not susceptible of more and less. For no one is said to be more rational or more mortal or less rational or less mortal. Indeed, even small children are similarly rational, but they are prevented by their instrument[208] from rational activities. In general, it should be known that those things are susceptible of more and less which are contraries and exist in conjunction with the same substrates, and which mix with one another. For instance, something white becomes more or less white than something white, since the same substrate sometimes becomes white, sometimes black, and these things mix with one another, I mean the white with the black, and it so happens that they become more pure in one place and mingled in another. In the case of substances, there is no more or less, since there is nothing contrary to substance.[209] Neither do the rational and the irrational exist in conjunction with the same substrate.

If someone were to say: 'why, then, did Aristotle say in the *Categories* that "substance is the one that is said in the most proper sense, primarily, and most of all"?[210] Indeed, he said "most of all" as if it were susceptible of the more and less'. We say, first of all, that this is said with regard to our knowledge; for he said that individual [substance] is primary and most of all because it is more familiar to us, and is the first to be apprehended. For from it, advancing in time and knowledge, we proceed to the second one as well, which is by genera and species. Therefore, even if one agreed that the more and the less is in them, it will not be in the horizontal ones, but in the vertical ones.[211] For a human being is not more human than a human being, or more rational, nor is a horse more of an animal than an ox, nor a human being [more of an animal] than these, but in the vertical ones, as I said, it is somehow possible to observe this. For those that are above are more clear, the more they partake of the superior things: for instance, rational is more so in the intellect, less so in the soul, and more so among the angels,[212] less so in the heavenly bodies, if they too are animate and rational, and if this is so, more so in them than in us.

Otherwise:[213] substance is more so in animal than in human being, and more in the latter than in Socrates. For since substance does not [accrue] immediately to Socrates, but through the intermediary of animal, and from the latter, once again, through the intermediary of human being, it is obvious that the things that participate in something primarily and immediately participate more than the secondary things that participate through an intermediary, and it has been well said that the horizontal [differences] are not susceptible of more and less, while the vertical ones are susceptible of them. For if the horizontal ones were susceptible of the more and less, they – I mean rational and irrational and mortal and immortal – would not have the same distance from the genus.

9,17 [Those that are per se are not susceptible of more and less, while those [differences] that are] accidental, even if they are inseparable, take on intensification and remission.

[He says this] instead of 'are susceptible of more and less'. These names have been taken metaphorically from strings, for in that domain a tightened string produces an intense sound, and a loosened one a lesser sound. Thus, the philosophers call 'intensification' an intense apprehension of a thing, and 'remission' a lesser one.

9,20 [For neither is the genus predicated more or less of that of which it is the genus, nor are the differences of the genus, by which it is divided,] for these are the [differences] that complete the account of each one.

The differences that are completive of the substance; but these are also completive of definitions. Definitions of the same thing are always the same, for a human being is not sometimes a rational animal and sometimes not, but always identical, not susceptible of intensification or remission.

9,22 [while the being of each thing is one and the same, not admitting intensification or remission, while being hooked-nosed or snub-nosed] or being coloured in some way [are both intensified and relaxed].

That is, being black or white, for these are intensified and slackened. For one thing is more white or more black than another. 15

9,24 Thus, since three species of differences are observed, and some of them are separable, others inseparable, and again, of inseparable ones, some are per se, and others accidental; [again, of the per se differences, some are those by which we divide genera into species, and others by which the things that are divided are specified. For instance, [of] all the differences of animal being, such as animate and sensitive, rational and irrational, mortal and immortal, the [difference] of animate and sensitive is constitutive of the substance of animal. For animal is an animate, sensitive substance, while the difference of mortal and immortal, and that of rational and irrational, are divisive differences of animal, for it is through them that genera are divided into species. Yet these divisive differences become completive of the genera, and constitutive of the species; for animal is sectioned by the difference of rational and irrational, and again by the difference of mortal and immortal. But the differences of mortal and rational become constitutive of the human being, those of rational and immortal of god, those of irrational and mortal of the irrational animals. Thus, since both the difference of animate and inanimate and of sensitive and insensitive are divisive of the highest substance, the [difference] of animal and sensitive, taken together with substance, produce animal, while [the difference of] animate and insensitive produce plant. Since, then, the same ones, taken in one way, become constitutive, and [taken in] another way, become divisive, all of them are called specific.]

Porphyry promised to teach about the matters at hand in a more logical way. 20
Here too, however, he wishes to teach, from the differences, some things that contribute to the definitional and divisional method. Thus, he says that of specific differences some are constitutive, others divisive, not different ones in each case, but the same ones become constitutive in one respect, divisive in 99,1 another, when they are taken up in different ways. For rational and irrational,

and mortal and immortal, are differences of animal, and they are divisive, for animal is divided into them. But when the ones that can be combined are taken together, such as rational and mortal, they become differences that are constitutive of the human being, for they constitute and complete its nature. It is thus clear that the divisive differences are useful for the divisive method, since it is by them that the divisions of genera into species take place, while the constitutive ones [are useful] for the definitional [method], since definitions are from genera and differences such as these.

It should be known that when they are combined, these [differences] produce four combinations,[214] three of which exist and one of which is non-existent. For instance, let there be rational and irrational, mortal and immortal. Now rational and mortal exists, for it is a human being, while a god is rational and immortal, a horse is irrational and mortal, but there is nothing irrational and immortal. There is debate about the remaining combination, I mean that of irrational and immortal, whether it exists and there is something irrational and immortal, as the poet seems to say about Scylla:

'But it is an immortal evil',[215]

or not. For some say that there is an immortal genus of irrational demons, which occupy a lesser rank, and which we try to avert. Others say that this genus is also mortal, for that which is immortal is necessarily also rational.

Let us move on to substance, and we will find the same things. Here too, there are two oppositions, animate and inanimate, sensitive and insensitive, and when they are combined, only three combinations exist, while the remaining one is non-existent. For what is animate and sensitive is an animal, what is animate and insensitive is a plant, what is inanimate and insensitive is a stone, but nothing is inanimate and sensitive. For that which has sense, has a fortiori a natural soul. For where it is natural, it is not necessarily sensitive as well, but where it is sensitive, it is necessarily natural as well.

These, at any rate, are the divisive differences of genera. For as some things are only species, and others both genera and species, so it is with differences. For of specific differences, some are only divisive – those of the most generic things; others are only constitutive – those of the most specific things; while others are both constitutive and divisive, i.e. those of subordinate things. For the differences of substance, I mean body and incorporeal, are only divisive of substance, but by no means constitutive. The differences of human being, such as rational and mortal, are only constitutive of the human being, whereas those of the intermediary ones, such as those of animal, mortal and immortal, rational and irrational, are both constitutive and divisive.[216] For[217] contrary [differences] are divisive of animal, such as mortal and immortal,[218] and likewise rational and irrational, for animal is divided into them. The same holds true of rational and irrational. The subordinate ones are constitutive of the species: for rational and mortal are constitutive of the human being, rational and immortal of angel,[219] irrational and mortal of the horse, while those of irrational and mortal [are constitutive] of irrational animals. Porphyry omitted irrational and immortal, since it is a matter of dispute whether such substances exist or not. For as I said, there are the irrational demons, occupying a lesser rank in the All and assigned to punishing deserving souls, and they are considered by some to be immortal, by others to be mortal.

10,19 The greatest usefulness of these is for the divisions of genera, [and for definitions, but not of the accidental inseparable ones, or a fortiori of the separable ones]

He added 'the greatest', because often, when we are at a loss for such differences owing to human weakness, we take up some of the accidental ones.

For instance, in the case of a crow, we take black instead of a difference, and in the case of a swan [we take] white; as when defining a horse, we say it is an irrational animal capable of neighing, we take the property, which is adventitious, instead of an essential difference, since it is not possible to discover an essential difference between a horse, for instance, and a donkey.

10,22 Defining them, we say: the difference is that by which the species exceeds the genus.

Having enumerated the meanings of 'difference', and said which meaning the philosophers most discuss, he wishes to give a description of it. Thus, he says that the difference is that by which the species exceeds the genus. For human being exceeds animal by rational and by mortal. Yet Porphyry raises a difficulty on the basis of this definition, and solves it. Prior to the difficulty, however, he takes up two clear axioms, so called by the Peripatetics because they have their trustworthiness in themselves.[220] These axioms are as follows: first, that nothing comes into being from what does not exist in any way; thus, a counting board has come into being out of wood, which was existent in one sense – for it was wood – but in another sense was non-existent, for it was not a counting board yet. If it were, it would not have needed a carpenter to make it; and stones are existents in one sense, as stones, but in another sense are not existents, because they are not yet a house. Yet how could something come into being from what does not exist in any way? Second, that it is not possible for contraries to be together in the same substrate at the same time, for contraries tend to annihilate one another.

These things having been stated beforehand, the difficulty proceeds in this way: the differences must accrue to the species either from the genus, in which they pre-exist, or from what does not exist in any way. But each of these is absurd; for if the differences are in the genera, contraries will be in the same thing at the same time – mortal and immortal, rational and irrational – which is absurd. For they cannot come from something else, because there is not anything else between the genus and the species, unless it is the differences. Clearly, then, this argument is most difficult.

Having raised the difficulty, however, he solves it in a Peripatetic way. For Porphyry says that contraries cannot be in the same thing at the same time in actuality, but they can be potentially. In order for what is said to become clear, let us say the following: it is one thing to be something potentially, and another to be something in actuality; for what is said to be potentially is incomplete and has not been brought to actuality, but is capable and is suitably disposed to be brought to actuality. For example, a child is potentially literate, for he can become literate, and cold water is said to be potentially hot. This, then, is what is [said to be] potentially. Said to be literate in actuality is he who has already been perfected in the knowledge of literacy according to his disposition, and has imparted the doctrines of reading and writing; and cold water is said to be potentially hot, while water that has been heated is said to be hot in actuality. He says, then, that it is impossible for contraries, such as cold and hot, to be present to something simultaneously in actuality, but it is possible [for them to be present] potentially. For lukewarm water is neither hot nor cold in actuality, but it is both potentially; and an infant potentially has both virtue and vice, and matter is potentially all the contraries. If, then, the genus occupies the position of matter, as he says subsequently,[221] it will clearly have all the contrary differences within it potentially. There is also another way in which it is possible for contraries to be in one thing: if it has one in actuality and the other potentially. For what is cold in actuality is potentially hot, if it is of such a nature as to change into something hot. He said this because there are some things that are receptive of only one of the opposites. For ice, which is cold, could never become hot, nor could fire receive the contrary cooling. Air, however, and water, are receptive of each of the contraries alternatively, for contraries can be present simultaneously in the same thing potentially. For if it did not have both potentially, it would not change into both in actuality; but since it has the contraries potentially, this is why it changes into both alternatively. Thus, he says, genera also have contrary differences potentially, and they do not come into being out of what does not exist in any way, nor are contraries in the same thing in actuality. This is the solution used by those from the Peripatos, and it is the one Porphyry gave, since, as has already been said, he is writing the book to be useful for Aristotle's *Categories*.

It should be known that the Platonists oppose this solution. Indeed, they say that the differences are in the genera in actuality, and they say that one must not be afraid to suppose that rational and irrational, mortal and immortal are in the genera in actuality. To demonstrate this, they use the following arguments. In the first place, they say that rational is not contrary to irrational, nor mortal to immortal; for contraries destroy one another, but not only are these not destructive of one another, but they bring each other into existence. For rational and immortal bring mortal and irrational into existence: for god, being immortal and rational, brings into existence mortal and irrational things, and human being, who is rational, becomes the protector and saviour of the irrational, and angels, who are immortal, are the protectors and guardians of mortals. Thus, rational and irrational are not contraries, nor are mortal and immortal. But if they are not contraries, it is not impossible for these things to be together in the genus, since the irrational faculties – I mean ardour and desire and sensation and the rational life – are observed together in one animal, i.e. the human being. They then say that although they are contraries, there is nothing absurd about them being in the same genus in actuality, since they are not as in an underlying body, but in some incorporeal – for the genus is an incorporeal – but contraries can be in incorporeals. Contraries cannot be in some underlying body, because both tend to participate in the substrate. But since the body is divisible, it cannot receive things that are mutually destructive simultaneously and in the same respect. In the case of the incorporeals, this does not occur. Indeed, nature also possesses the rational formulae of all contraries and brings them into existence. For instance, the eye simultaneously projects the rational formulae of white and black, and the soul has simultaneously and at the same time the rational formula of contraries – of good and bad, cold and hot – since the knowledge of contraries is one.[222] Thus, nothing absurd follows from the argument that says that the differences are in the genera in actuality. Likewise, we cannot corporeally and at the same time make a triangle and a square and a sphere on a tablet, since the impressions are obliterated by one another, but in the soul we possess all these things without confusion, whence we project them without confusion and show the first theorem and the second and the third, and about the sphere and the square and the triangle. Thus, in the case of incorporeals, it is possible for contraries to be together in actuality. In addition, if the differences exist potentially in the genera, what made them be in actuality in the species? For everything that exists potentially is brought to actuality through something that is such in actuality. For cold water, which is potentially hot, becomes hot in actuality through fire, which is hot in actuality, and a child, who is potentially literate, becomes literate through a person who is literate in actuality. If, then, the differences are in the genera potentially, but are brought to actuality, they will need something else that has the differences in actuality. But there is nothing else besides them; therefore, the differences are not potentially in the genera.

Again, all that is potentially is imperfect, while that which is in actuality is perfect. If, then, the species have the differences in actuality, but the genera potentially, the most specific things will be the most perfect and honourable of all things, while the most generic will be the most imperfect and dishonourable of all; which is absurd, for effects would be more perfect and powerful than causes. It is therefore necessary for the differences to be in the genera in actuality.

Is the argument of the Peripatetics entirely to be rejected? Not at all, we say. For since genera are threefold, as we have often said,[223] the Platonists spoke about those that are before the many – for the differences exist in actuality in the genera that are before the many, since there the rational formulae of all things are in actuality – while the Peripatetics [speak] about those that are in the many. For it should be known that nature journeys from the more universal things to the more particular, and brings the particulars into existence beforehand potentially in the things that are more universal: for instance, from deposited sperm she first creates a piece of flesh in the womb, as the doctors say, which is a body. But the body is a universal. Yet as a body it is in actuality, but as an animate being it is potentially, for it is not yet animate in actuality. Yet when, having been nourished, it grows and is ensouled, it is said to be animate in actuality, but an animal potentially, since it has not yet received sensation and motion. Once it participates in these things, it becomes an animal in actuality. When it is expelled and participates in reason (*logos*), it becomes rational (*logikon*) in actuality. Behold, then: in the genera that are in the many, the differences are observed potentially, and the natural philosophers do well to speak in this way. Hence, since he had proposed to expound this work not as a contribution to Platonic studies but to Aristotelian ones, for this reason Porphyry made use of the solution of the Peripatetics.

We have already stated everything in advance, and the rest of the text is clear. Let us read it, then,[224] and if anything should come up, we will clarify it.

> **11,2** [For human being has more than animal, i.e. rational and mortal,] for it is not the case that animal is neither of these; [if it were, whence would the species derive differences?]

That is, [it is not the case that] it does not participate.[225] One must understand something like the following: if animal did not participate in rational and mortal, whence was it able to receive the species?

> **11,3** Nor [does it have] all the opposite [differences]

Otherwise, contraries would exist at the same time.

> **11,4** [otherwise the same thing will have opposites at the same time,] but as they consider [it has all the differences of the things beneath it potentially, but none of them in actuality. Thus, neither does anything come to be out of not-being, nor will opposites be in conjunction with the same thing at the same time.]

Since Porphyry is not saying what he believes as a Platonist, he said, 'as the Peripatetics consider', for when they speak about nature they rightly maintain in this way that universals first have particulars in potency, and thus they advance to actuality.

11,7 They also define it as follows: [a difference is that which is predicated qualitatively[226] of several things that differ in species. For rational and mortal are said to be predicated of human being in what-kind-of-thing a human being is, not in what-he-is. For when we are asked what a human being is, it is appropriate to say 'an animal', but when they inquire what kind of animal, we shall appropriately respond 'rational' and 'mortal'.]

10   Here, he states a complete description, taken from the division of words, which says that of words, some are meaningless, others meaningful.

11,12 For since things are made up of matter and form [or at least of things that are analogous to matter and form, as a statue is made of bronze as its matter, and its figure as its form]

He now gives the reason why the genus is predicated essentially,[227] while the difference [is predicated] qualitatively.[228] He says, then, that all beings either consist of matter and form in the proper sense of the terms, or have a
15   constitution analogous to matter and form. Indeed, to all natural things there is a substrate, which they call matter in the proper sense, and it is bereft of beauty and form. There is also form in the proper sense, that which sets [matter] in order and comes to be within it. This is how matter and form in the proper sense are conceived in natural things, and what is analogous [is conceived] in artificial things. For instance, a statue comes to be out of bronze;
20   therefore, the bronze is called matter, not in the proper sense, but analogously. For the bronze is not formless, but because it is spread out before the craftsman and receives the form of the statue, as does matter in the proper sense, for this reason it is called matter. Figure is also said to be analogous to the form, since it stamps its mark on the bronze. It is because some one matter underlies
107,1 natural things that everything transforms into one another.

But it would be impossible for all things to transform into one another if there were not one common matter underlying all things. That is certainly how bronze objects can transform into one another, since they have a common matter: for instance, from a cauldron into a statue. Things that do not have one matter cannot
5   transform into one another, for a drawing-tablet could never come to be out of a cauldron. But water comes to be out of air, and air out of water, and fire out of air, because their underlying matter is one. It is clear that when it has received cold and moisture it becomes water, [when it has received] warmth and dryness it

becomes fire, and likewise for the other [elements]. Thus, all natural things derive from matter in the proper sense and form, such as a human being, a horse, and so on, while artificial things are made of what is analogous to matter, for instance wood, and of what is analogous to form, [i.e.] such-and-such a figure. He says, therefore, that the genus plays the part of matter, and the differences [play the part] of form. For just as with respect to their substance bronze implements, for instance, do not differ at all from one another, but the difference comes to be with regard to the figure, so with regard to the genus, according to which we are animals, a human being, a horse, a dog, and the others do not differ at all, but they do differ with regard to the differences. For animal, once it has received rational and mortal, produces a human being, and again, having received irrational and mortal, it produces a horse. Thus, the genus is analogous to matter, while the differences [are analogous] to form. Since, then, matter provides being to each thing, while form [provides] being of such-and-such a kind, the genus is rightly predicated essentially, since it is analogous to matter, and the difference [is predicated] qualitatively, in that it is analogous to form.

> **11,15** [so] the common and specific [human being consists of an analogue of matter, i.e. the genus, and of the difference as its shape, while the whole of it, rational mortal animal, is a human being, as is the statue in the other case.]

The universal [human being] is common, while the singular is specific.

> **11,18** They also describe [such differences] as follows: the difference is of such a nature as to separate what is beneath the same genus. [For rational and irrational separate human being and horse, which are beneath the same genus, animal. They also give it as follows: the difference is that by which each thing differs. For a human being and a horse do not differ in genus, for both we and the irrational beings are mortal animals, but when rational is added it distinguishes us from them. And both we and the gods are rational, but when mortal is added it distinguishes us from them.]

For when rational and mortal is added, it separates human being from horse.

> **12,2** [Working out what concerns the difference,] they say [that the difference] is not just any one of the things that separate [...what is beneath the same genus...]

For it is not just any difference: it is neither the one [said] in common nor the one [said] properly, nor sitting and standing, nor snub-nosed and hook-nosed that separates, but the one [said] most properly, i.e. the constitutive one: [the fact of] being receptive of intellect and knowledge. For this belongs only to human beings: not to god, insofar as he is superior to all knowledge, nor to irrational animals, since they are not naturally suited for it. Again, [human beings are not receptive] of this particular knowledge – for if it is of grammar alone, you are including the grammarian, but of all [knowledge].[229]

12,3 [but that which contributes to being and that which is a part] of the essence and what is a part of the thing.[230]

[He says this] instead of 'and to the definition'; for in Aristotle, the essence (*to ti ên einai*) signifies the definition – as among the grammarians 'wrath' [signifies] 'anger', since the definition signifies the essence (*to ti estin*) and the being (*to einai*) of each thing.[231] Whatever is a part of the definition, distinguishes, for 'receptive of intellect and science' becomes a part of the definition. This is why this difference distinguishes human being from the others.

12,4 For being of such a nature as to travel by water is not [a difference of human being, although it is a property of human being. For we would say that of animals, some are of such a nature as to travel by water, others not, separating from the others, but being of such a nature as to travel by water was not completive of the substance, nor was it a part of it, but it is a mere suitability thereof, since they are not like the differences that are properly said to be specific. Those differences would be specific which produce another species, and those that are taken up in the essence. This is enough on the subject of the difference.]

By 'travel by water',[232] he does not mean to swim or to be transported on the water – for this is how irrational animals and inanimate things travel by water – but to navigate; for this a property of human beings. Yet human beings are not characterized by navigating, for if this were so, those who do not navigate would not be human beings.

On the property

12,13 They divide the property into four. [Indeed, there is what occurs to some species alone, although not to all of it, as healing or doing geometry occurs to human beings; and what occurs to the entire species, as being a biped [occurs] to human beings; and what [occurs to a species] alone, to all of it, and at a certain time, as to all human beings [there occurs] the fact of turning grey in old age. The fourth one is that in which there coincides [the fact of occurring to a species] alone, to all of it, and always, as capable of laughing [occurs to a human being].]

Having completed the discussion of the difference, he now discusses the property, for this was what was consequent according to the aforementioned order. For having discussed the substantial [words],[233] he necessarily discusses the adventitious ones as well. He begins with the property, since it is a borderland; for it has aspects in common with the essential ones, insofar as the property properly so called belongs [to its subject] alone, to all of it, and always, as the essential ones do – for these too belong to all the things to which they belong, and [they do] always. Yet it also has aspects in common with accidents, in that as the latter are separated from their substrate in thought, so the property is separated in thought. Again, according to the same type of teaching, he first enumerates the meanings, and thus says which one the philosophers are concerned with. In a way, then, he divides the property into four, saying as follows: the property either belongs to one species alone, or not to it alone; and if to it alone, then either to all of the species or not to all of it; and if not to it alone, again, either to all or not to all, either always or not always. This is the division.

One meaning, the first one, is what occurs accidentally to one thing alone, but not to all of it, as to human being [there occurs] practising medicine, philosophy, astronomy, geometry, or some such thing. The second one is what [occurs] to all [of a species], but not only to it, as being a biped [occurs] to human beings: for it belongs to human beings, but not only [to human beings]: after all, being a biped belongs to winged creatures as well. Third is that which [belongs to a species] alone and to all of it, but not always but at a certain time, as turning grey occurs to human beings in old age: [it occurs] to them alone and to all [human beings], but they do not turn grey always, but in old age. Fourth is that in which there coincides [the fact of belonging to something] alone, to all, and always: for instance, capable of laughter [belongs] to human beings, and capable of neighing to horses, and capable of barking to dogs. Each of these is said according to potentiality, not to actuality; for it is not said to be

109,1

5

10

15

20

capable of laughing or neighing insofar as it laughs or neighs, but insofar as it is naturally suited [to do so]. For this is the property in the proper sense – that which belongs to [a species] alone, and to all of it, and always.

Porphyry applied this property in a loose sense to the other meanings, and in general, taking the property said in a more common sense, he divided it into four. Thus, since there are three oppositions from which the meanings of the property were taken, once these are combined with one another, several relationships come about between them, some of which are non-existent and some of them existent, as is shown by those who have made drawings.[234]

12,19 [For even if he does not always laugh, he is said to be capable of laughing not because he always laughs, but because he is of such a nature as to do so.] This always belongs to him as connatural.

By saying 'connatural', he indicated potentiality and the fact of having a natural tendency, not actuality. For even if we do not always laugh, we are said to be always capable of laughing, for we have laughing potentially, and we always have a natural tendency to laugh. We are therefore capable of laughing, although we do not always laugh; for it is one thing to laugh, and another to be capable of laughing; and neighing is one thing, and being capable of neighing is another.

On the accident

12,24 The accident is what occurs and departs without the destruction of the substrate.

Of the things that pertain to the teaching, the accident has the last rank; it remains to be discussed. It should be known that he did not teach about it in accordance with the customary instruction. For in the case of the other words, he first enumerated their various meanings, then stated which one the philosophers are concerned with. Here, however, he does not do this, but immediately states the description of the accident, knowing that philosophers are concerned with all the meanings of 'accident'. Yet if an accident occurs and departs without the destruction of the substrate, it is clear from this that accidents are not bodies.[235] For if they were bodies, when added to bodies they could obviously increase them, while when removed they could diminish them. But if they do not damage bodies either when added to them or when removed from them, they are incorporeals.

Another argument: if they were bodies, one place would contain several bodies, which is impossible. For if an apple has fragrance, colour, and sweetness, and if these were bodies, they could not have a single place, which is impossible, for it is impossible for a body to traverse another body. That separable accidents do not damage the substrate when they occur to it and depart from it is clear, for sitting and standing, being warmed and being cooled occur and depart without destroying the substrate. Do the inseparable ones also depart without damaging the substrate, I mean being snub-nosed and hook-nosed, and the blackness in a crow? We say that these things can also be separated, in thought if not in actuality. For whether you think of a nose as straight or curved, it nevertheless remains a nose.

Some problems are customarily raised against the given definition. They say, as has already been stated, that the definition does not fit with all the accidents, but the separable ones, I mean[236] the fact of 'occurring and departing'. For it is impossible for the black in an Ethiopian or in a crow to depart without the destruction of the substrate. Yet we already said that although it does not depart in actuality, the crow and the Ethiopian [can be] white in thought, but animal cannot be separated from a human being even in thought. For at the same time as we think of a human being as not being an animal, we destroy him, whereas by thinking of a crow not being black, or an Ethiopian, we do not destroy its substance as a crow or a human being. Indeed, even if someone removed a crow's wings, it would nonetheless still be a crow, and if you think of an Ethiopian as white, he is nonetheless still a human being, so that even if inseparable [accidents] do not depart in actuality, they do so in thought.

This problem is also raised: in what sense is it said that they 'occur and depart without the destruction of the substrate'? For when fever occurs, it destroys a human being. We say that just as when strings are tightened and loosened, it may happen that harmony is dissolved, but the substrate is not destroyed; so here too, when excessive heat or cold occur, or something like them, it may happen that the due proportion and harmony in an animal are destroyed, but the substrate, that is, the body, is preserved. For the substrate of heat or cold is not simply animal, but body. But the latter is a compound of

112,1 cold, hot, dry, and wet contraries – 'for if the human being were one thing', says Hippocrates, 'he would not be ill, but if he were ill, then what cures him would be one as well'[237] – mixed with one another and adjusted together into unity and friendship. Yet an animal's body is not made up only of the aforementioned
5 contrary qualities, but also of the substrate of some qualityless body, three-dimensional according to its own rational formula,[238] in which all quality comes into existence. Yet no quality conflicts with its own substrate or destroys that in which it has its subsistence, for by destroying its substrate, it destroys itself along with it: for when that in which it has its existence is destroyed, it
10 must be destroyed along with it, since it cannot exist by itself. But nothing is destructive of itself, for quality conflicts with quality, not with substrate and body. Thus, it is impossible for fever or, in general, any other quality to destroy its own substrate; for everything desires to exist. At any rate, when one of these contrary qualities out of which the body is mixed happens to be in excess, the
15 harmony of the entire body must be destroyed.

For by striving to seize the substrate, since it is preserved in it, [one of the qualities] destroys the [quality] that is in conflict with it, so that, having expelled it, it might seize its place, like those who fight over a common piece of land. For each strives, by repelling its opposite number, to come into possession
20 of the land. Thus, for instance, when hot and cold are in conflict over the same substrate, insofar as neither one predominates, their substrate is in a state of due proportion, but when one of them predominates, its opposite, having been destroyed by the predominant one, retreats, while the substrate suffers no effect, nor is it destroyed by the predominant quality. Thus, by fever the
25 harmony and optimal mixture of the qualities in the body are destroyed, but the body itself, which was the substrate for the qualities, is not destroyed.

Perhaps someone may object to what has been said that the substrate for
113,1 fever is not simply the body, but the body, tempered in a certain way, of an animal, which perishes when fever or a chill, or something like them, supervenes upon it excessively. For fever is not just any excessive heat, such as the one that is in iron or in fire, but that which is in the body of an animal. Indeed, when the
5 latter is destroyed, the fever is destroyed along with it, since it has its being therein. We solve this problem from the beginning, in this way. Motions and changes take place in four categories: they are either in substance, or in quantity, or in quality, or in the category of where. Change in substance produces

coming-into-being and corruption, for coming-into-being is change from not-being to being, while corruption is [change] from being to not-being. [Change] in quantity is increase and diminution; in quality it is alteration, whitening, blackening, heating, and the motions according to the rest of the qualities. Then there is change in place, which they call locomotion. Now if coming-into-being is substantial change leading from not-being to being, then the opposite one to it is therefore destruction, which leads from being to not-being, and it too is a change in substance. Thus, if fever destroys the substrate, it would not be an accident but a change in substance. For since coming-into-being and destruction are not alteration, but do not take place without alteration, when a moderate alteration takes place, [such as] heating or cooling, so that it does not destroy the due proportion of the animal, then such a quality is an accident, which also departs without destroying the substrate. Yet when it is further intensified, so as to destroy the due proportion of the temperament of the substrate, then, for the rest, such a thing is henceforth not an alteration, nor an accidental change, but [a change] of substance itself. Thus, not every fever destroys the substrate, but an excessive one, which is not an accident, but a change towards not-being.

They also raise problems about baldness, for they say that it destroys the substrate, i.e. the hair. It should be known, however, that it is not hair that acts as the substrate for baldness, but the head, and the latter is not destroyed.

> **12,26** [Sleeping, then, is a separable accident, while] being black [has occurred] inseparably to crows and Ethiopians, [but a crow can be conceived as white and an Ethiopian as having thrown off his colour, without destruction of the substrate.]

He did well to say 'to crows and Ethiopians', for there are many black things that are whitened. But he said that inseparable accidents can also be separated in thought, while differences in the most proper sense cannot [be separated] even in thought. For it is not possible to conceive of a human being apart from rational, since he would not even be a human being, nor of angels [without] immortal, for they would no longer be angels.

> **13,3** [They also define [it] as follows:] an accident is what can belong or not belong to the same thing.

He gives another description of the accident, which is more precise than the previous one; for to say 'what can belong or not belong to the same thing' fits better with inseparable ones as well.

> **13,4** Or that which is neither a genus, nor a difference, nor a species, nor a property, but always exists in a subject.

He gives another description of the accident, which can also be given in the case of the [other] four words, by elimination of the rest. After all, a genus is that which is neither species, nor difference, nor property, nor accident, and the same holds true of the rest. But he did not define those [words] in this way, since the subsequent words were unknown; now, however, having taught them all, he rightly defined the accident in this way. But since the elimination of the four not only introduces the accident, but also the goat-stag and many other things,[239] he added that they always have their being in a subject.

> **13,5** but always exists in a subject[240]

Since he said what it is not – for he carried out the description by negation, saying that it is neither a genus nor the rest, he also states what it is: that it exists in a subject.

> **13,10** Common to all of them is the fact of being predicated of many things, [but the genus [is predicated] of species and individuals, and likewise the difference; while the species [is predicated] of the individuals beneath it; the property [is predicated] of the species of which it is the property, and of the individuals beneath it; and the accident [is predicated] of species and of individuals.]

These three things are observed in all realities: substance, sameness, and otherness. By substance, I do not mean the one that is opposite to accidents, but the existence (*huparxis*) of each thing, through which they are called beings. They also have sameness: for since the principle of all things is one, all things must have some commonality with each other. Again, since all beings are also many, they must have some otherness, so that they may be many; for wherever there is a plurality, there is otherness as well. Thus, in the case of the five things under discussion as well, one must seek substance, sameness, and otherness. Substance has already been mentioned, for he stated their existence. He now discusses identity and sameness: in what respect they have something in common, and in what respect they differ. Those who are more clever by nature can pay attention to these things on the basis of what has already been said, but since he is writing the book to one of the more superficial readers – this is clear from the fact that he has written the superficial theorems to him – he states these things, having selected them from what has been said. First of all, he states the common things that are constant attributes of them all, so that he may then compare each one of them to the other four, and state in what respect they have something in common, and in what respect they differ.

It should be known that if, when certain terms are present in some way, we wish to learn how many differences they make of the combinations with one another, we must use a method such as the following:[241] one must take the number [of terms] less one, and multiply it by the [number] that was given at the outset, then divide the result by two, and say that is the number of combinations that come into existence. For instance, the words that are now being combined with one another are five in number. Take the [number] that is less than five by one, i.e. four, and make four times five, which makes twenty. Take half of this, which is ten, and say that that is how many combinations and aggregations there are of the five words with one another. We take the [number] that is less by one, since nothing is compared with itself, but one thing with another. We multiply them by one another, since we are seeking a comparison with each another. We take half the resulting number, since from the resulting multiplication it happens that the same things are compared with each other twice. For each of the five is multiplied by the remaining four: for instance, the genus [is multiplied] by the next four, and again, the species by the genus and the remaining three, and it so happens that the same comparison of each thing is carried out twice. This, then, is why we take half of the resulting number.

13,20 [For animal is predicated of horses and oxen, which are species, and of this horse and this ox, which are individuals, while irrational is predicated of horses and oxen and the particulars; while the species, such as human being, [is predicated] of the particulars alone; and the property, such as capable of laughter, [is predicated] of human being and the particulars; and black [is predicated] of crows and particulars, since it is an inseparable accident; and moving [is predicated] of human being and horse, since it is a separable accident,] but primarily of individuals, and in the second instance of the things that contain the individuals as well.

In this passage, Porphyry states something very necessary, for he says: both genera and differences are predicated of species and of individuals – for a human being and Socrates are said to be animal – but they are predicated primarily of species, and in the second instance, through them, of individuals as well. For since a human being is an animal, Socrates is also an animal, and since a human being is rational, Socrates is rational too. Properties and accidents are also predicated of species and of individuals – for a human being and Socrates are said to be capable of laughing, and a human being and Socrates are [said to be] white – but primarily of individuals, and in the second instance of species as well. For it is not because the universal human being is capable of laughing that we say all the particular [human beings] are capable of laughing – for the universal human being is incorporeal and is not such as to be capable of laughing – but by the fact that particular human beings are capable of laughing. In general, he is talking about those [universals] that are in the many or over the many.[242]

13,23 Common to the genus and the difference is the fact that they contain species.

After comparing the five [words] to one another together, and stating in what respect they have something in common and in what respect they differ, he wishes to take each of them and compare it to the remaining four, and show in what respect one of the many has something in common with the four, and in what respect it differs.

13,23 Common to the genus and the difference is the fact that they contain species.[243]

He now takes each one and compares it individually with each of the rest, one by one. He first compares the genus to the difference, and states in what respect they have something in common, and in what respect they differ.

**14,3 [For the difference also contains species, although it does not contain all those that the genus contains. For rational, although it does not contain irrational things, as animal does, does contain human being and god, which are species.] Whatever is predicated of the genus as a genus [is also predicated] of the species beneath it. Everything [that is predicated] of the difference qua difference will also be predicated of the species that comes from it. For substance and animate are predicated of the genus animal, as of a genus, but these things are also predicated of all the species beneath animal, as far as the individuals. And making use of reason is predicated of rational, which is a difference, but it will be predicated not only of rational, but also of the species beneath rational.   15

For whatever is predicated of animal, is also [predicated of] the species and individuals after animal. Similarly for the difference. Is it the case, then, since genus is predicated of animal – for we say that animal is a genus – that it will therefore be predicated of the species and the individual? For if this is so, then human being and Socrates are a genus, which is not so; and since 'genus' has two syllables, then human being does too. It must therefore be said that this   20 was why Porphyry added in common 'as a genus' instead of 'as a thing', for it was not as having a relation. For genus, two-syllabled, and all such things indicate the relation of animal. Thus, whatever is predicated of animal qua animal – for this is what 'as a genus' indicates – is necessarily predicated of the species and the individuals as well. 'Genus', in contrast, is not predicated of   25 animal as of animal, but relationally. For not only is animal said to be the genus of human being, and horse, and the rest, but also colour is [said to be] the genus of white, black, and the others. You will find things to be likewise in the   118,1 other categories: thus, the genus of animal is not predicated as of an animal, but as having assumed a relation of a certain kind to what is beneath it, and therefore it will not be predicated of species and individuals. The same argument applies to the difference: whatever is predicated of the difference as a difference, and not as indicating a relation, [is predicated] also of all the   5 species beneath it.

14,10 Also common is the fact that if [the genus or the difference] is eliminated, [that which is beneath them is also eliminated; for just as if animal does not exist if there is no horse or human being, so, if rational does not exist, there will be no animal that makes use of reason.]

There are two rules for things that are prior by nature: the fact of co-eliminating but not being co-eliminated, and the fact of being entailed but not entailing.[244]

14,14 Proper to the genus is also the fact that it is predicated of more things   10 than the difference [the species, the property, and the accident: for animal [is predicated] of human being, horse, bird, and snake; four-footed [is predicated] only of those things that have four feet; human being [is predicated] only of individuals; and capable of neighing [is predicated] only of horse and of particulars.]

Having stated what the genus and the difference have in common, he now states how they differ from one another. Here, the differences must be taken in two senses, for it has been stated[245] that differences are observed in two senses: either as constitutive and completive of species or else as divisive of genera. One must therefore, he says, take not the constitutive ones – for they are no longer as differences of genera, but as [differences] of species – one must, therefore, take the divisive ones, for these are of the genera. In general, one must take the divisive ones, for animal is of wider extension than they, since it is of lesser extension than the completive ones.

14,18 And the accident, likewise, [is true] of fewer things

And yet the accident is included in more things than the genus; black, for example, [does not apply] to animals alone, but to inanimate objects as well. How, then, can it be 'of lesser extension'?[246] We say that things that are beneath the same genus, such as the accident that is in animals, are of lesser extension than animal; for black does not belong to all animals, and the [accident] that is in plants is of lesser extension than plant.

> **14,20** In addition, the genus contains the difference potentially [for of animal, one part is rational, the other irrational. In addition, genera are prior to the differences beneath them, for they co-eliminate them, but are not co-eliminated. For when animal is eliminated, rational, and irrational are eliminated along with it; but differences no longer co-eliminate the genus. Indeed, even if all are eliminated, animate sensible substance, which we have seen animal is, can be conceived. In addition, the genus is predicated essentially, the difference qualitatively, as has been said.]

It has already been stated,[247] following the Peripatetics, that differences exist potentially in genera prior to the species that are beneath them.

> **15,4** In addition, there is one genus for each species, [such as animal for human being, while there are several differences, such as rational, mortal, receptive of intellect and science, by which it differs from the other animals.]

Another difference between the genus and the difference: the former is one, while there are several of the latter for each species.

15,6 And the genus resembles matter, [but the difference resembles shape.]

It has already been said[248] that the genus that is in the many, and especially the natural one, resembles matter, while the difference [resembles] form.

15,7 But while other common [and peculiar] things pertain [to the genus and the difference, let these suffice]

He says that they also have other common and peculiar features, but these nevertheless suffice. Also common to them is the fact of being substantial, for just as the genus is substantial, so is the difference. Also common to them is the fact of being predicated synonymously, for just as the genus is predicated synonymously of the things beneath it, so is the difference. Peculiar to each, apart from what has been said, is the fact that the genus, such as animal, does not combine with another genus to complete something, but differences do combine and make something: for rational combines together with mortal, receptive of intellect and science, and so on, and completes human being.

15,10 The genus and species have in common, as has been said, the fact of being predicated of many.

Having compared the genus to the difference, and having stated what they have in common, and in what respect they differ, he now compares the genus to the species, and states what they have in common.

15,11 Let the species be taken as species, [but not as genus as well, if the same thing is both species and genus.]

'As species' was placed rightly, so that you do not take the most specific one – for this is no longer predicated of many things – or the subordinate one. For as subordinate, it is both species and genus of what is after it, and it is found once again to be a genus. Yet even if it is subordinate, take it as a species, and no longer as a genus, so that you may carry out a comparison between species and genus, and not between two things, both of which are a genus.

15,12 Also common to them is the fact that they are prior [to that of which they are predicated, and the fact that each is a kind of whole.]

This is why he gave first place to the common feature that says that it is predicated of many: so that he could say that it is also prior to that of which it is predicated.

15,16 [They differ in that the genus contains the species, while the species are contained, and do not contain the genera; for the genus has wider extension that the species.] In addition, the genera must act as pre-existent substrates, [and produce the species when given shape by the specific differences. Hence, the genera are prior by nature, and they co-eliminate, but are not co-eliminated, and when the species exists, the genus also necessarily exists, but when the genus exists, the species does not necessarily exist. And the genera are predicated synonymously of the species beneath them, but the species are no longer [predicated synonymously] of the genera.]

Animal, as has been said, acts as a prior subject like matter, and when it has taken on rational and mortal in addition, it makes human being. Animal is a genus, while human being is a species. Genera are thus prior by nature. There are two rules, as we have already said,[249] by which what is prior by nature is distinguished: first is the one that says that what is prior is that which co-eliminates but is not co-eliminated. For instance, when animal is eliminated, it co-eliminates human being, but when human being is eliminated, it does not co-eliminate animal. The genus, then, is prior by nature to the species. The second rule is the one that says that what is entailed but does not entail is prior by nature. For instance, if human being exists, then animal is necessarily entailed as well, but if animal exists it is not necessary for human being to be entailed as well. Here too, the genus is prior by nature to the species; for if the genus exists, it does not entail the species as well, whereas if the species is postulated, it entails the genus as well.

15,22 [In addition, the genera exceed by their inclusion of the species beneath them, while] the species exceed the genera [by their proper species. In addition, neither can the species be most generic, nor can the genus be most specific.]

For the species have the differences that complete them in act.

16,2 Common to the genus and the property is that they follow the species. [For if something is a human being, it is an animal, and if it is a human being, it is capable of laughing. Also [common is] the fact that the genus is predicated equally of species, and the property of the individuals that participate in them. For a human being and an ox are animals, and Anytos and Meletos are capable of laughing.]

Having compared the genus to the species, he now compares it to the property. What is said to 'follow' is either the greater to the less, necessarily, as animal does to human being – for what is a human being, is an animal as well – or the equal to the equal, as capable of laughing, again, [follows] human being: for what is a human being is capable of laughing.

16,6 Also common is that fact that the genus <is predicated> synonymously [of its proper species, and the property of that of which it is the property.]

Indeed, it was because of this kinship that we said[250] that the property is on the borderland between substantial and adventitious things, and that it comes closer to the substantial ones.

16,9 They differ in that the genus is prior, and the property posterior. [For an animal must exist, then be divided by differences and properties. The genus is predicated of several species, while the property [is predicated] of one species, of which it is the property. And the property is counter-predicated of that of which it is the property, while the genus is not counter-predicated of anything: for it is not the case that if something is an animal, it is a human being, nor that if it is an animal, it is capable of laughing; but if it is a human being, it is capable of laughing, and vice versa. In addition, the property belongs to the entire species of which it is the property, and of it only, and always; while the genus [belongs] to the entire species, of which it is the genus, and always, but not to it alone.]

Having said what they have in common, he now says in what respect they differ. By 'prior' he means not in time, but by nature.

16,17 [In addition, properties, when they are eliminated, do not co-eliminate the genera,] but genera, when they are eliminated, co-eliminate [the species] of which they are properties, [so that when the things of which they are the properties are eliminated, they too are co-eliminated.]

When genera are eliminated, the properties are also eliminated, by means of the species. For when human being is eliminated, capable of laughing is eliminated along with it. Rightly so, for if when the species are eliminated the properties are also eliminated, but when the genera are eliminated the species are also eliminated, it is all the more true that when genera are eliminated, the properties will also be eliminated.

> **17,4**[251] Common to genus and accident is, as has been said, the fact that they are predicated of many, whether they are separable or inseparable. After all, moving [is predicated] of many, and black of crows, Ethiopians, and some inanimate objects.] The genus differs from the accident [in that the genus is prior to the species, but accidents are posterior to the species. For even if an inseparable accident is taken, that to which it occurs is prior to the accident.]

Of things that differ the most, as in the case of genus and accident, it is difficult to state the commonality, since the commonality is scant; but the difference is easy [to state] – for the things that differ a great deal differ from each other in many respects – just as of the things that are nearest to one another, it is difficult to state the difference, but [to state] the commonality is easy. For instance, it is easy to state the commonality of a wolf and a dog,[252] and a dove and a tame pigeon, but the difference is not easy. Again, it is easy to say in what respect a human being differs from an ant, but hard to say what they have in common. In general, things that are far removed from one another and very different have the least commonality, but maximal difference; whereas those that are not very distant but are close to one another have acquired minimal difference, but a great deal of commonality. Since, then, this genus and the accident are maximally far from one another, their commonality is minimal, while their difference is great. Hence, Porphyry set forth a single commonality between them, but several othernesses.

> **17,7** [Also, what participates participates equally in the genus, but not equally in the accident,] for participation in accidents admits of intensification and remission, [but that of genera does not. Also, accidents subsist primarily upon individuals, but genera and species are prior by nature to individual substances. Also, genera are predicated essentially of what is beneath them, but accidents [are predicated] qualitatively or according to disposition. For if you are asked, what kind of thing is an Ethiopian? You will say, 'black', and [if you are asked,] how is Socrates disposed? You will say that he is sitting down or is walking.]

For human being and horse and the other species participate equally in animal (for they are equally animals), but bodies do not equally participate in white or black, for they are said to be more or less white and black.

> **17,14** [Thus,] how the genus differs from the other four [has been stated, but it also so happens that each of the other ones differs from the four. Thus, since they are five, and each one differs from the four, four times five, the total number of differences is twenty. Yet this is not the case, but since those that are successive are counted, the second [set] is lacking by one difference, since they have already been taken, and the third by two, and the fourth by three, and the fifth by four, the total of differences becomes ten: four, three, two, one. For the genus differs from the difference, the species, the property and the accident; hence, the differences are four.]

Here, Porphyry wishes to show how many relations arise from the comparison of the five with one another. For he said that the relations that arise are not twenty, as one might suppose, since each of the five is compared twice to the remaining four, and he imparts the method, which we have already set forth beforehand,[253] by which we discover how many relations arise from the terms at hand, by their comparison to one another. He says, as has already been stated by us, that he who has set forth the number of terms must multiply by the [number] that is less by one, and take half the result, and say that that is how many relations arise. For instance, in the case of the five [terms] at hand, one must multiply five by [the number that is] less [than five] by a unit, i.e. four, and the result is twenty. Then [one takes] half of these, and the result is ten. This, then, is how many mutual relations come about of the five of them. The reason why we do things in this way is the following: it is necessary to compare each of the five to the remaining four. This, then, is why we take five times four, and the result is twenty relations. But since it so happens that we include the same relations twice, this is why we make the half. For in comparing the genus to the remaining four, it is clear that we compare it to the difference as well. If, then, we compare the difference to the remaining four, it so happens that we compare the genus to the difference twice. The same holds true of the rest. There is another rule, by which we learn how many relations arise of the terms set forth.

When there are some terms and they are added to others, for each term, as many relations are added as there were terms present. For instance, there is no relation of the first [number], but if another term is added, one relation comes about, since there was one term present. Again, if another [number] is added, two relations are added, as many as were the terms present. Thus, there come to be three relations in all.

If another term is added, three relations are added, and the relations come to be six in all. If another term is added, four relations are added, so that the relations of the five terms come to be ten in all.

In another way: each of the five must be compared to the remaining four. Therefore, when the genus is compared to the remaining four, it makes four relations, but the difference has already been compared to the genus, when he was comparing the genus (for it is the same); but when it is compared to the remaining three it makes three relations, so that seven come about. Again, the species has already been compared to the genus and to the difference, so that they too [have been compared] to it, but when it is compared to the remaining two it makes two relations, so that nine relations come about. Again, the property has already been compared to the genus, the difference, and the species, but when it is compared to the accident it makes one relation, so that they all come to be ten. The accident has nothing to be compared to, for it has already been compared to all, when they were being compared to it. It is clear, then, that all the relations come to be four, three, two, one: four of the genus, three of the difference, two of the species, and one of the property, so that all of them come to be ten. And the property has no longer been compared to the genus, for it has already been compared, when the genus [was being compared] to it.

17,23 [How the difference differs from the genus has been stated, when it was stated how the genus differs from it.] It remains to say how it differs from the species. [Then it will be said how it differs from the species, the property, and the accident, and they come to be three. Again, how the species differs from the difference has been stated, when it was said how the difference differs from the species. How the species differs from the genus was said when it was said how the genus differs from the species. Then it will be said how it differs from the property and the accident: for there are two of these differences as well. How the property differs from the accident will be left, for how it differs from the species and the difference and the genus was said beforehand in their difference towards it. Thus, four differences of the genus with regard to the others having been taken, but three of the difference, two of the species, and one of the property with regard to the accident, the total of them will be ten, four of which – those which were of the genus with regard to the others – we have already demonstrated.]

For the relation of the genus to the difference is the same as that of the difference to the genus, both of their difference and of their commonality, and it is no longer compared to the genus, but to the things that come after it.

18,11 Common to the difference and the species [is the fact of being participated equally. For particular human beings participate equally in human being, and in the difference of rational: for Socrates is always rational, and Socrates is always a human being.]

He now moves on to the common and proper features of the difference and the species and the others, and with these he concludes his discussion.

18,16 Proper to the difference is the fact of being predicated qualitatively [while [proper to] the species is the fact of [being predicated] essentially. For even if a human being is taken as something qualified, he would not be a qualified in an absolute sense, but insofar as the differences, when added to the genus, gave him subsistence. In addition, the difference is often observed in the case of several species, as four-footed [is observed] in the case of several animals that differ in species, while the species is [observed] only in the case of the individuals under the species. In addition, the difference is prior to the species associated with it, for when human being is eliminated, rational is eliminated along with it, but when human being is eliminated, it does not eliminate rational, as long as god exists. In addition, a difference is combined with another difference, for rational and mortal were combined for the existence of human being.]

He solves in advance the difficulty one might have raised; for he says: 'why is the species predicated essentially, but the difference qualitatively, although a human being is also said to be an animal of a certain kind?' For we say, what is Socrates? An animal. What kind of an animal? A human being. Thus, the species is also predicated qualitatively. However, he says that the species is qualified not in an absolute sense, but insofar as it participates in the differences. For species possess the fact of being predicated essentially from the genera, but that of [being predicated] qualitatively from the differences. For when asked what kind of animal, we say, 'rational [and] mortal'. Thus, the differences possess by themselves the [fact of being] qualified, while the species possess it through the differences.

19,2 [But one species is not combined with another, so as to engender some other species] for an individual horse mates with an individual ass [with a view to the generation of a mule, but horse in the absolute sense combined with an ass would not produce a mule. The difference and the property have in common the fact that they are participated equally by the participants: for rational beings are equally rational, and beings capable of laughing [are equally] capable of laughing. The fact of being present always and to each thing is also common to both: for even if a two-footed being is mutilated, 'always' is said with regard to natural tendency, since what is capable of laughing possesses [the characteristic of] 'always' by virtue of natural tendency, not by virtue of always laughing.]

For what is rational in an absolute sense, combined with what is mortal in the absolute sense, makes a human being, while the universal human being, combined with something else, does not produce anything. But if a mule comes about from a horse and an ass, it is not from the universal ones, but from the particular ones; for it is this [individual] horse which, when it mounts an ass, produces a mule.

Otherwise: when the differences come together to engender one species, they are not affected by each other at all, and each maintains its own substance. For instance, rational, mortal, and receptive of intellect and science came together to engender the one species of human being, and they were not damaged by any of them. Yet when a horse and an ass come together and produce a mule, since they are not species but individuals, they do not maintain their nature unmixed in the mule, for something else besides both of them has come into being, with the substance of each of them having perished. Thus, one species does not come together with [another] species.

19,12 [Proper to the difference is that fact that it is often said of several species, as for instance rational [is said] of god and of man, while] the property is said of one species [of which it is the property. And the difference follows the things of which it is the difference, but it does not reciprocate; while properties are convertible with that of which they are properties, because they reciprocate.]

[He means] the [property] that belongs to each thing, and always, and to it alone.

126,1

> **20,3** [Common to the difference and the accident is the fact of being said of several things, and common to the inseparable accidents is the fact of being present always and to each thing; for two-footed is always present to all crows, and likewise black. They differ in that the difference contains, but is not contained, for rational contains human being, while accidents contain in a way, by being in many things, and in a way are contained, by the fact that substrates are receptive not of one accident, but of several.] The difference cannot be intensified [or diminished, while accidents accept the more and the less.]

For nothing is more or less rational than what is rational, but we would say that one black thing is more or less black [than another]. But if one thing is more rational than another, we say 'less' and 'more', yet we signify something different by 'rational'. For we are not seeking rational substance, but the rational disposition in studies, which is a propensity of the soul.

5

> **20,5** Contrary differences are unmixed, [but contrary accidents could be mixed together]

For rational and irrational do not combine, but black and white, when mixed together, make grey. Capable of laughing is said in the sense of what naturally tends to laugh.

10

127,1

> **20,17** [Such, then, are the commonalities and properties of the difference and the other [words]. In what respect the species differs from genus and difference has been stated in the [passage] where we said in what respect the genus differs from the other ones and in what respect the difference differs from the others. Common to species and property is the fact of being convertible with one another. For if [something] is a human being, it is capable of laughing, and if it is capable of laughing, it is a human being. It has often been stated that capable of laughing is to be taken in accordance with what naturally tends to laugh; for the species are equal to what participates in them, and the properties of which they are properties. The species differs from the property in that] the species can be the genus of other things, [while it is impossible for the property to be proper to other things.]

For instance, animal is a species of animated, but the genus of human being and horse.

20,18 And the species subsists prior to the property, [while the property accrues to the species: for the human being must exist in order for it to be capable of laughing. In addition, the species is always present to the substrate in act, but the property [is present only] sometimes and potentially. For Socrates is always a human being in act, but he does not always laugh, although he always has a natural tendency to be capable of laughing. In addition, those things of which the definitions are different are themselves different. Pertaining to the species is the fact of being beneath the genus, and being predicated essentially of many things that differ in number, and all such things, while [pertaining] to the property is the fact of being present to one [species] alone, and always, and to all of it. Common to species and accident is the fact of being predicated of many things, while the other commonalities are few, because the accident and that to which it occurs are most distant from one another.]

For first the human being must exist previously, then, in this way, [the characteristic] capable of laughter [must exist].

21,10 [The properties of each: of the species, being predicated essentially of the things of which it is the species; of the accident, [being predicated] qualitatively or dispositionally.] And the fact that each substance participates in one species, but several accidents, [both separable and inseparable.]

For instance, Socrates participates in one species, i.e. that of human being, but in several accidents, such as hook-nosedness,[254] blackness, and whiteness.

21,15 [And species are conceived prior to accidents, although they are inseparable, for the substrate must exist, in order that something occur to it, while accidents tend to be last-born and have an adventitious nature.] And participation of the species is equal.

For Socrates and Plato are equally human beings, but not equally black or white.

Notes

1. cf. Chrysippus, *SVF* 2.99, who specifies that this is the more perfect part of grammar, after learning how to read and write, and the opening sentence of Dionysius Thrax, *Ars Grammatica*.
2. cf. Dionysius of Halicarnassus, *De Imitatione*, in L. Radermacher and H. Usener (eds), *Dionysii Halicarnasei quae extant*, vol. 6 (Leipzig: Teubner, 1929, repr. 1965), pp. 197, 200, 202–16; Olympiodorus, *in Gorgiam* 9.2.11. Sopater, *Scholia ad Hermogenis status seu artem rhetoricam*, in C. Walz (ed.), *Rhetores Graeci* (Stuttgart: J.G. Cottae, 1835), vol. 5, p. 17 ff. attributes the definition to Publius Hordeonius Lollianus (fl. 142 CE).
3. cf. Pseudo-Galen, *Definitiones Medicae*, vol. 19, pp. 350–1 Kühn.
4. Reading *hupokeimena men* with Busse *in apparatu*, as suggested by Jonathan Barnes, instead of *hupokeimenon*.
5. cf. Plato, *Theaetetus* 176A–B.
6. Homer, *Odyssey* 4.379; 4.468.
7. Homer, *Odyssey* 8.325; Hesiod, *Theogony* 46; 111; 633, etc.
8. Homer, *Iliad* 5.441–2; cf. Elias, *in Isag.* 16,19 ff.; David, *Prolegomena* 34,21–2. These later commentators make explicit what Ammonius(?) only hints at: the attribution to the gods of a divine triad of properties: knowledge, power, and will; cf. Proclus, *Platonic Theology* 1.15, and references in H.D. Saffrey and L.G. Westerink (eds), *Proclus. Théologie platonicienne*, 6 vols (Paris: Les Belles Lettres,1968–97), vol. 1, p. 148, n. 1, to which one must add the passages in his commentary on the *Republic* where Proclus derives the triad of divine knowledge, power, and goodness from Book 10 of Plato's *Laws* (*Leges* 901D2–E3); cf. Proclus, *in Rem publicam* 1,27,13 ff.; 1,41,2 ff.; 1,167,10 ff. (where Proclus cites the same Homeric texts as does his student Ammonius); Proclus, *Elements of Theology* prop. 121. For echoes of this triad of divine properties in the Arabic tradition, see E. Wakelnig, 'What Does Aristotle Have To Do with the Christian Arabic Trinity? The Triad "Generosity-Wisdom-Power" in the Alexandrian Prolegomena and Yaḥyā ibn ʿAdī', *Le Muséon* 130.3–4 (2017), 445–77.
9. cf. Elias, *in Isag.* 14,4 ff.; David, *Prolegomena* 31,30 ff.; Augustine, *City of God* 1.22. The epigram is by Callimachus (in R. Pfeiffer (ed.), *Callimachus*, 2 vols (Oxford: Oxford University Press, 1987), vol. 2, no. 23 = *Anth. Gr.* 7.471).

10 Literally, 'release oneself' (*exagein*); it is the same term that is used in the Platonic quote below.
11 Again, the Greek word used is *exagein*; see previous note.
12 Plato, *Phaedo* 62B, translation by H.N. Fowler, *Plato. Euthyphro, Apology, Crit, Phaedo, Phaedrus*, LCL (Cambridge, MA.: Harvard University Press, 1960).
13 cf. Porphyry, *Sentences* 8.
14 cf. Hippocrates, *de Flatibus* 1.26.
15 An enigmatic claim. In what may be a fragment of Porphyry's commentary on the *Physics*, preserved in the *Lesser Book of Salvation* by the medieval-Islamic author Miskawayh, we read that snow can accidentally heat other things: 'for the cooling induces condensation and constriction, so that the heat is retained, and something cooled is heated'. Translation by P. Adamson, 'Porphyrius Arabus on Nature and Art: 463F Smith in Context', in G. Karamanolis and A. Sheppard (eds), *Studies on Porphyry* (London: Institute of Classical Studies, 2007), pp. 141–63, at p. 162.
16 Aristotle, *An. Pr.* 24b19–20.
17 cf. Aristotle, *Rhet.* 1356b12–27.
18 cf. Plato, *Alcibiades* 1 113D ff.
19 i.e. the quantity of syllables.
20 An odd claim, which may be based on Plato, *Timaeus* 88C.
21 cf. Euclid, *Elements* 1, def. 4.
22 Archilochus, fr. 211 West.
23 cf. Homer, *Iliad* 23.712.
24 Homer, *Iliad* 15.412.
25 Reading *aidion* with the MSS, instead of Busse's *aidiôn*.
26 Deleting *philosophian* at 9,22, following Busse's suggestion *in apparatu*.
27 i.e. the fixed stars and the planets.
28 Note the belief in the animation of the heavenly bodies.
29 The following text (10,10–11,5) is signalled by the editor as an addition; yet it seems to be present in all manuscripts.
30 Reading *eilêkhe* with MS Vat. gr. 207, instead of Busse's *eilêphe*.
31 The reference is to the drawing of geometrical figures on a tablet, the *abakion*, that was covered with wax.
32 This is the end of the passage designated by Busse as an addition.
33 Deleting *gar* at 11,23, following a suggestion by Jonathan Barnes.
34 Euclid, *Elements* 1, def. 15.
35 cf. Aristotle, *DA* 1.1, 403b3 ff.
36 This is one of the few times Plotinus (*Enneades* 1.3.3) is quoted (approximately) by later Greek authors; cf. the references given by P. Henry, *Études plotiniennes. I. Les états du texte de Plotin* (Paris: Budé, 1938), p. 345.

37 Odd-times-even are numbers that are even, but become odd when divided by a power of two; see below, n. 42.
38 In other versions of this anecdote (Quintilian, *Institutio oratoria* 1.10.32; Iamblichus, *Life of Pythagoras* 112; Boethius, *On Music* 1.1; Sextus Empiricus, *Adversus mathematicos* 6.8; Cicero, *de Consiliis Suis* fr. 10.3, in C.F.W. Mueller (ed.), *M. Tullii Ciceronis. Scripta quae manserunt omnia*, 16 vols (Leipzig: Teubner, 1898), vol. 3), Pythagoras orders the flautist (sometimes male, sometimes female) to change his playing from the Phrygian to the spondaic mode. This must be the meaning of Ammonius(?)' odd turn of phrase 'turn the flute around (*strephein ton aulon*)'.
39 cf. Aristotle, *Cat.* 4b20.
40 Etymologically, 'to do geometry' (*to geometrein*) means 'to measure the earth'.
41 cf. Aristotle, *Cat.* 4b36 ff.
42 An even-times-even (*artiakis artios*) number, according to Euclid (*Elements* 7, def. 8), is one that is measured by an even number an even number of times, e.g. 64; an odd-times-even (*perissartios*) number (e.g. 24, 48, 40) is one that is measured by an odd number an even number of times (Euclid, *Elements* 7, def. 10).
43 [Pythagoras], *Carmen Aureum* lines 9–10, (modified) translation by J.C. Thom (ed.), *The Pythagorean Golden Verses* (Leiden: Brill, 1995), p. 95. In his commentary, Hierocles presents a different version, reading *lagneiês te* ('and lust') instead of *kai philotêtos*.
44 Isocrates, *ad Demonicum* 16.
45 [Pythagoras], *Carmen Aureum* lines 40–4, translation (slightly modified) by Thom, op. cit., p. 97.
46 Apollonius of Rhodes, *Argonautica* 1.944.
47 Reading *diorthoutai* with MS E.
48 Plato, *Timaeus* 47B.
49 Here, Busse omits a lengthy passage preserved by MS M, which he claims has been interpolated from the commentaries of David and Elias. I have followed his lead.
50 The author thus ends his general introduction to philosophy, and begins his introduction specific to Porphyry's *Isagôgê*.
51 Plato, *Cratylus* 437A.
52 The horses of Achilles, offspring of the West Wind and the harpy Podargê; cf. Homer, *Iliad* 16.149; 19.400.
53 The Greek word here is *anêgagon*. The verb *anagein* can mean both 'raise', as in the previous line, and, in logic, 'reduce'. On the ambiguities this sometimes entails in Aristotle, see P.H. Byrne, *Analysis and Science in Aristotle* (Albany NY: SUNY Press, 1997), p. 23 ff.

54 Although angels are not absent from pagan theology, their appearance here is strongly suggestive of Christianity.
55 cf. Aristotle, *Cat.* 10a27 ff.
56 The editor Busse brackets this paragraph as if it were inauthentic, without giving his reasons.
57 cf. Simplicius (*in Cat.* 8,9–13), who lists the *skopos*, the book's usefulness, the reason for the title, its place in the reading order, whether the book is genuine, and how it is divided into chapters. The question of which part of philosophy the treatise is to be ranged under is said to be optional.
58 The Greek word is *mathêmata*. Elsewhere this word clearly means 'mathematics', and it may do so here, but it is hard to imagine that Ammonius(?) thought Porphyry was a teacher of mathematics.
59 If we retain the reading Tauros, the reference must be to Lucius Calbenus Tauros of Beirut, a second-century CE Middle Platonist. It seems unlikely he would have written on Aristotle's predicables, but Baltes (H. Dörrie and M. Baltes, *Der Platonismus im 2. und 3. Jahrhundert nach Christus*, Der Platonismus in der Antike 3 (Stuttgart: Frommann-Holzboog, 1993), p. 259) suggests Taurus may have claimed that the *quinque voces* were already to be found in Plato.
60 i.e. the *Categories*. Reading *eikotôs oun pro autôn tattetai* with MS M; *pro autou* with MSS DE. Busse suggests <*ouden*> *pro autou in apparatu*: 'nothing is ranged before it'.
61 This is the first of several indications that Ammonius(?) was not the first to have commented on the *Isagôgê*.
62 i.e. to philosophy.
63 Thus, we have, in descending order of comprehensiveness, statement (*logos*) => compound statement => syllogism => demonstration.
64 Reading *hôs* instead of *kai*, as suggested by Busse *in apparatu*.
65 Reading, with MS Vat. gr. 207, *ouk êgnounto ho ti dêlousi hai tôn <philosophôn> pragmateiai*, instead of Busse's incomprehensible *enoounto dêlon hoti hai tôn philosophôn pragmateiai*.
66 Porphyry, *Isag.* 1,7–8.
67 Porphyry, *Isag.* 1,3–4.
68 cf. Simplicius, *in Cat.* 18,15 ff., quoting Adrastus.
69 A Hellenistic forgery, accepted since the time of Iamblichus as a work by Plato's companion Archytas, by which Aristotle's *Categories* was supposed to be inspired.
70 cf. Aristotle, *An. Pr.* 29b34 ff.
71 On this concept, see Alexander of Aphrodisias, *in An. Pr.* 7,1–2 and the translation in this series by J. Barnes and S. Bobzien, *Alexander of Aphrodisias. On Aristotle Prior Analytics 1.1–7* (London: Duckworth, 1991), p. 49, n. 46.

72 Oddly, the objectors interpret the Greek *ontos anankaiou*, 'it being necessary', as a predication, in which 'being' is the subject and 'necessary' the predicate.
73 For the homonymy of 'dog', see, for instance, Ammonius, *in Cat.* 38,13–14; for Ajax, Ammonius, *in Cat.* 16,2 ff.
74 cf. Aristotle, *Int.* 17b16 ff.
75 This appears to be a kind of attempt at etymology: *prosdiorismos* comes from the verb *horizein*. In fact, of course, it comes from *prosdiorizein*.
76 In other words, when saying 'it being necessary' (*ontos anankaios*), Porphyry left 'being' (*on*, genitive singular *ontos*) unquantified, which means he meant to quantify 'being' as particular ('some being').
77 i.e. of the necessary, the contingent, and what obtains.
78 i.e. the accident and what obtains.
79 i.e. substance and the contingent.
80 The *editio princeps* here adds a long development which appears to derive from the commentary of David, as Busse points out in his apparatus.
81 cf. Porphyry, *Isag.* 8,8 ff.
82 Reading *tou anthrôpou*, with the MSS, instead of Busse's *tou hupokeimenou*.
83 cf. Aristotle, *Top.* 139a24 ff.
84 Plato, *Phaedrus* 265E.
85 Reading *horistikou* with MS V instead of Busse's *horistikês*, at the suggestion of an anonymous reader.
86 Reading *to zôion kai to logikon kai to thnêton* with MS Vat. gr. 207, instead of Busse's *to zôion to logikon kai to thnêton*.
87 Plato, *Phaedrus* 245C ff.
88 The following passage (36,15–38,4) looks very much like an alternative version, thus adding to the general impression that this work is more of a collection of scholia than a work by Ammonius.
89 Reading *analuei* with MS Vat. gr. 207 and the *editio princeps*, instead of Busse's *poiei*.
90 Reading *ho diaieretikos* instead of Busse's *hê diairetikê*.
91 Supplying [*enantioutai*], with the *editio princeps*.
92 i.e. the analyser (reading *ekeinos de dialutikos* instead of Busse's *ekeinê de dialutikê*).
93 At 37,6, I read *kaitoi tautês* instead of Busse's *kai tauta*.
94 cf. Aristotle, *Phys.* 202a19; 248a22: uphill and downhill are the same thing, but their account (*logos*) is different.
95 Reading *pleionôn haplôn*, with most MSS, instead of Busse's *pleionôn*.
96 Reading, with MS Vat. gr. 207, *Oukoun ho analuôn ean eis ta pleiona analuêi, pseudos men ara to ton analutên eis haploun analuein to suntheton*.

97 Reading *to de eskhaton eis hen*, with most MSS, instead of Busse's *to de eskhaton ou*.
98 Reading *en huphêi logou* with most MSS, instead of Busse's *en hupokeimenôi*, but the text is probably corrupt.
99 The words 'as in Galen's works', and 'as the *Demonstration*', absent from every MS except D, may well be marginal glosses.
100 i.e. the *Posterior Analytics*. See below, n. 193.
101 Several meanings of the verb *stokhazomai* and the noun *stokhasmos* are in play here. In Porphyry's text the verb means 'to aim at'; but it can also mean 'to guess'. Finally, *stokhasmos* was a technical term in rhetoric, where it can mean 'conjecture', or debate about whether or not a particular act was committed.
102 Alain de Libera has written extensively on this passage of the *Isagôgê*, its Greek and Latin interpreters, and the doctrine of the triple universal that arises from it: *La querelle des universaux. De Platon à la fin du Moyen Âge* (Paris: Seuil, 1996), pp. 103–5; *L'art des généralités. Théories de l'abstraction* (Paris: Aubier, 1999), pp. 193–202. Also see R. Sorabji, *The Philosophy of the Commentators 200–600 AD. A Sourcebook*, 3 vols (London: Duckworth, 2004), vol. 3, p. 132 ff.
103 On the goat-stag (Greek *tragelaphos*, Latin *hircocervus*) see, for instance, Plato, *Republic* 488A; Aristotle, *Int.* 16a; *An. Pr.* 49a24; 92b7.
104 For this translation of *hupostasis*, cf. LSJ s.v. B.II.2: substance, actual existence, reality.
105 cf. Antisthenes, fr. 50, in F. Decleva Caizzi, *Antisthenis fragmenta* (Milan: Istituto Editoriale Cisalpino, 1966).
106 Reading *ti de esti ta huphestôta*, with MS Vat. gr. 207, instead of Busse's *ti de esti 'peri ta huphestôta'*.
107 For the history of the famous image of the signet ring and the wax, see S. Fortier, 'Ammonius on Universals and Abstraction: An Interpretation and Translation of Ammonius' *In Porphyrii Isagogen* 39, 8–42, 16', *Laval théologique et philosophique* 68.1 (2012), 21–33.
108 The Greek here reads: *tou apomaxamenou*. See Fortier, 'Ammonius on Universals and Abstraction', 28.
109 On the notion that the Platonic Forms are present within the intellect of the Demiurge, see, for instance, C. Militello, *I commentari all' Isagoge di Porfirio tra V e VI secolo* (Roma: Bonanno, 2010), pp. 91–2.
110 Busse prints *ou gar hôs hê phusis alogôi dunamei poiei*: 'for he [i.e. the Demiurge] does not make things like nature, by an irrational power'. Yet a couple of pages later (44,6–7), the author declares that nature does *not* make things irrationally, but does so according to some rational principle (*logos*). I therefore prefer to read, with MS Vat. gr. 207, *ou gar hê phusis alogôi dunamei [phusin] poiei*.

111 Reading *kataginesthai* instead of Busse's *kekhrêsthai*.
112 cf. Ammonius, *in Int.* 2,9–25.
113 Aristotle, *Int.* 17a2–3.
114 Reading *pan hoti entheôreitai en tois kath' hekasta* with MS Vat. gr. 207, instead of Busse's conjecture *pan hoti an theôrêtai*.
115 The *Parmenides* comes later in the school curriculum, as dealing with theological issues; in fact it was the last dialogue to be studied.
116 Reading *genos*, with most MSS, instead of *meros*, attested only by the second hand of F.
117 Reading *parekhein*, with MS Vat. gr. 207, instead of Busse's *ekhein*.
118 In other words, the preliminary questions having been covered, Porphyry, and consequently Ammonius(?), now begins his discussion of the treatise's subject-matter.
119 This embryological scheme, with its gradual development of ascending levels in the Aristotelian hierarchy of kinds of souls, merits comparison with that of Porphyry in the *ad Gaurum*; see the translation in this series by J. Wilberding, *Porphyry. To Gaurus On How Embryos Are Ensouled and On What Is in Our Power* (London: Bloomsbury, 2011). Unlike Porphyry, Ammonius(?) does not explicitly mention the vegetative stage, although it may be equivalent to the initial stage at which the soul is 'vivified and animated'.
120 Busse points to Aristotle, *Top.* 108a18; 139b19 ff.
121 i.e. Sirius.
122 Perhaps, instead of the reading of the MSS *diakrinei/diakrinetai tous karpous*, one should read *diaphtheirei tous karpous*, 'the dog ruins the fruits'. A poem in the Greek Anthology (*Anth. Gr.* 9.256) speaks of the caterpillar as *kuôn dendrôn karpophthoros*, 'dog destructive of the fruit of trees'.
123 The marine dog was probably a kind of shark. On the homonymy of 'dog', see, for instance, Simplicius, *in Cat.* 29,8 ff.
124 cf. Aristotle, *Phys.* 5.1, 225a14–15.
125 Euripides, *Phoenician Women* 470. 'When it is said in Euripides', attested only by MS D, may well be a marginal gloss. The other MSS read *hôs hotan eipômen*, 'as when we say'.
126 It is odd to find Ammonius(?) attributing what corresponds to the first imposition of names to Nature, rather than to mankind, or a council of sages at the dawn of history. See Porphyry, *in Cat.* 57–8.
127 Homoeomeries are substances whose parts are synonymous with the whole; see Aristotle, *GC* 1.1, 314a20.
128 Plato's five 'greatest kinds' (*megista genê*); see Plato, *Sophist* 249D–55E.
129 i.e. Porphyry.

130 cf. Aristotle, *Phys.* 1.6, 189a11 ff.
131 For instance, of Heracles to his descendants (one to many), or of the descendants to one another (them to them). The Greek is as awkward as its English translation.
132 Again, using Porphyry's examples, the relation of Tantalus to Orestes (one to one), or of Thebes to Pindar (cause to effect).
133 The *onomatothêtai* are usually thought of as a group of sages who get together at the dawn of history to impose names on things; it is odd, therefore, to see them placed as late in history as the descendants of Heracles. Previously (50,16 ff.), we have seen the author speak of *Nature* as the inventor of names.
134 Repetition of the Porphyrian lemma, which is rather frequent in our commentary, seems to be another sign of the sloppy and/or hybrid nature of its composition.
135 i.e. the genus.
136 cf. Aristotle, *Top.* 112a19.
137 cf. Alexander of Aphrodisias, *in Top.* 381,25–6.
138 The Greek word is *hupographê*: literally, a 'sub-painting' or 'something painted underneath'.
139 Reading *peri tou haplôs genous poioumetha ton logon tou panti genei epharmosai dumanenou*, with most MSS, instead of Busse's *peri tou haplôs genous poioumetha ton logon ton panti genei epharmosai dumanenon*.
140 It is noteworthy that the author here seems perfectly oblivious of the objections by Plotinus (*Enneades* 6.1.2–3, following Nicostratus) that there cannot be one common genus of the sensible and the intelligible, since they stand in a relation of prior to posterior. On the response to this argument, which seems to come from Porphyry's lost major commentary on the *Categories* and is preserved in Dexippus, *in Cat.* 40,19–41,3; also see P. Hadot, 'The Harmony of Plotinus and Aristotle according to Porphyry', in R. Sorabji (ed.), *Aristotle Transformed* (Ithaca, NY: Cornell University Press, 1990), pp. 125–40.
141 cf. Plato, *Cratylus* 399C.
142 cf. Aristotle, *DA* 1.1, 403a30–b2 (although Aristotle's term for 'anger' here is *orgê*, rather than *thumos*, as in our text); Nemesius, *On the Nature of Man* 20.
143 cf. Philoponus, *in An. Post.* 109,8 ff.; *in Phys.* 228,15 ff.
144 Omitting 'but species' (*all' eidê*), with MS Vat. gr. 207. Individuals (*ta atoma*) cannot, I presume, be construed as species.
145 On these typical examples of meaningless words, see David Blank's translation: *Ammonius. On Aristotle On Interpretation 1–8* (London: Duckworth, 1996), p. 148, n. 154.
146 What follows (59,4–8) seems to provide an alternative division; the passage is missing from MS Vat. gr. 207, and I have bracketed it with curly brackets. In

fact, this section of the commentary presents several slightly divergent versions, of which the most complete and coherent seems to be the one presented at 60,7.
147 Omitting *hoti* at 59,20 with Busse *in apparatu*.
148 cf. above, 17,7.
149 Omitting *hôs ta eidê tôn atomôn*, which is a conjecture by Busse.
150 The Greek *eidos* can mean either 'species' or 'form', and our author is playing upon both meanings here.
151 Busse postulates a lacuna here.
152 Literally, 'in the what-is-it'. On the difficulty of translating this expression, see A. de Libera and A.-P. Segonds, *Porphyre. Isagoge* (Paris: Vrin, 1998), pp. 40–2.
153 The Greek reads, *en tôi hopoion ti estin*, literally 'in the what-kind-of-thing-is-it'.
154 Porphyry, *Isag.* 2,15–17; cf. Aristotle, *Top.* 1.5, 102a31–2.
155 The following lines are a paraphrase of Porphyry, *Isag.* 2,17 ff.
156 Presumably, what is meant is that of the initial division of words into meaningless and meaningful, the entire branch of meaningless words is left out of consideration.
157 Reading *en tôi pôs ekhei* with most MSS, instead of Busse's *pôs ekhon esti*, literally 'in-the-how-is-it-disposed'. This was the third of the four Stoic categories; see Sorabji, *Philosophy of the Commentators*, vol. 3, pp. 90–1.
158 Homer, *Odyssey* 19.361–475.
159 Typical examples of polyonyms, or identical things with many names; cf. Ammonius, *in Cat.* 16,6; Simplicius, *in Cat.* 38,26.
160 Porphyry, *Isag.* 2,28–3,1.
161 Our author here skips Porphyry's discussion of the difference between the genus and the property, *Isag.* 3,1–5.
162 MS p here adds a rather confused paragraph on the difference between genus, species, and property, which I omit, following Busse.
163 MS V here adds a rather lengthy passage on subordinate genera. See Appendix of Variant Readings.
164 Another repeated lemma; see n. 134 above.
165 Porphyry, *Isag.* 3,14–15.
166 The Greek word is *êthiliotês*. LSJ's definition ('folly, silliness') does not fit with this or many other occurrences. The contrast between *êthiliotês* and *akolasia* seems to go back to Speusippus; cf. fr. 81b, in L. Tarán (ed.), *Speusippus of Athens: A Critical Study with a Collection of the Related Texts and Commentary*, Philosophia Antiqua 39 (Leiden: Brill, 1981).
167 i.e. definitions.
168 cf. above, 41,10 ff.
169 This explanation seems to contradict Ammonius' viewpoint in his commentary on the *Categories* (*in Cat.* 40,22–41,11), where he claims that Porphyry dealt with

ante rem universals in the *Isagôgê*. See Militello, *I commentari all' Isagoge di Porfirio*, pp. 97–8; R. Sorabji (ed.), *Aristotle Re-Interpreted: New Findings on Seven Hundred Years of the Ancient Commentators* (London: Bloomsbury, 2016), p. 381.

170 cf. Ammonius, *in Cat.* 16,27; *in Int.* 10,4.
171 cf. Ammonius, *in Int.* 10,3–4.
172 cf. above, at 69,25.
173 Another double lemma, although here the author seems to have first given a theoretical treatment or general survey of the chapter on the species, before moving on to a lemma-by-lemma commentary.
174 Porphyry quotes this verse from Euripides' lost tragedy *Aeolus*, fr. 15, in J.A. Nauck (ed.), *Euripidis tragoediae. Euripidis perditarum tragoediarum fragmenta*, vol. 3 (Leipzig: Teubner, 1869). *Eidos*, the Greek word for 'species', can also mean 'form' or 'external appearance', as in this case.
175 Omitting *to eidos* at 71,24, following Busse in his apparatus.
176 A common theme among the commentators; cf. Simplicius, *in Cat.* 126,5–31; Dexippus, *in Cat.* 3.3, 67,8–68,12.
177 Plato, *Timaeus* 53C ff. At 72,18, I excise *legôn*, following Busse *in apparatu*.
178 Euclid, *Elements* 1, prop. 46. I restore this reference to Euclid, which Busse omitted although versions of it are found in several MSS, including Vat. gr. 207.
179 Reading *oude touto ex anagkês* at 73,6 with MSS D, V, and Vat. gr. 207.
180 Here, the original square is divided into two rectangular areas by a median.
181 Proclus (*in Euclidis* 104,18; 113,7) classes the semicircular angle as mixed, and the scholiast to Euclid (*Sch. in Eucl.* 1,1,445–8) speaks of the angles of semicircles as consisting of a straight line and an arc.
182 cf. Aristotle, *Cat.* 7b15.
183 See above, 70,25–71,1.
184 Porphyry, *Isag.* 4,11–12.
185 cf. Porphyry, *Isag.* 5,21–3.
186 In other words, the original first division of substance is into corporeal and incorporeal; but Porphyry chose to ignore the incorporeal in the present context, and further divided only the corporeal.
187 Reading *diakheontai* (Busse, *in apparatu*) for the unlikely *hêdontai* of the MSS.
188 Porphyry, *Isag.* 5,17–20.
189 Porphyry, *Isag.* 5,17–18.
190 cf. Porphyry, *Isag.* 5,21–2.
191 cf. Homer, *Iliad* 1.544, and in several other passages.
192 cf. above, 49,5 and note.
193 The author's reference is somewhat obscure. Busse cites Plato, *Philebus* 16C; *Politicus* 262A–C; *Sophist* 266A–B; *Sophist* 219 ff.

194 Busse points to Aristotle, *An. Pr.* 43a25 ff.; *Metaph.* 6.15, 1039b28. Yet these passages do not come from the *Demonstration*, by which the ancients meant the *Posterior Analytics*. The reference is more probably to a passage such as Aristotle, *An. Post.* 75b30 ff.
195 Herodotus, 1.47.
196 Reading *epeidê prostithemenos autôi ho tôn anthrôpôn arithmos kai tôn hippôn*, with MS Vat. gr. 207, instead of Busse's *epeidê prostithemenos autêi ho tôn anthrôpôn arithmos*.
197 Note that the author here leaves open the possibility, contrary to Aristotelian orthodoxy, that the universe may have had a beginning. If the author is really Ammonius, was this a concession to the Christians in his audience?
198 Reading *êdunanto*, with MS Vat. gr. 207, instead of Busse's *edunato*.
199 See above, 45,2 ff.
200 Following the suggestion of an anonymous reader, I read *to gar leukon katholou estin* with the *editio princeps*, instead of Busse's *to gar katholou esti leukon*.
201 As usual, the author begins with a brief overall consideration of the chapter (*theôria*), before moving on to a lemma-by-lemma commentary (*praxis*).
202 Porphyry, *Isag.* 8,19–20.
203 i.e. there are some animals that are neither standing nor sitting.
204 The Greek reads, *en tais tou pôs ekhein heterotêsi*: 'and always in respect of diversities in what he is like', according to the translation of Barnes. But the Greek *pôs ekhein* refers to the third Stoic category, sometimes rendered as 'disposition' or 'modality'.
205 In the text of the *Isagôgê* as edited by Busse, the order of these two adjectives is reversed: 'for of differences, some make [a thing] of another sort (*alloion*), and others [make it] something else (*allo*)'.
206 Homer, *Odyssey* 16.181.
207 Presupposed here is a scheme of chiasmic logic, in which four characteristics are placed each at the corner of a square: separable, inseparable, making something other (*allo*), and making something of a different sort (*alloion*). The six possible combinations of these four terms are then examined.
208 i.e. the body.
209 Aristotle, *Cat.* 3b24–5.
210 Aristotle, *Cat.* 2a11.
211 By horizontal (*kata platos*), the author means entities that belong to the same ontological level (two human beings, for instance, or horse, man, and ox); while by vertical, he means entities at different ontological levels (intellect, soul, angels, etc.).
212 As we have seen (above, n. 54), the author's frequent mention of angels, which play only a subordinate role in pagan Neoplatonism, seem to be a clear indication

213 The Greek reads *kai allôs*: a phrase used to introduce various possible interpretations that is common in scholia; less so in written commentaries.
214 As we have just seen, four terms in fact produce six possible combinations, but presumably the combinations 'rational and irrational' and 'mortal and immortal' are omitted as contradictory.
215 Homer, *Odyssey* 12.118.
216 With MSS F, V, and Vat. gr. 207, I omit the following words that translate the Greek printed by Busse: 'because they have something prior to them, situated higher'. This is likely to be a rather inept explanatory gloss.
217 Busse remarks, without giving his reasons, that the next ten lines do not seem to be by Ammonius.
218 Once again, with MSS F, V, and Vat. gr. 207, I omit the Greek words, included by Busse, that may be translated as, 'for animal is divided into these'.
219 For Porphyry (*Isag.* 10,15), it is a god that is defined by immortal and rational. Once again, the author's substitution of 'angel' for 'god' is no doubt significant.
220 In this etymology, the word *axiôma* is derived from *axiopiston oikothen*. The 'axioms' in question are those stated by Porphyry at *Isag.* 11,5–6; cf. below, Ammonius(?)' commentary ad loc.
221 cf. Porphyry, *Isag.* 11,19.
222 cf. Aristotle, *Top.* 8.13, 163a3.
223 See above, 41,10 ff.; 68,25 ff.
224 A clear indication of the oral nature of this text.
225 That is, it is not the case that animal does not participate in rational and mortal. I thank my anonymous readers for helping me to clarify this point.
226 Literally, 'in-the-what-kind-of-thing-is-it' (*en tôi poion ti estin*).
227 Literally, 'in the what-is-it' (*en tôi ti estin*).
228 Literally, 'in the what-kind-of-thing-is-it' (*en tôi hopoion ti estin*).
229 The author's point seems to be as follows: the definition of human being is 'capable of receiving intellect and knowledge' (cf. *Top.* 112a19). But, one might wonder, 'what kind of knowledge?' The answer must be 'knowledge in general', for if the knowledge in question were a particular kind of knowledge – say, the knowledge of grammar – then the definition in question would define not a human being as such, but a grammarian.
230 Ammonius(?)' lemma: *Kai tou ti ên einai kai ho tou pragmatos esti meros* – differs slightly from the text of the *Isagôgê* as edited by Busse: *Kai ho tou ti ên einai tou pragmatos esti meros*.

231 The Greek phrase *to ti ên einai* is, of course, an Aristotelian technical term, notoriously difficult to translate, but meaning roughly 'essence'. Here Ammonius(?) analyses it as consisting of *to ti estin* (another Aristotelian term meaning 'essence'), and *to einai*, or being.

232 The Greek verb *pleô* usually means 'to sail', but I have chosen a broader meaning to convey a mode of transport by water than can be carried out by animals or inanimate objects as well.

233 i.e. the genus, species, and difference.

234 Reading *dia tôn grapsantôn* with MS Vat. gr. 207, instead of Busse's *dia tôn hupogrammatôn*. The allusion is to diagrams illustrating divisions.

235 As was the view of the Stoics, for instance.

236 Reading *to ginesthai legô* with MSS F, V, and p ('fortasse recte', according to Busse).

237 An imprecise quotation of Hippocrates, *On the Nature of Man* 2.11.

238 On the three-dimensional, qualityless body as substrate, cf. Philoponus, *in Phys.* 156,13; 579,4; *de Aeternitate Mundi* 409,22; 413,6–434,2.

239 In other words, the negative definition 'by elimination of the other words' (i.e. genus, species, property, and difference) might also apply to such non-existent *entia rationis* as the goat-stag.

240 Note the repetition of the lemma, which adds to the impression that we have to do, at least in this part of the commentary, with a collection of scholia rather than the work of a single author.

241 For this method, cf. Simplicius, *in Cat.* 45,11 ff.; Philoponus, *in Phys.* 250,29 (who refers to it as 'the method transmitted in the *Isagôgê*').

242 A reference to the last two kinds of universals enumerated in the discussion of the triple universal, above, 39,14 ff., corresponding to physics and logic respectively.

243 See n. 134 above.

244 These two concepts have not been introduced as *kanones* in this work, but they are presented in Ammonius, *in Cat.* 74,20. This remark would thus seem to be useless for students who have not yet read the *Categories* or commentaries on it. Yet it seems to be referred to below, at 120,15 ff.

245 cf. 55,19; 58,1 ff.; 98,22; 99,1–9; 100,4–19.

246 While Busse's text of the *Isagôgê* and Ammonius(?)' lemma read *ep' elattonôn*, 'of fewer things', the comment implies that its author read *ep' elatton*, 'of lesser extension'.

247 cf. Porphyry, *Isag.* 11,2–5; Ammonius(?), *in Isag.* 104,13–22.

248 cf. 57,25; 102,18.

249 See 118,7.

250 See 109,1–3.
251 The author (or authors?) provides no comment whatsoever on the section of the *Isagôgê* entitled 'On the Commonality of the Genus and the Accident', Porphyry, *Isag.* 16,19–17,2. Instead, he jumps directly to the section 'On the Difference between the Genus and the Accident'.
252 The MSS add *kai hippou*, 'and a horse', but it is hard to understand why it would be easy to state the commonality between a dog and a horse, so I prefer to delete these words.
253 cf. 115,22 ff.
254 Earlier (7,2; 92,17), Socrates has been described as snub-nosed, as he almost always was described in the Greek tradition. This contradiction may be interpreted as yet another indication of the heteroclite nature of the present commentary.

Appendix of Variant Readings

I append a selection of alternative readings, which Busse decided not to include in the text. Their provenance is as follows: D = Firenze, Biblioteca Medicea Laurenziana, Plut. 10.26 (12th cent.); V = Vienna, Österreichische Nationalbibliothek, phil. gr. 139 (14th cent.); p = the *editio princeps*, Venice: sumptibus Nicolai Blasti, 1500. In what follows, page numbers refer to Busse's edition, while the letters indicate the respective manuscript or edition from which the variant reading is taken (folios not indicated).

at p. 23,24 Busse: D

Here is the end of the prolegomena to philosophy and to the *Isagôgê*. Is time within time, or not within time? In time. If it is in time, what is its nature? For things that are in something are of another nature, as a grain of wheat is in a medimnos,[1] but not in time. But if this is so, time is timeless, which is absurd. Time is in time as a part in a whole. This pertains to the theologian.

23,24: V

A word is a discourse of the philosophers, which announces and articulates[2] nouns and verbs or, as it were, a distribution of what are the ten most generic genera among the philosophers, since all the ten categories are divided and distributed and uttered by the five words of the philosophers, and without these a philosophical noun or verb cannot be announced.

25,4: V

What is useful is something other than what is necessary. Necessary is living and breathing, since one cannot exist without breathing. But if something is needful (*khreiôdês*), it is not necessary as well: for what is needful is putting on clothing and shoes, but it is not necessary, since it is possible for a human being and an animal to exist without these things. In short, what is necessary is observed in conjunction with the very existence of substance, while what is needful [is observed] in conjunction with such-and-such a way of life of it.

66,12: V

'from those which are predicated as of species'. Why did he say 'as of species and genera'? Because of subordinate genera and species. Therefore, the same things are said to be both genera and species. This, then, is why he said 'as of species', because they are not always species, but sometimes genera as well. 'As here' indicates the species and the property properly so called, or the most specific and the [property] that belongs [to its subject] alone, always, and to each one. For the subordinate species is predicated of things that differ in species, as animate, which is a species of body. Thus, the property, too, which occurs to the entire species, although not to it alone, is said of things that differ in species, [as for instance] two-footed [is said] of human beings and of birds.

125,22: DVp

he says there are commonalities of the difference and the property: that of being equally participated and that of always belonging to the things to which they belong. For neither is Socrates more rational than Plato, nor is he more capable of laughing. For although we say one being is more or less rational than another, we mean something else by 'rational' and 'more rational' in that case. For then we are not seeking rational substance, but the rational habitude in studies, which is a propensity of the soul. Human beings are always rational, and always capable of laughing: but [they are] 'always' [so] not in the sense of laughing, but in the sense of natural tendency. He also states two othernesses: the difference contains several species, while the property is present to only one species; and that although the difference follows the species, it is not convertible with it. For if something is a human being, it is rational, but it is not the case that if something is rational, it is a human being. The property, by contrast, both follows and is convertible: for if something is a human being, it is capable of laughing, and if something is capable of laughing, it is a human being.

125,22: p (continuing the previous)

On the commonality and the difference between the difference and the accident

> Common to the difference and the accident is the fact of being said of several things

There are two commonalities of the accident and the difference: the fact of being said of several things, and the fact of always being present to the species, but the former fits with both separable and inseparable things, while the latter [fits] only with inseparable ones. For a human being is not always sitting, but a crow is always black. There are three othernesses: for the difference contains the species, for rational has a greater extension than human being, while accidents are both contained and contain. For insofar as black fits not only with an Ethiopian, but also with a crow and other things, it contains, while insofar as the Ethiopian can also be receptive of other accidents, it is contained. He said [in a way], because they neither contain in the proper sense of the term, nor are they contained in the proper sense of the term.

126,2: p

For Socrates is not more rational than another, unless it be by [amount] of learning alone, which is a capacity of the soul, but not by rational substance, as we have already said. Accident, in contrast, is susceptible of the more and the less, for one Ethiopian can be more black than another.

127,4: p

On the commonality of the species and the property

Common to the species and the property is the fact of being mutually predicated of one another. For having completed the account of the differences, he moves on to the species, and says that that whereby the species differs from and has something in common with the genus and the difference has been stated when it was being compared to them. Therefore, that whereby it differs from and has something in common with the property and the accident will be stated. Now, there are two commonalities between the species and the property: that of reciprocating, and that of being mutually predicated of one another. For if something is a human being, it is capable of laughing, and if something is capable of laughing, it is a human being. [By] capable of laughing, however, he means not laughing but being of such a nature as to laugh. And also [the fact that] the species share equally in that of which they are species, and the properties in that of which they are properties. For all are equally rational according to the essential account, and all are equally capable of laughing. But there are several othernesses, that the species can be the genus of other things; for instance, animal is a species of animate, but genus of human being and horse.

On their differences

But the species differs from the property. By species, he means the subordinate one, not the most specific. But the property cannot be a property of something else. And the species is prior to the property, for human being and capable of laughing must [previously] exist. But the property is posterior to the species. In addition, the species is always present to the substrate in act, for Socrates is always a human being, but the property is not always [present] in it, but it is always capable of laughing potentially. In addition, those things whose definitions are different are themselves different. This fits with the other four: after all, we can also say of the genus and the others that of those things whose definitions are different, they too are different.

127,5: p

On the commonality of the species and the accident.

Of the species and the accident. He states one commonality of the species and the accident, but several differences. He also states the reason why he stated one commonality, but several differences: [it is] the one we too stated earlier, that the things that differ the most have scarcely any commonalities, but several differences. On the contrary, things that are closely joined to one another have very few differences, but several commonalities. Common to both of them is the fact of being said of several things; after all, human being is predicated of Socrates, Alcibiades, and the rest, and black of an Ethiopian and a crow, and many other things.

On their difference

Properties of each of them. It is a property of the species to be predicated essentially, of the accident to be predicated qualitatively or dispositionally. For having been asked, 'what kind of an Ethiopian?', we say 'he is healthy' or 'he is sick'. Species, although it is said qualitatively, participates in the differences, as we said previously. In addition, each substance participates in one species, but several accidents, such as hook-nosedness, snub-nosedness, blackness. In addition, the species is prior, the accident posterior: for the human being must exist, then black.

Notes

1 A measure of volume, equivalent to 51.84 litres in ancient Attica, but its quantity varied considerably according to place and time.
2 The Greek word is *diatranôtikos*, a hapax.

Bibliography

Adamson, P., 'Porphyrius Arabus on Nature and Art: 463F Smith in Context', in G. Karamanolis and A. Sheppard (eds), *Studies on Porphyry* (London: Institute of Classical Studies, 2007), pp. 141–63.

Athanassiadi, P., *Damascius. The Philosophical History* (Athens: Apamea Cultural Association, 1999).

Barnes, J., *Porphyry. Introduction* (Oxford: Clarendon Press, 2003).

Barnes, J., and Bobzien, S., *Alexander of Aphrodisias. On Aristotle Prior Analytics 1.1–7* (London: Duckworth, 1991).

Blank, D., *Ammonius. On Aristotle On Interpretation 1–8* (London: Duckworth, 1996).

Blank, D., 'Ammonius Hermeiou and His School', in L. Gerson (ed.), *The Cambridge History of Philosophy in Late Antiquity* (Cambridge: Cambridge University Press, 2010), pp. 654–66.

Blank, D., and Kretzmann, N., *Ammonius. On Aristotle On Interpretation 9 with Boethius. On Aristotle On Interpretation 9* (London: Duckworth, 1998).

Busse, A. (ed.), *Ammonii in Porphyrii Isagogen sive quinque voces*, CAG 4.3 (Berlin: Reimer, 1891).

Byrne, P.H., *Analysis and Science in Aristotle* (Albany, NY: SUNY Press, 1997).

Chiaradonna, R., 'Porphyre de Tyr, Isagogè', in R. Goulet (ed.), *Dictionnaire des Philosophes Antiques*, vol. Vb (Paris: Presses du CNRS, 2012), pp. 1335–43.

Decleva Caizzi, F., *Antisthenis fragmenta* (Milan: Istituto Editoriale Cisalpino, 1966).

de Libera, A., *La querelle des universaux. De Platon à la fin du Moyen Âge* (Paris: Seuil, 1996).

de Libera, A., *L' art des généralités. Théories de l' abstraction* (Paris: Aubier, 1999).

de Libera, A., and Segonds, A.-P., *Porphyre. Isagoge* (Paris: Vrin, 1998).

Dörrie, H., and Baltes, M., *Der Platonismus im 2. und 3. Jahrhundert nach Christus*, Der Platonismus in der Antike 3 (Stuttgart: Frommann-Holzboog, 1993).

Erismann, C., 'Isagogè: la tradition latine médiévale', in R. Goulet (ed.), *Dictionnaire des Philosophes Antiques*, vol. Vb (Paris: Presses du CNRS, 2012), pp. 1344–9.

Fortier, S., 'Ammonius on Universals and Abstraction: An Interpretation and Translation of Ammonius' *In Porphyrii Isagogen* 39, 8–42, 16', *Laval théologique et philosophique* 68.1 (2012), 21–33.

Fowler, H.N., *Plato. Euthyphro, Apology, Crito, Phaedo, Phaedrus*, LCL (Cambridge, MA: Harvard University Press, 1960).

Gertz, S., *Elias and David. Introductions to Philosophy with Olympiodorus. Introduction to Logic* (London: Bloomsbury, 2018).

Hadot, I., *Athenian and Alexandrian Neoplatonism and the Harmonization of Aristotle and Plato*, trans. M. Chase (Leiden: Brill, 2015).

Hadot, I., et al., *Simplicius. Commentaire sur les Catégories. Fascicule I: Introduction, première partie* (Leiden: Brill, 1990).

Hadot, P., 'The Harmony of Plotinus and Aristotle according to Porphyry', in R. Sorabji (ed.), *Aristotle Transformed* (Ithaca, NY: Cornell University Press, 1990), pp. 125–40.

Henry, P., *Études plotiniennes. I. Les états du texte de Plotin* (Paris: Budé, 1938).

Hugonnard-Roche, H., 'Porphyre de Tyr: Tradition arabe', in R. Goulet (ed.), *Dictionnaire des Philosophes Antiques*, vol. Vb (Paris: Presses du CNRS, 2012), pp. 1453–60.

Huh, M.-J., 'Le premier commentaire de Boèce à l'Isagogè de Porphyre, introduction, traduction et commentaire', PhD diss., Institute of Philosophy, Leuven, 2013.

Kühn, K.G. (ed.), *Claudii Galeni opera omnia*, 22 vols (Berlin: De Gruyter, 1821–33).

Mansfeld, J., *Prolegomena. Questions To Be Settled before the Study of an Author, or a Text* (Leiden: Brill, 1994).

Matthews, G., and Cohen, M., *Ammonius. On Aristotle Categories* (London: Duckworth, 1991).

Militello, C., *I commentari all' Isagoge di Porfirio tra V e VI secolo* (Roma: Bonanno, 2010).

Mueller, C.F.W. (ed.), *M. Tullii Ciceronis. Scripta quae manserunt omnia*, 16 vols (Leipzig: Teubner, 1898).

Nauck, J.A. (ed.), *Euripidis tragoediae. Euripidis perditarum tragoediarum fragmenta*, vol. 3 (Leipzig: Teubner, 1869).

Pfeiffer, R. (ed.), *Callimachus*, 2 vols (Oxford: Oxford University Press, 1987).

Rabe, H. (ed.), *Joannes Philoponus. De aeternitate mundi. Contra Proclum* (Leipzig: Teubner, 1899).

Radermacher, L. and Usener, H. (eds), *Dionysii Halicarnasei Opuscula*, 2 vols (Leipzig: Teubner, 1929).

Saffrey, H.D. and Westerink, L.G. (eds), *Proclus. Théologie platonicienne*, 6 vols (Paris: Les Belles Lettres, 1968–97).

Sorabji, R. (ed.), *Aristotle Transformed: The Ancient Commentators and Their Influence* (Ithaca, NY: Cornell University Press, 1990).

Sorabji, R., *The Philosophy of the Commentators 200–600 AD. A Sourcebook*, 3 vols (London: Duckworth, 2004).

Sorabji, R., 'Divine Names and Sordid Deals in Ammonius' Alexandria', in A. Smith (ed.), *The Philosopher and Society in Late Antiquity: Essays in Honour of Peter Brown* (Swansea: Classical Press of Wales, 2005), pp. 203–13.

Sorabji, R. (ed.), *Aristotle Re-Interpreted: New Findings on Seven Hundred Years of the Ancient Commentators* (London: Bloomsbury, 2016).

Tarán, L. (ed.), *Speusippus of Athens: A Critical Study with a Collection of the Related Texts and Commentary*, Philosophia Antiqua 39 (Leiden: Brill, 1981).

Tardieu, M., *Les paysages reliques* (Louvain and Paris: Peeters, 1990).

Thiel, R. and Lohr, C. (eds), *Ammonius Hermeae. Commentaria in quinque voces Porphyrii* (Stuttgart: Frommann-Holzboog, 2002).

Thom, J.C. (ed.), *The Pythagorean Golden Verses* (Leiden: Brill, 1995).

Wakelnig, E., 'What Does Aristotle Have To Do with the Christian Arabic Trinity? The Triad "Generosity-Wisdom-Power" in the Alexandrian Prolegomena and Yaḥyā ibn 'Adī', *Le Muséon* 130.3–4 (2017), 445–77.

Walz, C. (ed.), *Rhetores Graeci*, 9 vols (Stuttgart: J.G. Cottae, 1832–6).

Watts, E.J., *City and School in Late Antique Athens and Alexandria* (Berkeley, CA: University of California Press, 2006).

Watts, E.J., *Riot in Alexandria: Tradition and Group Dynamics in Late Antique Pagan and Christian Communities* (Berkeley, CA: University of California Press, 2010).

Wilberding, J., *Porphyry. To Gaurus On How Embryos Are Ensouled and On What Is in Our Power* (London: Bloomsbury, 2011).

English–Greek Glossary

able (be): *dunamai*
abstain: *apekhomai*
absurd: *atopos*
accept: *paralambanô*
accident: *sumbebêkos*
accomplish: *teleô*
account: *apodosis*
accusation: *enklêma*
accustomed (be): *ethô*
achieve: *ekprassô*
achieved (be): *katorthoomai*
acquaintance: *empeiria*
acquire: *ktaomai*
act as a prior subject: *proupostrônnumi*
acting: *poiein*
activity: *energeia*
actuality: *energeia*
add: *prostithêmi*
add an additional specification: *prosdiorizomai*
added (be): *proserkhomai, proskeimai*
address (v.): *agoreuô, prosagoreuô, prosphôneô*
adjacent (be): *parakeimai*
admit: *prosdekhomai*
adorn: *epikosmeô*
advance: *prokoptô*
adventitious: *epeisodiôdês, epousiôdês*
affected (being): *paskhein*
after the many: *epi tois pollois*
aggregate: *athroisma, sunkrisis*
agree: *homologeô, sunkhôreô*
aim at: *stokhazomai*

akin: *sungenes*
alone: *monos*
alteration: *alloiôsis*
ambiguous: *amphibolos*
analogous: *analogos, analogeô*
analogous (be): *analogeô*
analyse: *analuô*
analysis: *analusis*
ancient: *palaios, presbus*
angel: *angelos*
anger: *orgê*
angle: *gônia*
angry: *thumikos*
animal: *zôion*
animate (adj.): *empsukhos*
animate (v.): *zôopoieô*
announce: *mênuô*
answer (v.): *apokrinomai*
ant: *murmêx*
apparition: *phantasma*
appear: *phainomai*
appellation: *prosêgoria*
appetitive: *orektikos*
apple: *mêlon*
apply: *prosagô*
apprehend: *katalambanô*
approach (n.): *epibolê*
approach (v.): *proseimi*
appropriate (adj.): *deon, oikeios*
appropriately: *prepontôs*
ardour: *thumos*
argument: *epikheirêma, logismos, logos*
arithmetic: *arithmêtikê*

armed (be): *hoplizô*
around the heart: *perikardios*
arrive: *hêkô*
art: *tekhnê*
artery: *artêria*
articulated (adv.): *diêrthrômenôs*
artificial: *tekhnêtos*
ascend: *anagô, anatrekhô*
ascent: *anabasis*
ask: *erôtaô*
ass: *onos*
assimilate: *exomoioeô*
assimilation: *homoiôsis*
assume: *hupolambanô*
assume beforehand: *prolambanô*
assumption: *lêmmation*
astral: *astrôios*
astronomy: *astronomia*
at hand: *prokheiros*
attempt: *enkheirêsis*
attend: *ephistanô*
attract: *ephelkô*
attribute (v.): *aponemô*
attributes (n.): *prosonta*
authentic: *gnêsios*
avert: *apotrepomai*
awaken: *diegeirô*
axiom: *axiôma*

bad: *kakos*
bald, baldness: *phalakros, phalakra*
barking (capable of): *hulaktikos*
be (to): *huparkhô*
before the many: *pro tôn pollôn*
begin: *arkhomai, eisballô*
being: *einai, on*
being-in-a-position: *keisthai*
belly: *gastêr*
belong (v.): *huparkhô*

biped: *dipous*
black: *melas*
blackening: *melansis*
blackness: *melania*
blame (v.): *memphô*
blameworthy: *psektos*
bleed: *phlebotomeô*
blind (go): *tuphlôttô*
blood: *haima*
body: *sôma*
body-loving: *philosômatos*
bond (n.): *desmos*
bone: *ostoun*
book: *biblion*
borderland: *metaikhmion*
bridge: *gephura*
bright: *phôteinos*
bring: *proagô*
bring into existence beforehand:
    prohuphistamai
bronze (n.): *khalkos*
bronze (adj.): *khalkeos*
burn (v.): *kaiô*
butcher: *mageiros*

call (v.): *kaleô, prosagoreuô, prosphôneô*
calm (v.): *koimizô*
camel: *kamêlos*
carpenter: *tektôn*
carpentry: *tektonikê*
carry out: *poieomai*
case: *ptôsis*
category: *katêgoria*
cauldron: *lebês*
cause: *aitia, aition*
cease: *pauô*
cease to exist: *apollumi*
celestial: *epouranios*
censorious: *philaitios*

censure: *diabolê*
centaur: *hippokentauros*
centre: *kentron*
chain (v.): *katadeô*
champion: *prostatês*
chance: *tukhê*
change (v.): *metaballô*
change (n.): *metabolê*
change along with (v.): *summetaballô*
chapter: *kephalaion*
character: *êthos*
characterized (be): *kharaktêrizomai*
child: *paidion, pais, teknon*
choice: *eklogê, proairesis*
circle: *kuklos*
circular: *diallêlos*
circumference: *periphereia*
circumscribe: *perigraphô, periorizô*
city: *polis*
clarify: *saphênizô*
clarity: *saphêneia*
clear (adj.): *dêlos, enargês, saphês, tranês*
clothed (be): *enduomai*
co-eliminate: *sunanaireô*
coextensive (be): *exisazô*
cognitive: *gnôstikos*
coincide: *suntrekhô*
cold: *psukhros*
coldness: *psukhrotês*
collect: *sullegô, sunagô*
colour: *khroia, khrôma*
combination: *sumplokê, suzugia*
combine: *sumplekô, sunkrinô, suntithêmi*
come first: *prôteuô*
come to be: *ginomai*
come together: *suneimi*
come up: *prospiptô*
common: *koinos*
commonality: *koinônia, koinotês*

companion: *hetairos*
compare (v.): *paraballô*
comparison: *parabolê*
complete (adj.): *anendeês*
complete (v.): *sumplêroô*
completive: *sumplêrôtikos*
composition: *sunthesis*
compound (adj.): *sunthetos*
compound (n.): *sunkrima*
comprehend: *perilambanô*
comprehension: *noêsis*
conceive: *ennoeô, epinoeô*
concept: *ennoia, epinoia*
conceptual: *ennoêmatikos*
concerned (be): *kataginomai*
concerning motion: *metabatikos*
concise: *suntomos*
conclude: *katapauô, sumperainô*
conclusion: *sumperasma*
concomitant (be): *parepomai*
concourse: *sundromê*
conflict (v.): *makhomai*
confuse: *sunkheô*
conjunction: *sundesmos*
consider: *nomizô*
consideration: *theôria*
consist (in): *sunkeimai*
consistent: *akolouthos*
conspicuous: *ekdêlos*
constitute: *sunistêmi*
constitution: *sustasis*
constitutive: *sustatikos*
contact (v.): *sunaptô*
contain: *periekhô*
containing: *periektikos*
contingent: *endekhomenos*
continuous: *sunekhes*
contract (v.): *stenoomai, sustellô*
contrary (adj.): *enantios*

contrary (be): *enantioomai*
contribute: *sumballomai, sunteleô*
conversation: *sunousia*
convert: *antistrephô*
convertible (be): *antikatêgoreisthai*
cool (v.): *psukhô*
cooling (n.): *psuksis*
copulative: *sumplektikos*
corporeally: *sômatikôs*
count (v.): *aparithmeô*
countless: *murios*
coupled (be): *sunduazomai, suzeugnumi*
craftsman: *tekhnitês*
create: *dêmiourgeô*
crow: *korax*
cultivate: *periepô*
cure (n.): *iama*
cure (v.): *iaomai*
curved: *kampulos*
customary usage: *sunêtheia*

dagger: *makhaira*
daily: *hêmerinos*
damage (n.): *blabê*
damage (v.): *blaptô, diaphtheirô, lumainomai*
dark: *skoteinos*
dative: *dotikos*
deal with: *dialambanô, pragmateuomai*
death: *teleutê*
declaratory: *apophantikos*
declare: *apophainomai*
decline (v.): *paraiteô*
deep (adj.): *bathus*
defence: *apologia*
defend onself: *apologeomai*
deficiency: *elleipsis*
define: *horizô*
definiendum: horiston

definition: *horismos, horos*
definitory: *horistikos*
deliberately: *exepitêdes*
demiurge: *dêmiourgos*
demon: *daimôn, daimonion*
demonstrate: *apodeiknumi*
demonstration: *apodeixis*
demonstrative: *apodeiktikos*
depart: *apoginomai*
deposit: *kataballô*
depth: *bathos*
descend: *hupokateimi, katapheromai, kateimi*
descent: *katabasis*
describe: *hupographô*
description: *hupographê*
desirable: *ephetos*
desire (n.): *epithumia*
desire (v.): *ephiêmi, oregomai*
destroy together: *sumphtheirô*
determinate: *aphôrismenos, hôrismenos*
diagonal: *diametron*
dialectic: *dialektikê*
differ: *diallattô, diapherô, diistêmi*
different: *diaphoros*
different sort (of): *alloios*
difficult: *duskherês*
dimension: *diastasis*
diminish: *meioô*
diminution: *meiôsis*
disagree: *diaphôneô*
disbelieve: *apisteô*
discover: *heuriskô*
discovery: *heuresis*
discrete: *diôrismenos*
discuss: *dialegô*
dishonourable: *atimos*
disorder: *akosmia*
disparage: *diaballô*

disposed (be): *diatithêmi*
disposition: *hexis*
disproportion: *ametria*
dissimilar parts (of): *anomoiomerês*
distance: *apostasis*
distant: *porrô*
distinguish (v.): *antidiaireô, diakrinô, diastellô, diorizomai*
distinguishing (n.): *diastolê*
divide (v.): *diaireô, merizô*
divine: *theios*
divisible: *diairetos, meristos*
division: *diairesis*
divisive: *diairetikos*
do: *draô, prattô, rezô*
doctor: *iatros*
dog: *kuôn*
dominate: *krateô*
double: *diplasios*
doubt (v.): *endoiazô*
dove: *phatta*
downhill: *katantes*
drawing-board: *abakion*
dry: *xêros*
dryness: *xêrotês*

eager: *prothumos*
earth: *gê*
easy: *eukherês, eumarês, rhadion*
economical: *oikonomikos*
effect: *aitiaton*
element: *stoikheion*
eliminate: *anaireô*
emulation: *zêlon*
enclose: *perikleiô*
encompass: *sumperilambanô*
encourage: *protrepô*
end (n.): *telos*
end up: *teleutaô, teleô*

endure: *diarkeô*
enmattered: *enulos*
ensoul: *psukhoô*
entail: *suneispherô, sunephelkomai*
enter: *eiserkhomai*
entitle: *epigraphô*
enumerate: *aparithmeô*
equal: *episês, isos*
equilateral: *isopleuros*
equine: *hippeios*
equivalent (be): *isodunameô*
error: *hamartêma*
essence: *to ti ên einai, ti estin*
essentially: *en tôi ti estin*
establish: *diatassô*
esteem (held in): *endoxos*
eternally moved: *aeikinêtos*
ethical: *êthikos*
Ethiopian: *aithiops*
etymology: *etumologia*
even (adj.): *artios*
evident: *phaneros*
examine: *episkopeô, exetazô, prokheirizomai*
example: *hupodeigma, paradeigma*
exceed: *huperballô, huperkeimai, perisseuô*
excess: *huperbolê*
excessive (be): *peritteuô*
exchange (v.): *ameibô*
exegete: *exêgêtês*
exhort: *parakeleuomai*
exist: *huparkhô, huphistêmi*
existence: *huparxis*
expedient (be): *sumpherô*
expel: *exôtheô, ekkrinô*
experience: *paskhô*
explain: *exêgeô*
explanation: *exêgêsis*

extended: *diastatos*
extraordinary: *xenoprepês*
eye: *ophthalmos*

face (n.): *ôps, prosôpon*
faculty: *dunamis*
fall beneath: *hupopiptô*
fallible (be): *ptaiô*
false (be): *pseudomai*
falsehood: *pseudos*
familiar: *gnôrimos*
familiar (be): *sungignôskô*
fashion (v.): *anaplassô*
fatal: *olethrios*
father: *patêr*
fatherland: *patris*
fear (v.): *phobeomai*
fever: *puretos*
fight (v.): *polemeô*
fig tree: *sukê*
figure: *skhêma*
figure in relief: *ektupôma*
final cause: *hou heneken*
finite: *peperasmenos*
fire: *pur*
first: *prôtos*
fit (v.): *arariskô, epharmozô, harmozô*
flesh: *sarkion, sarx*
follow: *hepomai*
food: *opsa*
foot: *pous*
form: *eidos*
formless: *aneideos*
four-footed: *tetrapous*
fragrance: *euôdia*
free (be): *apallassomai*
friend: *philos*
fruit: *karpos*
function: *ergon*

gaze (v.): *athreô*
genealogy: *genealogia*
general: *holoskheres*
generate (v.): *gennaô*
generated: *gennêtos*
generation: *genesis*
generative: *gennêtikos*
generic: *genikos*
genitive: *genikos*
genus: *genos*
geometer: *geômetrês*
geometry: *geômetria*
geometry (practise): *geômetreô*
give: *didômi, apodidômi*
give birth: *tiktô*
glad (be): *terpomai*
go abroad: *ekdêmeô*
go over: *eperkhomai*
go through: *diexerkhomai*
goal: *skopos*
goat: *tragos*
goat-stag: *tragelaphos*
god: *theos*
good (adj.): *agathos, khrêstos, spoudaios*
grammar: *grammatikê*
grammarian: *grammatikos*
greater: *meizôn*
grey: *phaios*
greyness: *glaukotês*
grow upon: *prosphuô*
gymnasium: *gumnasion*
gymnastics: *gumnastikê*

habituate: *ethizô*
habituation: *sunethismos*
hair: *thrix*
half: *hêmisu*
hand: *kheir*

happen: *sumbainô*
harmony: *harmonia, sumphônia*
hasten: *speudô*
have: *ekhô*
head: *kephalê*
heal: *hugiazô*
health: *hugeia*
healthy (be): *hugiainô*
heat (n.): *kauma, thermê, thermotês*
heat (v.): *thermainô*
heating: *thermansis, thermasia*
heavenly: *ouranios*
hesitate: *okneô*
hexagon: *hexagônon*
homonym: *homônumia*
homonymous: *homônumos*
homonymy: *homônumia*
honour (v.): *timaô*
honourable: *entimos*
hookedness: *grupotês*
hook-nosed: *grupos*
horse: *hippos*
horseness: *hippotês*
hot: *thermos*
house: *oikos*
house-builder: *oikodomos*
how many: *posos*
human: *anthrôpeios, anthrôpinos*
human being: *anthrôpos*
humble: *meionektês*
humility: *meionexia*
humour: *khumos*

ice: *krustallos*
idea: *dianoêma, idea*
identical: *tauton*
identity: *tautotês*
ignorant of (be): *agnoeô*
ill (be): *noseô*

illuminate: *phôtizô*
illumination: *ellampsis*
image: *eikôn*
imagination: *phantasia*
imitation: *mimêma, mimêsis*
immobile: *akinêtos*
immortal: *athanatos*
immortality: *athanasia*
impart: *paradidômi*
imperative: *prostaktikos*
imperfect: *atelês*
imperfection: *ateleia*
implication: *akolouthia*
impose: *epitithêmi*
impossible: *adunatos*
impression: *tupos*
in a certain way: *toiôsde*
in a disorderly way: *ataktôs*
in the many: *en tois pollois*
in the most proper sense: *idiaitata*
in vain: *matên*
inanimate: *apsukhos*
incommensurable: *asummetros*
incorporeal: *asômatos*
increase (v.): *auxanô, auxomai*
increase (n.): *auxê, auxêsis*
indefinitely: *aprosdioristôs*
indicate beforehand: *prosêmainô*
indifferent: *adiaphoros*
individual: *atomos*
indivisible: *adiairetos*
induction: *epagôgê*
infallible: *aptaistos*
infant: *brephos*
inferior: *katadeês*
infinite: *apeiros*
infinity: *apeiria*
infringe: *paratrepô*
innate: *sumphutos*

iron: *sidêros*
irrational: *alogos*
insensitivity: *êlithiotês*
inseparable: *akhôristos*
isosceles: *isoskeles*
instil: *empoieô*
instrument: *organon*
intellect: *nous*
intelligence: *phronêsis*
intelligible: *noêtos*
intend: *mellô*
intense: *sphodros*
intensification: *epitasis*
intensify: *ekteinô, epiteinô*
intermediate: *mesos*
interrogative: *pusmatikos*
introduce: *eisagô, eispherô, komizô*
introduce by way of a prelude: *proanakrouomai*
introduction: *eisagôgê*
introductory: *eisagôgikos*
investigate: *episkeptomai, historeô, skopeô*
invisible: *aoratos*

join (v.): *epizeugnumi*
joining: *epizeuxis*
joint: *arthron*
journey (v.): *hodeuô*
judge (v.): *dikazô*
judgement: *krisis*
just: *dikaios*
justice: *dikaiosunê*

kill: *exagô*
kinship: *sungeneia*
know: *ginôskô, gnôrizô, oida*
knowable: *epistêtos*
knower: *epistêmôn*

knowledge: *epistêmê, gnôsis*
knowledge (object of): *gnôston*

labour (v.): *mokhtheô*
lack: *endeia*
lacking: *endees*
ladder: *klimax*
land: *khôriôn*
last (adj.): *eskhatos, hustatos*
last year: *perusin*
last-born: *husterogenês*
laugh: *gelaô*
laughing (capable of): *gelastikos*
law: *nomos*
lead: *agô*
learn: *manthanô*
leave: *katalimpanô*
left (adj.): *aristeros*
left behind (be): *hupoleipô*
legislate: *nomotheteô*
legislative: *nomothetikos*
length: *mêkos*
lengthy: *polustikhos*
lesser: *meiôn*
life: *bios, zôê*
limit (v.): *perainô, peratoô*
line: *grammê, stathmê, stikhos*
list (v.): *aparithmeô, katarithmeomai*
live (v.): *zô*
logic: *logikê*
look (v.): *blepô*
loosely: *katakhrêstikos*
loosen (v.): *dialuô*
love: *philia*
lukewarm: *khliaros*
lung: *pneumôn*

magnitude: *megethos*
maintain: *presbeuô*

make: *poieô*
manifest (v.): *diaphainomai*
many: *polloi*
many times as many: *pollaplasios*
marine: *thalattios*
master: *despotês*
mathematical: *mathêmatikos*
mathematics: *mathêma, mathêmata, mathematikê*
matter: *hulê*
meaning: *sêmainomenon*
meaningless: *asêmos*
measure: *metron*
mechanical: *banausos*
medicine: *iatrikê*
medicine (practise): *iatreuô*
mention (v.): *mimnêskô, mnêmoneuô*
mere: *psilos*
metaphor: *metaphora*
method: *methodos*
milk: *gala*
mingle: *epimignumi*
minimal: *oligostos*
misshapen: *duseidês*
mistaken (be): *hamartanô*
mix (v.): *kerannumi, mignumi*
mixed: *miktos*
mobile: *kinêtos*
moderate (adj.): *metrios*
moderately (adv.): *summetrôs*
moisture: *hugrotês*
moment: *kairos*
monad: *monas*
mortal: *brotos, thnêtos*
motion: *kinêsis*
move: *kineô*
mule: *hêmionos*
multiplication: *pollaplasiasmos*

multiply: *plêthunô, pollaplasiazô, poluplasiazô*
multitude: *plêthos*
music: *mousikê*
mythology: *muthopoiia*

name (n.): *onoma*
name (v.): *onomazô*
name-imposer: *onomatothetês*
navigate: *nautillomai*
near (be): *sunengizô*
necessary: *anankaios*
necessity: *anankê*
necessity (of): *pantôs*
need (v.): *deomai*
negation: *apophasis*
neglect: *kataphroneô*
neigh: *khremetizô*
neighing (capable of): *khremetistikos*
never: *oudepote*
nickname: *epônumia*
nomenclature: *onomasia*
non-existent: *asustatos*
nose: *rhis*
notice: *ephistêmi*
notion: *hupolêpsis, noêma*
nourish: *trephô*
novel (adj.): *kainos*
number: *arithmos*
nurse: *trophos*
nutritive: *threptikos*

object (n.): *skeuos*
object (v.): *enistêmi, epilambanomai*
obscure: *asaphes*
obscurity: *asapheia*
observe: *theaomai, theôreô*
obtain: *porizomai*
obtaining (adj.): *huparkhon*

obvious: *prodêlos*
occupy: *epekhô*
odd: *perittos*
odd-times-even: *perissartios*
of similar kind: *homoioeidês*
of such-and-such a kind: *toionde*
old age: *gêras*
olive tree: *elaia*
omit: *paraleipô*
only: *monôs*
opinion: *doxa*
opposite (adj.): *antikeimenos*
opposite (be) (v.): *antikeimai*
opposition: *antithesis*
optative: *euktikos*
optimal mixture: *eukrasia*
order (n.): *kosmos, taxis*
order (v.): *keleuô*
order (in good): *eutaktôs*
ostentation: *philotimia*
other: *heteros*
otherness: *heterotês*
outline (in form of): *eskiagraphêmenos*
outstanding (be): *huperekhô*
overcome: *nikaô*
ox: *bous*
oyster: *ostreon*

painting: *graphê*
parent: *goneus*
paronymous: *parônumos*
part (n.): *meros, morion*
partake: *apolauô*
participate: *metekhô*
participation: *metokhê*
particular: *merikos, kata meros*
parts (having many): *polumerês*
parts (with similar): *homoiomerês*
passion: *pathos*

path: *hodos*
pay attention: *prosekhô*
pedagogical: *didaskalikos*
pentagon: *pentagônon*
perceive: *aisthanomai*
perception: *aisthêsis*
perfect (adj.): *teleios*
perfect (v.): *teleioô*
perfection: *teleiôsis, teleiotês*
perpetual: *aidios*
philosopher: *philosophos*
philosophy: *philosophia*
philosophy (practise): *philosopheô*
phraseology: *phrasis*
pigeon: *peristera*
pilot: *kubernêtês*
place (n.): *khôra, topos*
place (v.): *tassô, tithêmi*
place before (v.): *protassô*
placing around: *perithesis*
plane: *epipedos*
please (v.): *areskô*
plumb line: *kathetos*
plural: *plêthuntikos*
poet: *poiêtês*
point: *sêmeion*
political: *politikos*
position: *epokhê, thesis*
possession: *kathexis*
possible: *dunaton*
possible (be): *endekhomai*
posterior (adj.): *husteros*
pot-bellied: *progastôr*
potentially: *dunamei*
power: *dunamis*
practical: *praktikos*
practise: *askeô, epitêdeuô*
pray: *eukhomai*
precede: *proêgomai, protereuô*

predicate: *katêgoreô*
predominate: *epikrateô*
pre-exist: *prohuparkhô*
prelude: *proaulion*
premise: *protasis*
present (be): *keimai, pareimi, prokeimai*
present (v.): *paristêmi*
preserve (v.): *sôzô, diasôzô*
pre-subsist: *prohupokeimai,
  prouphistêmi*
presuppose: *proepinoeô*
prevent: *empodizô, kôluô*
preventing: *kôlutikos*
primarily: *proêgoumenôs*
primary: *prôtos*
principle: *arkhê*
prior: *proteros*
privation: *sterêsis*
problem: *aporia*
proceed: *probainô, proeimi,
  proerkhomai*
procure: *peripoieô*
produce: *apoteleô*
producing: *peripoiêtikos*
profess: *epangellomai*
project: *proballomai*
prologue: *prooimion*
promise (n.): *huposkhesis*
promise (v.): *hupiskhneomai*
prompting (n.): *hupothêmosunê*
proof: *deixis*
propensity: *epitêdeiotês*
proper: *idios, kurios, oikeios*
properly: *kuriôs*
property: *idion, idiôtês*
proportion: *summetria*
propose: *protithêmi*
protector: *kêdemôn*
provide: *parekhô*

provide technical treatment beforehand:
  protekhnologeô
providence: *pronoia*
providence (exercise): *pronoeomai*
providential: *pronoêtikos*
proximate: *prosekhês*
punish: *kolazô*
pure: *katharos*
purpose: *prothesis*
pursue: *meteimi*

qualified: *poion*
qualitatively: *en tôi hopoion ti estin*
quality: *poiotês*
quantified: *poson*
quantification: *prosdiorismos*
question: *zêtêma, zêtêsis*

rain: *ombros*
raise: *anagô, anapherô*
raise a problem: *aporeô*
range (v.): *tattomai*
rational: *logikos*
read: *analegô, entunkhanô*
reading: *anagnôsis*
reason: *logos*
rebuke (v.): *epiplêssô*
receive: *anadekhomai, apolambanô,
  dekhomai, epidekhomai, proslambanô,
  tunkhanô*
receive an impression: *anamassomai,
  apomassomai*
receptive: *dektikos*
reciprocate: *antistrephein*
recognize: *epiginôskô*
rectilinear: *euthugrammos*
reduce: *anagô*
refer: *anagô*
reject: *ekballô*

relation: *skhesis*
relationally: *skhetikôs*
relative: *pros ti*
relative disposition: *pôs ekhein*
relatively: *en tôi pôs ekhon, en tôi pôs estin*
relax: *diakheô*
reluctant: *oknêros*
remain (v.): *leipomai, menô*
remaining (adj.): *loipos*
remark (v.): *episêmainomai*
reminding: *hupomnêsis*
remission: *anesis*
remove: *aphaireô, exaireô*
repel: *apôtheô*
require: *khrêizô*
rest (n.): *stasis*
result: *apotelesma*
retreat (v.): *existamai*
return (v.): *hupostrephô*
reward (n.): *geras*
rhetoric: *rhêtorikê*
rhetorical: *rhêtorikos*
rhetorician: *rhêtor*
right (adj.): *orthos*
right-angled: *orthogônios*
ring: *daktulios*
rise: *anabainô, anerkhomai*
rock: *petra*
rooted (be): *rhizoomai*
ruined (be): *kakunomai*
rule (n.): *kanôn*
rule (v.): *arkhô*
run: *theô, trekhô*

sand: *psammos*
saviour: *sôtêr*
say: *phaskô, phêmi, legô*
say beforehand: *prolegô*
scalene: *skalênos*

scant: *oligos*
scar: *oulê*
scattered: *sporadên*
school: *diatribê, hairesis*
scientifically: *epistêmonikôs, epistêmonôs*
sea: *thalassa*
seal (n.): *sphragis*
section (n.): *tmêma*
section (v.): *temnô*
see: *horaô*
seed: *sperma*
seek: *zêteô*
seem: *dokeô*
select: *eklegomai*
self-existent: *authupostatos*
self-moved: *autokinêtos*
semicircle: *hêmikuklion*
semicircular: *hêmikuklios*
sensible: *aisthêtos*
sensitive: *aisthêtikos, êlithios*
separable: *khôristos*
separate (v.): *apokhôrizô, khôrizô*
series: *seira*
serve: *douleuô*
set forth: *ektithêmi, protithêmi*
set forth beforehand: *proektitêmi*
set in order: *kosmeô*
sex: *philotês*
shadowy: *skioeidês*
shape (n.): *morphê*
shapely: *eueidês*
share (v.): *koinoneô*
shelter: *skepasma, skepê*
shift (v.): *methistêmi*
shod (be): *hupodeomai*
short: *brakhus*
should (v.): *opheilô*
show (v.): *deiknuô, deiknumi, dêloô, diasapheô*

side: *pleura*
significant: *sêmantikos*
signify: *sêmainô*
silent (be): *siôpaô*
similar: *homoios, paraplêsios*
similarity: *homoiotês*
simple: *haplos*
sinew: *neuron*
singular (adj.): *henikos*
singular (n.): *kath' hekaston*
sit: *kathêmai, kathizô*
sitting: *kathêsthai, kathezesthai*
situated above (be): *epanabainô*
sketch (v.): *skiagrapheô*
sky: *ouranos*
slacken: *aniêmi*
slave: *doulos, oiketês*
sleep (n.): *hupnos*
small: *mikros*
snow: *khiôn*
snubness/snub-nosed: *simos*
solution: *epilusis, lusis*
solve: *epiluô, luô*
solve beforehand: *proepiluô*
son: *huios*
song: *melos*
soul: *psukhê*
sound: *psophos*
speak: *legô*
specific: *eidikos, eidopoios*
spend one's life: *diagô*
spend time: *diatribô*
sphere: *strongulon*
sponge: *spongos*
spontaneously: *autophuôs*
spread (v.): *epiphoitaô*
spread out (be): *hupostornumi*
square: *tetragônon*
stag: *elaphos*

stamp (v.): *sphragizô, tupoô*
stand (v.): *histêmi*
starting point: *arkhê*
state beforehand: *prokataballô*
statue: *andrias*
stone (adj.): *lithinos*
stone (n.): *lithos*
stop (v.): *lêgô*
store: *apotithêmi*
stored (be): *apokeimai*
straight: *euthus, orthios*
strike (v.): *tuptô*
string: *khordê*
strip off: *aposulaô*
strive: *spoudazô*
student: *akroatês, mathêtês*
study (v.): *enkuptô*
subdivide: *epidiaireô, hupodiaireô*
subdivision: *epidiairesis, hupodiairesis*
subordinate: *hupallêlos*
subsist simultaneously: *sunuphistêmi*
subsistence: *hupostasis*
substantial: *ousiôdes*
substrate: *hupokeimenon*
subtle: *glaphuros*
succeed: *diadekhomai*
suffice: *arkeô*
suitable: *epitêdeios*
suitable (be): *prepô*
summary (adj.): *kephalaiôdês*
superficial: *epipolaios*
superiority: *huperokhê*
supervene: *epigignomai, episumbainô*
suppose: *hupotithêmi*
surface: *epiphaneia*
surprised (be): *thaumazô*
surprising: *thaumastos*
swan: *kuknos*

swim: *nêkhomai*
sweet: *glukus*
sweetness: *glukutês*
sword: *xiphos*
syllable: *sullabê*
syllogism: *sullogismos*
synonym: *sunônumon*
synonymously: *sunônumôs*

take: *lambanô*
take care: *epimeleomai*
take in certain sense: *metalambanô*
teach (v.): *didaskô*
teacher: *didaskalos*
teaching: *didaskalia*
temperament: *krasis*
temperance: *sôphrosunê*
tend: *hormaô, pephuke*
tent: *skênê*
terminology: *lexis*
terrestrial: *khersaios*
theological: *theologikos*
theology: *theologia*
theorem: *theôrêma*
theoretical: *theôrêtikos*
think: *noeô, oiomai*
think up in addition: *prosepinoeô*
thing: *khrêma, pragma*
thought: *dianoia, noêsis*
threefold: *trittos*
three-pronged spear: *triaina*
time: *khronos*
title: *epigraphê*
toil (v.): *talaipôreô*
tone: *tonos*
touch (concerning): *haptikos*
trace (n.): *ikhnos*
train (v.): *meletaô*
training: *meletê*

transgress: *parabainô*
translation: *phora*
transported (be): *pheromai*
traverse: *khôreô*
treatise: *pragmateia*
treatment: *paradosis*
triangle: *trigônon*
true: *alêthês*
true (to be): *alêtheuô*
truly: *ontôs*
trustworthy: *axiopistos*
truth: *alêtheia*
turn (v.): *strephô*
turn grey: *polioomai*
twofold: *dittos*

unable (be): *adunateô*
unbridled: *eklutos*
unclear: *adêlos*
underlie: *hupokeimai*
understand: *dioraô, eklambanô, parakoloutheô*
understanding: *katalêpsis*
undertake: *enkheireô*
unextended: *adiastatos*
unitive: *sunaptikos*
unity: *henôsis*
universal: *katholikos, katholou*
unknown: *agnôstos*
unmixed: *eilikrinês*
usage: *khrêsis*
use (v.): *khraomai*
use loosely (v.): *katakhraomai*
useful: *khrêsimos*
useful (be): *khrêsimeuô*

vanity: *kenodoxia*
vein: *phleps*
verb: *rhêma*

vice: *kakia*
virtue: *aretê*
vital: *zôtikos*
vocative: *klêtikos*
voluntary: *proairetikos*

walk (v.): *hodoiporeô, peripateô*
walking upright: *orthoperipatêtikos*
wall: *toikhos*
war-trumpet: *salpinx*
water: *hudôr*
wax (piece of): *kêrion, kêros*
way: *tropos*
weakness: *astheneia*
wear (v.): *pherô*
well-known: *poluthrullêtos*
wet: *hugros*
when: *pote*
where: *pou*
white: *leukos*
white lead: *psimmuthion*
whiten: *leukainomai*
whiteness: *leukotês*
whitening: *leukansis*

whole (adj.): *holos*
will (n.): *boulêsis*
wing: *pteron*
winged: *peteinos*
wisdom: *sophia*
wise: *sophos*
wish (v.): *boulomai, thelô*
wish to die (v.): *thanataô*
without a conception: *anennoêtos*
without confusion: *asunkhutôs*
without relation: *askhetos*
woman: *gunê*
wood: *xulon*
wooden: *xulinos*
word: *muthos, phônê*
work out: *exakriboô*
wrath: *mênis*
write (v.): *graphô*
writing: *sungramma*

yesterday: *khthes*
young: *neos*

zoophyte: *zôophuton*

Greek–English Index

Note: Some very common technical terms, such as *ousia*/substance; *genos*/genus; *eidos*/form or species; *diaphora*/difference; and *idion*/property have not been indexed.

abakion, drawing-board, tablet, 2,3; 101,15.16; 107,5
adelphos, sibling, 50,2
adêlos, unclear, 23,2; 75,5
adiairetos, indivisible, 9,25
adiaphoros, indifferent, 37,24
adiastatos, unextended, 18,22
adunateô, be unable, 12,17
adunatos, impossible, 7,30; 11,9; 25,5.20; 72,6; 76,7; 83,6; 86,7.8.24; 87,6; 102,15; 103,21; 107,1; 110,24.25; 111,10; 112,11
aeikinêtos, eternally moved, 14,5.9; 35,21; 74,15.17
aêr, air, 102,25; 107,5.6
agapaô, be content within, 55,13
agathos, good, 24,2.3.10.11; 104,4
agnoeô, be ignorant of, 1,6; 21,13; 76,10
agnoia, ignorance, 4,26
agnôstos, unknown, 17,27; 20,16; 85,19; 87,7; 114,19
agora, market, 20,1
agoreuô, address, 20,14; 60,9
agô, lead, bring, refer, 11,19; 15,8; 17,8; 56,17; 59,21; 63,13; 104,14; 113,13.14
aidios, perpetual, 3,4; 9,17; 17,4.6; 86,28
aiskhunô, feel shame, 15,22
aisthanomai, perceive, notice, 75,26; 79,11
aisthêsis, (sense-)perception, sensation, 11,17; 40,9; 48,5; 63,14; 79,5; 99,27; 103,22; 105,6
aisthêtikos, sensitive, capable of sensation, 18,1; 28,2; 77,20; 79,8; 84,15; 90,13; 99,23.25.27.29
aisthêtos, sensible, perceptible, 40,17; 42,21; 45,10; 65,19; 78,23
aithiops, Ethiopian, 111,9.12.17; 114,3

aitia, cause, reason, 8,28; 11,7.10; 21,9; 31,21; 46,5; 76,25.26; 87,23; 91,24; 106,12; 123,6
aitiatikos, accusative, 91,8
aitiaton, effect, 50,8.9; 53,10; 104,25
aition, cause, 22,7; 50,7.8; 53,10; 104,25
akairos, inappropriate, 2,18; 10,15
akallês, without beauty, 106,16
akatêgorêtos, acategorical, 60,9
akhôristos, inseparable, 11,27; 12,2.7.8.10–12.22.23; 13,6; 41,8; 42,10.20.23; 92,5.10.18.20.25; 95,15.20.23.24; 111,2.18; 114,4.11
akinêtos, immobile, 14,5.7
akoê, sense of hearing, ear, 13,10; 26,6
akolasia, licentiousness, 67,23
akolastos, licentious, 68,1
akolouthia, implication, 27,2.13.17; 69,17
akolouthos, consistent, consequent, 10,10; 26,19
akolouthôs, accordingly, 47,5
akosmia, disorder, 16,9.11.12
akosmos, disorderly, 16,9.10
akouô, listen, 41,24
akra, extreme terms, 80,6
akribês, exact, 76,27; 114,10
akribôs, accurately, 25,16
akroatês, student, 38,17; 39,5; 69,19
akron, extreme term, 16,7
alêtheia, truth, 43,11; 49,14; 74,9; 96,2
alêtheuô, be true, speak the truth, 43,12.14.15; 44,20
alêthês, true, 44,2; 72,20.21; 73,3; 88,20
algeô, be ill, 112,2
alloioô, alter, 20,10
alloios, of a different sort, 93,2–4.6.8; 94,11.21; 95,1.2.3.17.20.23.24
alloiôsis, alteration, 113,10.17.18.22

allos, other, 65,15
allotrios, extraneous, 54,10
allôs, otherwise, 72,2; 97,16; 123,23; 125,13
alogos, irrational, 10,2; 24,6; 26,18; 30,6; 32,11.22; 34,5.14; 42,1; 44,6; 58,11; 70,16; 78,2; 85,4; 92,21.22; 93,5.7; 94,6; 95,8; 97,24; 99,2.12.13.14.15.16.19; 100,9.13.15.16.18; 101,2.26; 103,11.13.16–21; 107,16; 108,6.17; 126,8
ameibô, exchange, pass, 74,11; 77,23
amelei, indeed, 104,1; 111,15; 113,4
ameres, partless, 7,15
amesôs, immediately, 12,21; 79,17.18; 97,17,19
amethodos, unsystematic, 35,9
ametokhos, not participating, 105,16
ametria, disproportion, 67,19
ametros, excessive, 111,23; 113,1(adv.).2.24
ampelos, vine, 18,3; 85,17
amphiballô, hesitate, be in dispute, 53,23
amphibolos, ambiguous, 53,21
anabainô, rise, 37,12
anabasis, ascent, 70,25.27; 76,15.17.20
anadekhomai, receive, 57,2
anadromê, ascent, 17,9
anaginôskô, read, 21,13
anagkaios, necessary, 8,7; 24,14.16.19; 25,4.12; 26,18.21; 27,11.13.24; 28,7.13.14; 29,1; 109,2(adv.); 116,14
anagnôsis, reading, 21,9; 24,10
anagô, refer, raise, reduce, trace back, subsume, 13,1; 17,14.27; 18,4.6.8.17.20; 19,2.15.22.25.28; 20,2.3.8.25.27; 21,3.24; 23,19; 24,19; 63,1.2.4.5.16; 71,24; 77,3; 81,5; ascend, raise oneself up, 12,21.25; 13,5; 17,6; attribute, 46,2
anaireô, eliminate, 29,27; 72,5.6; 73,3; 82,8.9.14.20.21.22; 120,18.19; 121,16.17.18.19.20
anairesis, elimination, 114,16.20
anairetikos, tending to eliminate, 101,20
anaisthêtos, insensitive, 99,23.26
anakaleomai, restore, 7,12
anakeimai, lie down, 20,4
anakuptô, emerge, 21,21
analambanô, assume, 118,2
analegô, read, 24,21
analogeô, be analogous, 55,6; 107,17.20.21

analogizomai, calculate, 69,8
analogos, analogous, 106,14.19.20(adv.).23; 107,10
analuô, analyse, 36,2.8; 37,15.16.17
analusis, analysis, 34,20; 37,8.9.10.12.13; 38,2
analutikos, analytic, analyser, 36,1.7.10.19.25
anamassomai, receive an impression, 12,3; 42,12
anamimnêskomai, recollect, 10,21
anamphisbêtêtôs, indisputably, 23,8
anankê, necessity, it is necessary, 25,5; 48,16; 61,16; 62,2; 72,23; 73,19; 74,2; 76,3.8; 82,8; 104,25; 112,14; 114,7.8; *ex anankês*, necessarily, 65,11
anantes, uphill, 37,8
anaphainô, become apparent, 24,7; 61,9.14
anapherô, raise up, 24,15; 40,10
anaplassô, fashion, 40,3.4
anapnoê, breathing, 25,7
anapodeiktôs, without demonstration, 7,16
anateinomai, reach upwards, 24,4
anathreô, look up to, 57,16
anatrekhô, ascend, go back, 17,9; 81,9.11
anatrepein, overturn, 5,5
andrias, statue, 106,19.21; 107,3
aneideos, formless, 106,16.20
aneimi, go up, 87,13.14.19
anendeês, complete, 16,11
anennoêtos, without a conception, 31,20; 69,19
anepitatos, that cannot be intensified, 126,1
anepsios, cousin, 49,21
anerkhomai, rise, 19,10
anesis, remission, 98,6.12
anêr, man, 35,9; 81,10
angelos, angel, 18,20; 19,1; 32,14.19; 40,15; 62,15; 70,17; 97,14; 100,14; 103,18; 114,7; messenger, 43,8
aniêmi, slacken, 98,5.14; 111,22
anisos, unequal, 51,3.5
anodos, way up, 70,28
anomoioeidês, of a different kind, 63,18
anomoiomerês, of dissimilar parts, 81,19.21; 83,2.10.15.18.20
anô, upwards, above, 57,16; 67,9; 70,28
anôtatô, highest, top, 10,10
anôterô, higher, 52,4; 80,1

Greek–English Index

anôthen, from above, 37,10; 76,16
anthrôpeios, human, 85,23; 86,15; 100,23
anthrôpinos, human, 17,26; 52,23
anthrôpos, human being, 2,24; 5,2; 17,10;
  19,10; 32,3.10.14.23; 33,6.14.15; 35,6.15;
  36,5; 40,3.8; 47,11.16; 50,17; 52,7; 53,17;
  61,5.8; 62,14.15.16; 63,14;
  65,1.7.10.15.16.17.22.23.24; 68,7.8.9.13;
  69,8.9; 70,17.18; 78,2.3.6.7.15.24;
  79,1.2.13.18.19; 80,10; 81,4.18; 82,7.9;
  84,13; 85,17; 86,1.21; 88,19.23.24.25;
  89,6.9.11; 90,7.13.15.16; 93,22;
  94,6.12.15.16.18.19; 95,4.5.10;
  96,3.4.6.7.8; 97,10.11.17.19; 98,11;
  99,5.13; 100,8.9.14; 101,10; 103,18.23;
  107,9.14.16.27; 108,5.14.18.19;
  109,14.16.18.20; 111,12.13.15.17.21;
  112,1; 114,5.6; 116,16.18.21–5;
  117,18.19.26; 119,19;
  120,14.15.18.21.23; 121,6.7.17; 122,18;
  124,20; 125,1.9.10.15
anthrôpotês, humanness, 40,8
antidiaireô, distinguish as opposite, 25,1.5;
  30,1; 34,1
antikatêgoreomai, be convertible, 88,24
antikeimai, be opposite, 18,10; 73,7
antikeimenos, opposite, 102,23; 112,18;
  113,14; 115,5
antilambanô, grasp, 1,4
antilêpsis, apprehension, 98,6
antipeponthôs, opposed, 18,21
antistrephô, reciprocate, convert, 27,1; 65,4;
  75,2
antithesis, opposition, 95,18; 99,23; 109,27
antitupos, hostile, 78,1.9
anuô, accomplish, 7,31
aoratos, invisible, 10,24
aoristôs, indefinitely, 23,4
apallassomai, be free from, 38,18.21; 39,1;
  68,23
aparenklitos, undeviating, 9,1
aparithmeô, count, list, enumerate, 13,14;
  19,24; 47,7; 49,2.5; 52,17; 53,5; 54,3;
  69,20; 92,1; 101,7; 109,8; 110,13
apeiria, infinity, 20,29; 86,28
apeiros, infinite, 17,3; 18,12; 59,19.22; 60,5;
  85,2.22; 86,5–24.29; 87,4.5
apekhomai, abstain, 38,20; 39,10; 47,4
apekhô, be distant, 122,13

aperilêptos, what cannot be
  comprehended, 17,5.26; 59,19; 85,8
aphaireô, remove, 11,3; 86,9; 110,20;
  111,16; lay claim to, 54,10; 68,4
aphiêmi, give up, 21,14
aphoraô, look to, 34,6; 41,22; 42,18
aphorizô, assign, 100,18
aphôrismenos, determinate, 28,17; 77,2;
  92,9.19(adv.)
apisteô, disbelieve, doubt, 13,28; 21,17
aplanês, fixed, 10,7
apoballô, lose, 33,15
apoblepô, attend, 34,9
apoblêtos, to be rejected, 104,27
apodeiknumi, demonstrate, 7,32; 35,22;
  36,17; 62,6; 84,3
apodeiktikos, demonstrative, demonstrator,
  35,16; 36,10.14.17
apodeixis, demonstration, 22,8; 23,21;
  34,20; 35,16.19.23; 36,14; 37,3; 74,24;
  88,7; 103,12
apodidômi, give, 6,5; 37,7; 55,10.12;
  56,3.6.12.15.18; 57,8; 58,2.15; 62,1; 63,8;
  68,22; 74,8; 76,13.21; 77,8.10.11.14;
  78,16; 95,9; 101,9; 103,7; 106,12; 111,7;
  114,10.15; account for, 64,10.11; give an
  account of, 74,5; give a construction,
  91,15
apodidraskô, run away, 5,2
apodosis, account, construction, 6,28;
  61,19; 91,6.10.12
apoginomai, depart, be taken away, 33,1;
  110,17.26; 111,2.3.9.10.11; 113,20
apoios, qualityless, 112,5
apokeimai, be stored, 10,21
apokhôrizô, separate, 50,18; 60,22
apokrinomai, answer, 61,7; 66,17
apolambanô, receive, 46,14.16
apolauô, partake of, 97,13
apollumi, cease to exist, 31,18; lose,
  46,15.16
apologeomai, defend oneself, 76,2
apologia, defence, 72,14
apomassomai, receive an impression, 41,19
apomenô, remain, 60,2
aponemô, attribute, 12,9
apophainomai, declare, 43,14
apophantikos, declaratory, 43,4.11.24;
  44,13 (adv.); 45,13

apophasis, negation, 114,24
apoptôsis, disappearance, 13,22
aporeô, raise a problem, 23,2; 26,18.20; 37,21; 51,17; 52,16; 55,14; 56,13; 63,1; 101,11; 102,3; 111,7.18; 113,26; 124,18; be at a loss, 72,14; 100,24
aporia, difficulty, problem, 5,9; 56,22; 72,16; 81,7; 101,11.12.21; 102,3; 113,5
aporos, difficult, 102,2
aposôzô, maintain, 44,16
apostasis, distance, 97,23
aposulaô, strip off, 10,27
apoteleô, produce, 40,5; 98,5; 125,17
apotelesma, result, 21,6
apôtheô, repel, 112,18
apotithêmi, store, 10,27
apotrepomai, avert, 99,20
aprosdioristôs, indefinitely, 23,2; 28,18.23; 29,1
apsukhos, inanimate, 18,10.16; 70,15; 77,17; 99,23.26.27; 108,17; 118,20
aptaistos, infallible, 7,2.5
arariskô, fit, 9,13
areskô (*ta areskonta*), what one believes, 106,4
aretê, virtue, 67,20.22; 68,5; 102,17
aristeros, left, 19,28
aristotelikos, Aristotelian, 105,11
arithmêtikê, arithmetic, 7,4; 13,11; 14,17.21
arithmos, number, 14,14.17.19; 19,16.17; 59,6; 60,21; 62,19; 64,13.14.19; 65,2.3.4.6.14.18.21.24.25; 66,3; 70,4; 76,23; 78,13; 86,5.6.8.9.27.28; 87,3.4.11.25; 115,23; 116,5; 123,1
arkeô, suffice, 9,24; 119,11
arkhetupos, archetype, 42,18
arkhê, starting point, principle, 7,13; 10,14; 22,25; 23,21; 37,12; 45,7; 68,16; 80,21; 81,11; 84,2.3; 87,24; 95,14.5; 115,7; beginning, 87,9
arkhomai, embark upon, begin, 1,2.3; 16,2; 31,16; 71,5.7; 76,16; 95,13; 109,3
arkhô, rule, 47,19.21
artêria, artery, 81,20
arthron, joint, 35,8
artiakis artion, even-times-even, 14,14
artios, even, 13,17
artiôs, just now, 44,8; 56,22
asapheia, obscurity, 38,19; 48,23; 51,9

asaphês, obscure, unclear, 39,1; 52,11; 70,6; 74,13; 75,1.3.10–25
asêmos, meaningless, 59,1.10.13; 60,7.8; 106,10
askeô, practise, 9,20
askhetos, without relation, 34,4
asômatos, incorporeal, 12,25(adv.); 19,1; 40,11.13.14.18; 41,6.7.12; 42,19; 57,3; 70,14; 77,17; 78,23; 100,6; 103,25.26.29; 104,12; 110,21; 116,24
astheneia, weakness, 100,23
astronomeô, practise astronomy, 109,14
astronomia, astronomy, 2,9.14; 7,3; 13,11.31; 14,9.10
astrôios, astral, 48,25; 49,3; 82,1; 84,10
asummetros, incommensurable, 13,9
asunkhutôs, without confusion, 104,9
asustatos, non-existent, 95,19.21; 96,2.9; 99,11.25; 109,28
ataktôs, in a disorderly way, 68,1
ateleia, imperfection, 16,15
atelês, imperfect, 8,9; 102,7; 104,21.24
athanasia, immortality, 35,20
athanatos, immortal, 35,6; 43,15.21.23; 74,14.15.17.19; 95,9; 97,25; 99,2.12–16.19.21; 100,9.12.14.16.19; 101,26; 103,12.14.16.17.19.20; 114,7
athreô, gaze, 57,16
athroisma, aggregate, 86,3.4.19; 90,2.21
athroizô, take in the aggregate, 90,11
atimos, dishonourable, 104,24
atomos, individual, 32,1; 44,12; 58,2; 60,19; 61,22; 63,17; 66,10; 78,14; 79,18.19; 80,9.12; 85,17.23; 86,2.4.5.6.13–16.18.24.25.27; 87,7.19.21; 90,10.11.17.25; 91,1; 97,5; 116,15.17.20.22; 125,18
atoneô, weaken, 7,12
atopos, absurd, 31,7; 33,14; 56,20; 63,3; 75,21; 86,24; 101,24.26; 103,24; 104,5
aulêtria, female flautist, 13,25
aulos, immaterial, 52,6
aurion, tomorrow, 20,3
authis, in turn, 17,14
authupostatos, self-existent, 19,3; 70,8.12
autokinêtos, self-moved, 35,21; 74,14.15.16.19.21.22; 88,13.14
autophuôs, spontaneously, 8,28; 24,2

auxanô, increase (v.), 79,5; 105,5
auxê, increase (n.), 87,21
auxêsis, increase (n.), 113,10
auxêtikos, concerning growth, 77,19
auxomai, grow, increase, 18,9; 86,29; 87,20.24
axioô, think fit to, consider, 9,21; 15,13; 106,5
axiopistos, trustworthy, 101,13
axios, it is worth, 52,16; worthy, 75,2; deserving, 100,19
axiôma, axiom, 101,13.14

badizô, walk, 46,6
banausos, mechanical, 8,25
barus, heavy, 8,28
bathos, depth, 7,20; 38,16.21
bathus, deep, 38,21; 39,10; 47,4.5
bebaios, steadfast, 11,1
biblion, book, 20,15; 21,13; 22,2.5.11.23; 29,7; 36,11; 43,2; 103,8
bios, life, 15,4
blabê, damage (n.), 33,1
blaptô, damage (v.), 125,16
blepô, look, 52,5
blituri, example of a meaningless word, 59,1; 60,7
boulêsis, will, 11,18
boulomai, wish, tend, 10,23; 12,27; 17,5; 27,20; 31,16; 42,17; 51,5; 52,6; 58,12; 62,2.6; 67,14; 74,19.20; 75,5.7; 85,13; 87,14; 88,5.15; 98,20; 101,8; 103,27; 122,22
bous, ox, 29,4; 30,4; 32,10.15; 65,1.7; 85,17; 97,11
brakhus, short, brief, 38,11
brephos, infant, 102,17
brotos, mortal, 65,10

daimôn, demon, 70,17
daimonion, demon, 99,19; 100,18
daktulios, ring 12,5; 20,6; 41,13.18
deiknumi, show, 22,1; 28,23; 29,16; 55,1; 64,11; 66,11; 72,8; 74,19.20; 75,5.8.16.22; 81,16; 82,2; 83,21; 85,20; 86,12; 87,2; 97,11; 104,10; 117,7; 122,22; designate, 89,19
deiknuô, exhibit, prove, show, point to, 1,7; 63,11; 75,18.23

deixis, demonstrative reference, 63,15.16; proof, 74,9.19.23; 75,14.15.17.19.20.22.24.26
deka, ten, 123,5.22; 124,3
dekakhôs, in ten ways, 56,1
dekhomai, receive, 102,25; 103,29; 105,17; 107,6.16.17
dektikos, receptive, 54,15; 90,16; 95,11; 102,23; 103,1; 108,4.12; 119,18
deomai, need, require, 19,9; 22,14; 34,8; 82,17; 96,6; 104,19
deon, duty, 16,1; *to deon*, what is appropriate, 67,21.22
deontôs, appropriately, 6,12
deô, tie, 5,6
desmos, bond, 5,6
despotês, master, 50,12
deuteros, second, 71,27; 72,11; 74,11.12; 82,12; 97,20
dexios, right, 19,28
dêloô, show, indicate, 22,10; 29,11; 38,19.21; 45,20.21; 49,6; 51,6.13; 55,3; 63,8; 75,21; 77,1; 94,21; 96,11; 110,2; 117,22.5
dêlos, clear, 66,2; 75,17; 82,5; 86,2; 88,21; 102,19; 107,6; 110,18; 124,4
dêmiourgeô, create, 11,29; 41,24.25; 104,2
dêmiourgikos, demiurgic, 5,7
dêmiourgos, demiurge, 41,21.23; 42,17.20; 45,11; 63,15
di' holou, throughout, 40,18
diaballô, disparage, 74,10.24; 75,23
diabolê, censure, 75,2
diadekhomai, succeed, 46,10
diagô, spend one's life, 32,14
diaireô, divide, 7,27; 11,6.8.9.13.21; 13,10; 14,1.4.25; 15,2.21; 23,12; 35,13; 36,12.22; 48,20; 72,3.4.9; 73,4.7.12.20; 74,1; 80,18; 81,17.19.20; 82,2.4.5.20.23; 83,1.6.11.15.20.22; 84,22; 85,23; 99,4; 100,11; 109,10.26
diairesis, division, 7,28; 21,9; 34,20; 41,6; 59,8; 60,6; 61,16.18; 62,1.8.10; 63,4; 73,19; 76,22; 77,16; 78,5.22; 85,18; 93,1.11.14; 94,10.13; 99,8; 106,9; 109,12
diairetikos, divisive, 35,4; 36,12.16; 55,21; 58,6.10; 98,21.22; 99,1.3.7; 100,3.5.9.11; 118,14.17; divider, 35,12
diairetos, divisible, 7,25; 9,25
diakeimai, be in a state, 115,13

diakheô, relax, 78,1
diakrinô, distinguish, 53,13; 89,22–4; 95,15.17.18; 108,12.14; 120,16
dialambanô, deal with, 45,5.8.10.12; 46,3.20; 47,6
dialegô, discuss, 8,16; 9,28; 26,1; 28,20; 30,11; 43,22; 51,11; 80,19; 91,25; 109,1
dialektikê, dialectic, 34,17.18
diallattô, differ, 7,2; 38,3
diallêlos, circular, 74,9.18.22; 75,23.26
dialuô, loosen, 5,6
dialutikos, tending to dissolve, 37,1
diametron, diagonal, 72,4; 73,4; 74,1; diameter, 73,13.15
dianoêma, idea, 38,21
dianoia, (discursive) thought, 11,17; 12,4; 17,26.39; 41,17; 42,12; 69,2.8
diaphainomai, be made manifest, 32,8; 46,8
diapherô, differ, 10,4; 18,1; 32,7.9; 34,13; 37,10; 56,4.7.23; 57,8; 59,4.6; 60,17.18.20; 61,1–3.10.15.21.23; 62,12.19.20; 64,13.14.16.18.19.22; 65,2–4.12–14.20.21.25; 66,1–3.6; 70,4.24; 71,4.7; 74,6; 76,23; 78,12; 83,3.4.9.12.16; 84,11; 92,5.7.14.21; 93,22.23; 115,13.19; 117,6.8.13; 118,12; 120,1; 121,13; 122,2.4
diaphoros, different, 53,12; 56,9; 70,25; 71,3; 76,14; 81,23; 82,4; 83,22; 96,1; 110,13
diaphôneô, disagree, 42,22
diaphtheirô, damage, 25,3
diarkeô, endure, 25,4
diasapheô, show clearly, 31,8
diasôzô, preserve, 31,19
diastasis, dimension, 7,18
diastatos, extended, 18,18
diastellô, distinguish, disambiguate, 66,9; 71,14.17
diastolê, distinguishing, 6,21
diatassô, establish, 34,19
diatithêmi, be disposed, 13,22
diatribê, school, 46,10
diatribô, spend time, 13,3.4
didaskalia, teaching, instruction, 20,16; 23,18; 26,10; 31,12; 46,2.18; 48,15.19.22; 58,14; 64,6; 76,9; 109,8; 110,10
didaskalikos, pedagogical, 69,17

didaskalos, teacher, 22,13; 47,19; 50,11
didaskô, teach, 20,19; 22,6; 23,13.14.16.20; 26,7; 36,9; 45,1.20; 48,11.16; 62,2; 64,8; 69,3; 71,13.15.23; 76,4; 88,3.4; 98,19; 110,12; 114,19
didômi, give, 82,16
diegeirô, awaken, 13,20
diexerkhomai, go through, 41,10
diêrthrômenôs, in an articulated way, 55,4
diistêmi, differ, 122,4.10.11
dikaios, just, 8,19; 9,26
dikaiosunê, justice, 67,19
dikastikos, judicial, 15,11
dikazô, judge, 15,13.15.16
dikha, in two, 73,7.12; 115,24
dikhôs, in two senses, 91,21; 118,12.13
dioraô, understand, 5,3
diorizomai, distinguish, 51,11
diôrismenos, discrete, 14,3.12.17.18.21.23; 57,5
diplasios, double, twice, 13,15; 73,11.21; 86,22
diplasiôn, double, 73,21
dipous, biped, 109,16.17
dis, twice, 122,23; 123,9.12
disyllabos, having two syllables, 117,18.22
dittos, twofold, 5,10.11; 11,11.16; 69,24; 71,3; 81,19
dokeô, seem, be someone's view, 42,22; 44,4; 52,21; 83,16; 96,1
dotikos, dative, 91,6.16
douleuô, serve, 5,13
doulos, slave, 50,12
doxa, opinion, 11,17; 24,6; 34,19; 40,14; 44,1
draô, do, 20,9
dunamai, be able to, 83,15.20; 85,8; 90,3.19; 92,17; 94,13.15.17; 102,1.5; 103,26.28; 104,8; 112,9; 114,15; 115,13
dunamei, potentially, 27,6.9; 56,22; 102,52-2; 103,2.3.5; 104,13–20.23; 105,4.6.9; 106,6; 110,4; 119,2
dunamis, faculty, potentiality, power, 1,14; 42,2; 77,19.20.22; 79,7.8; 87,20.25.26; 103,22; 109,22; 110,2
dunaton, possible, 77,8; 91,14; 97,12; 102,15.20; 104,12; 111,13; 114,6
duseidês, misshapen, 70,1
duskherês, difficult, 122,3.9

eidikos, specific, 34,10; 70,3.6; 107,23;
  eidikôtatos, most specific, 70,18.20;
  77,15.16; 78,8.15.17; 79,1; 80,7.9.15.17;
  85,14.16.22; 86,12.13; 87,6.15.16; 100,4;
  104,23; 120,4
eidopoios, specific, 85,3; 94,8; 95,3; 96,13;
  98,21; 100,3
eidos, form, 6,16; 11,28; 12,3.12; 13,14;
  36,7.23; 52,2.9; 106,14.17.18.22;
  107,9.11.12.18.21; 119,9
eikêi, at random, 38,1
eikosi, twenty, 122,23; 123,4
eikotôs, rightly, reasonably, 11,13; 68,14;
  75,23; 87,23; 107,19; 121,18
eikôn, image, 42,18; 55,4
eikôs, reasonable, 41,12
eilikrinês, unmixed, 125,18
einai, being, 19,5; 82,17.22; 85,2; 107,18;
  108,11; 112,12; 113,5; 114,22; *to ti ên*
  einai, essence, 108,9
eiôthos, usual, 69,19
eisagô, introduce (v.), 22,24; 23,9.24; 26,6
eisagôgê, introduction, 20,22; 22,18;
  23,1.2.7.8
eisagôgikos, introductory, 13,10; 23,19; 47,3
eisballô, begin, 47,6
eiserkhomai, enter, come in, 41,15
eispherô, introduce (v.), 114,21
ekballô, reject, 59,17; 60,2
ekdêlos, conspicuous, 32,8
ekdêmeô, go abroad, 22,15
ekhô, have, 18,16; 20,11; 75,6.7.8.9.12;
  82,22; 83,2.11; 84,14.20; 86,1; 99,27;
  100,10; 102,19; 102,2; 104,1.9.19; 106,15;
  120,2; be able to, 19,2; 64,2; 105,17;
  110,4.19; *hôsautôs ekhô*, be in the same
  state, 17,19–20; *houtôs ekhei*, holds true,
  85,14; 91,8; *pôs ekhei*, how is it
  disposed, 66,17; *ekhein*, having
  (category), 20,7.12; 84,23
ekkrinô, expel, 105,7
eklambanô, understand, 34,25
eklegomai, select, 35,13.15; 61,19; 115,16
eklogê, choice (n.), 26,9
eklutos, unbridled, 13,24.26
ekprassô, achieve, 16,3
ekteinô, intensify, draw out, extend, 26,7;
  68,15; 113,21
ektithêmi, set forth, 94,10; 105,10; 122,15

ektupôma, figure in relief, impression, 12,5;
  41,13; 42,9; 44,2
elaia, olive tree, 18,4.5.6; 85,17
elaphos, stag, 40,4
elattôn, lesser, 87,21; 98,5; 116,3; 118,18;
  121,5; 123,1.4; *ep' elatton*, of lesser
  extension, 118,23.24
ellampsis, illumination, 46,7
elleipô, be deficient, 67,17; 68,6.9.19.21.23;
  69,10; 86,29
elleipsis, deficiency, 16,9; 68,5
empalin, vice versa, conversely, 44,16; 75,4;
  76,1; 87,25
empeiria, acquaintance, 1,12
empodizô, prevent, 96,16
empoieô, instil, 49,2
empsukhos, animate (v.), 18,1.8; 28,2;
  35,13; 70,15; 77,18; 78,9–11.17.22;
  79,3–8.11; 84,15; 88,28; 89,8.9.11;
  90,13; 97,15; 99,23.25.26; 105,4.5;
  127,2
en aporrhêtois, in secret, 5,1
en suntomôi, succinctly, 21,23; 66,11
en tôi hopoion ti estin, qualitatively, in the
  what-kind-of-thing-it-is, 61,7.8.11;
  62,21.22; 64,18; 66,7.15; 67,5; 106,13;
  107,20; 124,19; 125,1
en tôi pôs ekhon, relatively, 64,22; 66,7.16;
  67,5.7
en tôi pôs estin, relatively, 62,21.22; 67,5
en tôi ti estin, essentially, in the what-it-is,
  61,4.6.11.21.24; 62,20.22; 64,16.19; 66,8;
  70,2.4.22; 74,6; 76,23; 106,12; 107,19;
  124,19; 125,3
enantioomai, be contrary, 36,20; 41,12;
  103,9
enantios, contrary, 16,15.16; 19,4; 26,24;
  73,10; 96,18; 100,10; 101,19.21.25;
  102,4.14.18.20;
  103,1.4.6.14.20.21.23.26.27; 104,1.3.4;
  106,1; 111,27; 112,4.13
enargês, clear, 10,25; 101,12
endeês, lacking, 16,9
endeia, lack (n.), 16,8.14
endekhomai, be possible, 55,18.22.24;
  56,6.22; 57,8; 72,17; 73,6.20.23;
  101,20
endekhomenos, contingent, 25,1.21;
  27,11.13.15.16; 28,8.13.14; 29,23.26

endoiazô, doubt (v.), 49,8
endoxos, held in esteem, 21,19; generally admitted, 35,18
enduomai, be clothed, 25,2
energeia, activity, actuality, 11,12.16; 26,26; 33,15; 46,8.14; 87,1.8; 96,16; 102,7; 104,14.19.22.26; 106,7; 109,22; 110,3; 111,11; *energeiai*, in actuality, 102,4.7.11.14.15.16.21; 103,2.6.10.24; 104,6.12.14.15.16.17.18.30.31; 105,4.5.7.8; 111,4.18; 121,2
energeô, perform, 33,16
enistêmi, object (v.), 41,23; 112,26
enkheireô, undertake, 21,16
enkheirêsis, attempt, 4,26
enklêma, accusation, 2,18
enkuptô, study (v.), 4,18; 22,17
ennea, nine, 70,12
ennoeô, consider, conceive of, 41,13.20; 114,6
ennoêmatikos, conceptual, 69,1.4.6
ennoia, concept, 56,17.18; 69,5.10
enthumêma, enthymeme, 8,6
entimos, honourable, 104,23
entunkhanô, read, 38,14
enulos, enmattered, 10,18.23; 11,28; 12,12; 52,6
eoike, resemble, 52,14
epagôgê, induction, 8,5
epanabebêkos, higher, 80,17; 100,10
epangellomai, profess, 59,19
epanô, above, 89,15; 97,12
epeisodiôdês, adventitious, 33,7.18; 59,4; 121,10
epekhô, occupy, 35,26; 57,24; 99,20; 100,18; 102,21
eperkhomai, go over, proceed to, 15,25; 16,2; 20,29; 31,11; 51,10
epharmozô, fit, 55,16; 67,14; 77,15; 78,16; 114,11
ephelkô, attract, 24,8
ephetos, desirable, 16,18
ephexês, subsequent, 114,19; 116,8
ephiêmi, desire (v.), 24,2.5; 112,12
ephistanô, attend, 42,2
ephistêmi, notice, pay attention to, take into consideration, 9,8; 41,16; 115,14
epibolê, approach, 9,29

epidekhomai, be susceptible of, receive, 7,29; 13,9; 57,26; 96,13.17; 97,4.21.22; 98,3.12
epidiaireô, 93,1, subdivide
epidiairesis, subdivision, 9,27; 10,1
epigignomai, supervene upon, 53,14; 102,23; 113,1
epiginôskô, recognize, 10,21; 64,1.2
epigraphê, title, 21,9.23; 23,12
epigraphô, entitle, 23,1.2.11
epikheirêma, argument, 8,15
epikosmeô, adorn, 13,30
epikrateô, predominate, 112,20.21.22.23
epilambanomai, object (v.), 71,25
epiluô, solve, 72,15; 81,8; 101,12; 102,3; 113,5; 124,18
epilusis, solution, 26,20; 103,9; 105,12
epimeleomai, take care of, 4,13
epimignumi, mingle, 96,22
epinoeô, conceive, 21,10; 31,18; 40,1; 50,17; 53,21; 94,14.15; 95,1; 111,14.17
epinoia, concept, 11,26.27; 33,12; 39,15; 40,3.5.7; 41,4; 73,18; 94,13; 109,6.7; *epinoiai*, in thought, mentally, 109,6.7; 111,5.12.13.18; 114,5
epipedos, plane, 12,14
epiphaneia, surface, 7,19
epiphoitaô, spread (v.), 97,19
epi pleiston, further, 113,20
epi pleon, having greater extension, 28,4.5.6.8; 88,23; 118,17
epiplêssô, rebuke, 16,3
epipolaios, superficial, 115,14.15
episêmainomai, remark, point out, 51,10; 68,21; 81,14
episês, equal, equivalent, 27,1.10; 28,28; 29,12.13
episkeptomai, investigate, 3,17; 4,11; 85,13
episkopeô, examine, 42,25; 44,5
epistamai, know, 59,20
epistêmê, knowledge, science, 6,2; 9,5.6; 17,4.7; 23,7.9; 54,15; 59,20; 60,1; 85,7.10; 90,15; 95,10; 97,7; 104,5; 108,4.6.12; 119,18
epistêmonikôs, scientifically, 39,7; 59,19
epistêmonôs, scientifically, 39,4
epistêmôn, knower, 17,2; 19,14
epistêtos, knowable, 85,8

episumbainô, supervene, 54,21
epitasis, intensification, 98,6.12
epiteinô, tighten, intensify, 98,4; 111,21
epitêdeios, suitable, 3,28; 46,7; 102,8(adv.)
epitêdeiotês, propensity, 126,6
epitêdeuô, practise, make use of, 13,19.23
epithumia, desire (n.), 11,18; 13,27; 48,6; 103,22
epitithêmi, impose, 50,20
epizeugnumi, join, 73,2.4.8
epizeuxis, joining, 72,3
epokhê, position (astron.), 13,31
epouranios, celestial, 10,6
epousiôdês, adventitious, 33,20; 64,21; 101,3; 109,2
epônumia, nickname, 46,14
ergon, function, 21,16; 35,2.16
erkhomai, arrive, move on, 56,19; 90,14.16; 99,22
erôtaô, ask, 61,5.7; 66,16; 125,5
eskhatos, last, 10,17; 57,26
eskiagraphêmenos, in outline form, 64,7
ethizô, habituate, 10,23; 12,25; 15,19
ethô, be accustomed to, 54,8; 93,18; 110,2; 112,7
etumologia, etymology, 57,14
eueidês, shapely, 70,1
eukherês, easy, 20,19; 31,2
eukhomai, pray, 43,9.13
eukrasia, optimal mixture, 112,24
euktikos, optative, 43,5
eumarês, easy, 25,11.22
euôdia, fragrance, 110,23
euphuesterôs, more clever, 115,13
eutaktôs, in good order, 35,4; 36,12
eutheia, straight line, 9,2.3; 73,2.22; nominative case, 29,3.8
euthugrammos, rectilinear, 72,8.19
euthus, immediately (adv.), 110,15; straight, 79,17; 111,5
exagô, kill, release, 4,28; 5,2.3
exaireô, remove, 59,15.16; 62,5
exakriboô, work out in detail, 46,4
exepitêdes, deliberately, 39,13
exetazô, examine, 60,6
exêgeô, explain, 22,14
exêgêsis, explanation, 60,6
exêgêtês, exegete, 72,14
exisazô, be coextensive, 27,3; 88,23.24

ex isou, equally, 82,5
existamai, retreat, 112,22
exomoioeô, assimilate, 3,16
exôthen, external, 35,25
exôtheô, expel, 112,16
êlithios, insensitive, 67,23
êlithiotês, insensitivity, 67,23
êthikos, ethical, 15,2.4.6.17.18; 16,5
êthos, character, 15,4; 16,6

gala, milk, 19,8; 75,6.7.8.12.13
gastêr, belly, 15,20
gelaô, laugh, 33,14; 109,22; 110,3.4.5; 126,10
gelastikos, capable of laughing, 32,24; 88,24.25; 109,20; 110,3.4.5; 116,20.23.25; 117,1; 121,7.17; 126,10; 127,4
genealogia, genealogy, 80,20; 81,5.8
genesis, generation, 3,5; 48,4; 53,13; coming-into-being, 87,9; 113,8.13.17; 125,13.15
genikos, genitive, 29,5; 91,6.10.15; *genikôteros*, more generic, 31,18; 58,8; *genikôtatos*, most generic, 30,10; 58,5.13; 63,2.5; 70,9.17; 78,7.21.25; 80,6.14.15; 81,13; 84,22; 85,12.14.15.16; 87,15; 89,6.16; 100,3; 104,24
gennaô, generate, 8,3; 18,9; 48,23; 79,6
gennêtikos, generative, 77,20
gennêtos, generated, 17,3
genos, genus, 18,6.15.17; 19,2.15.25.29; 20,17; 22,5; 23,15; 28,16; 29,11.14.17.19.20; 31,12.20; 32,16; 33,3; 56,20; 93,11
geômetreô, practise geometry, 109,15
geômetrês, geometer, 7,15
geômetria, geometry, 7,4; 8,3; 13,11.18; 14,7.8.11
gephura, bridge, 13,5
geras, reward, 15,13
gê, earth, 14,7
gêras, old age, 109,18.19
ginomai, come to be, occur, become, result, 17,13; 33,23; 51,21; 72,17.23; 73,1; 85,2.19; 86,28; 87,7.8; 90,6; 94,20; 99,5; 101,14.15.19; 102,5; 103,5; 105,7; 106,17; 107,4.5; 109,28; 110,17.26; 111,1.9.19.20.23; 113,18; 115,24.26; 116,1.5.10; 122,23.26; 123,2.8.10.17.19.20.22.29; 124,5.7; 125,11

ginôskô, know, 17,12; 18,2; 21,15; 36,18; 47,12; 52,7; 76,8; 88,16
glaphuros, subtle, 26,20; 30,6
glaukotês, greyness, 92,14
glukus, sweet, 19,23
glukutês, 19,6; 110,23: sweetness
gnêsios, authentic, 21,18.20; 22,10.22
gnôrimos, familiar, 51,14; 71,8; 78,23; known, 85,13.15
gnôrizô, know, 37,24; 42,15
gnôsis, knowledge, 6,18; 9,21; 14,8.10.18; 17,1.4; 21,21; 31,6; 52,10.11; 97,5; 108,5
gnôstikos, cognitive, 3,10; 6,9; 11,12.17.20; 42,2(adv.); 43,8
gnôston, object of knowledge, 17,4
goneus, parent, 15,21
gônia, angle, 8,29
grammatikê, grammar, 1,11.12; 9,18; 19,27; 108,7
grammatikos, grammarian, grammatical, 19,27; 23,3; 36,4; 59,17; 108,7; 109,10; literate, 68,12.13.19; 102,9.11; 104,17.18
grammê, line, 7,21; 10,26; 11,2; 72,1; 73,15
graphê, painting, 55,6
graphô, write, 20,15; 22,17.18; 25,19; 46,19; 103,8; 115,15.16; paint, 55,3
grupos, hook-nosed, 58,4; 66,18; 92,15; 93,4.8.13; 94,17; 95,1; 96,5.6.7; 108,3
grupotês, hookedness, 92,14; 96,1; 111,3; 127,8
gumnasion, gymnasium, 13,30; exercises, 46,7
gumnastikê, gymnastics, 13,29
gunê, woman, 75,6.7.8

haima, blood, 57,19
hairesis, school of thought, 41,2
hama, simultaneously, 69,16
hamartanô, be mistaken, 6,20
hamartêma, error, 9,8
haplos, simple, 22,24; 23,19; 36,2.24; 38,22; 47,4; 49,10; 56,11(adv.); 68,15; 72,19; 73,16.17; 90,8; 111,26; 118,17(adv.); *haplôs*, in general, in an absolute sense, 88,22; 96,17; 122,9; 125,3.9
haptikos, concerning touch, 77,22
harmonia, harmony, 14,20; 111,22.24; 112,14.24

harmozô, adjust, fit, 69,23; 111,8; 112,3
henikos, singular, 91,1
hêkô, come, arrive, 16,19
hêmerinos, daily, 15,25
hêmikuklion, semicircle, 73,13.14.17
hêmikuklios, semicircular, 73,15
hêmiolios, one and a half, 13,16
hêmionos, mule, 125,11.12.17.18
hêmisu, half, 116,6.11; 123,2.5.10
henôsis, unity, 112,3
hepomai, follow, 13,26; 24,6; 35,10
hepta, seven, 123,27
hetairos, companion, 26,14; 46,6
heteromêkês, oblong, 73,9; *to heteromêkês*, oblong rectangle, 73,7.9.10.11.20
heteros, other, 65,12.19; *to heteron*, the other, 65,11
heterotês, otherness, 52,19; 92,3.4.5; 94,1; 115,4.8.9.10.12
heuresis, discovery, 25,24; 40,10; 46,2
heuriskô, find, discover, 18,23; 19,14; 22,15; 35,1; 41,5.7; 47,14; 51,2; 53,18; 55,16; 56,19.20; 60,4; 99,22; 101,4; 118,1; 120,6; 122,26
hex, six, 123,21
hexadaktulos, six-fingered, 16,11
hexagônon, hexagon, 72,9
hexakheir, six-handed, 16,11
hexis, disposition, 42,3; 102,12; 126,5
hêttôn, less, 96,14.15.17.19.23; 97,4.9.14.22.23; 98,3; 126,2.3.4
hippeios, equine, 86,1.16
hippokentauros, centaur, 39,15; 40,2.3
hippos, horse, 17,15.29; 27,28; 29,3; 30,3; 32,2.5.10.15.23; 35,7; 40,3.7; 53,17; 62,14.16; 65,1.7.22.23.24; 68,11; 78,18; 81,18; 82,7.10; 84,13; 85,17; 86,22; 90,14; 94,7; 95,4.5; 97,11; 99,14; 100,15; 101,2.4; 107,9.15.17.27; 109,21; 117,26; 122,18; 125,11.12.16; 127,2
hippotês, horseness, 40,7
histêmi, stand (v.), 20,4; 62,24; 92,6.7; 93,8.12; 94,20; *to hestanai*, standing, 33,2; 62,18; 93,4; 96,5; 108,3; 111,1
historeô, investigate, 22,15.18
hodeuô, journey, 12,22; 104,32
hodoiporeô, walk (v.), 21,14
hodos, path, 10,22; 20,22; 43,2

holos, whole, 81,18.21; 82,2.24; 83,2.3.5.8.11.13.17.19; 90,25; 91,1.4.9.10.11.12.13.14.15.16
holoskherês, general (adj.), 76,21
holôs, in general, 86,7; 112,11
homoioeidês, of the same kind, 63,17
homoiomerês, having similar parts, 52,3; 81,19.20; 83,1.6.19
homoios, similar, equal, 3,21; 4,13; 18,9; 63,19(adv.); 79,6.12; 81,21; 83,2.5(adv.).9.14; 86,1.12; 87,22(adv.); 117,16; 122,18.19(adv.); 123,13(adv.); 128,2(adv.)
homoiotês, similarity, 52,14; 53,6; 71,8
homoiôsis, assimilation, 3,8.19; 6,10; 11,11
homologeô, agree upon, 8,2; 28,12.28; 74,25; 75,4; 84,5
homologoumenôs, by common agreement, 95,19
homônumia, homonymy, 48,22; 71,14.16
homônumon, homonym, 48,19; 56,2.6; 84,8.16
homônumos, homonymous, 28,3.16; 29,24; 56,1.2.22; 57,12; 81,23; 82,3; 83,22; 84,6.15(adv.).21
hopôsoun, in some way, 115,10
horaô, see, 17,3; 57,17
horismos, definition, 1,5; 6,5.15.17; 34,20; 35,11.23.24; 36,14.15; 37,7.22; 54,7.8.9.18.23; 55,5.6.8.11.23.24; 56,4.5.14; 57,18; 58,2.14; 61,18; 64,11; 67,14.15; 68,2.7.20.22.23; 70,2; 77,1.6.7; 84,12.13.14.17.21; 85,9; 93,14; 95,9; 96,12; 98,10; 99,9; 101,11; 108,9.10.11.12; 111 7.8
horistikos, definitory, 35,9; 36,13.17.19; 37,3; 98,21; 99,9; definer, 36,10; 35,12
horiston, *definiendum*, 55,19; 67,16; 85,8
horizô, define, determine, 3,1; 4,14; 12,13.17; 28,1.20; 34,15; 36,13; 56,14; 57,18; 69,7; 74,7; 86,9.11; 87,6.7; 101,2; 114,20
hormaô, tend, 4,6; 8,28
horos, definition, 6,24; 23,10; 27,2.4; 54,6; 57,25; term, 36,8; 59,21; 88,9; 115,20; 122,26; 123,1.14-22; boundary, 67,16
hosautôs, likewise, identical, 86,2; 104,6
hosautôs ekhon, in an identical state, 26,22
hou heneken, final cause, 6,14

hôplisthai, be armed, 19,6
hôrismenos, determinate, 87,11
hôs etukhen, as chance would have it, 41,11
hôsanei, as if, 73,9
hudôr, water, 102,10.13.16.25; 104,15; 107,5; 108,16
hugeia, health, 6,3; 24,12
hugiainô, be healthy, 24,15; 62,24; 66,17
hugiazô, heal, 2,2
hugros, wet, 112,1
hugrotês, moisture, 107,7
huios, son, child, 15,16; 47,11; 50,14; 80,22; 90,18; 91,6
hulaktikos, capable of barking, 109,21
hulê, matter, 7,2; 10,26; 11,25.27; 12,1.2.4.12.13.17.22; 36,7.23; 41,8; 42,7.23; 52,2.9.21; 53,1; 57,18.24; 65,24; 102,18; 106,14.18.20.22.24; 107,2.3.4.6.9.10.11.17.18.20; 120,13
hupallêlos, subordinate, 10,6; 70,20; 78,6; 80,14.18; 91,19; 100,5.13; 120,5.7
huparkhon, obtaining, 26,22; 27,12.13; 28,8.13.15; 29,22.26
huparkhô, belong, 15,23; 29,4; 32,9; 55,11; 62,19; 63,11; 64,20; 65,3.5.7.9.11.15.25; 67,22; 69,24; 70,6.28; 72,20; 86,10; 92,11; 93,4; 101,16; 104,30; 116,25; 120,24; be, exist, 28,17; 32,24; 33,10.11; 43,16; 54,16; 56,7; 61,12; 62,4; 64,1.3; 90,7.10.16.19.23; 92,9; 96,3; 108,5; 109,4.5.11.16.17.24; 118,23
huparxis, existence, 26,24; 33,3; 34,8; 112,8; 115,6.11
huperballô, exceed, 69,10
huperbolê, excess, 68,5
huperekhô, be outstanding, 23,4
huperkeimai, exceed, 87,21
huperokhê, superiority, excess, 2,21; 6,26; 16,8.12; 86,10.11
huphistêmi, exist, cause to exist, have (extra-mental) existence, 12,1; 19,5-10; 28,11; 29,21; 34,7; 40,15.17.18.20.21; 41,1.5; 42,14; 69,16; 82,16; 103,17; 104,2; 112,6; 115,2
hupiskhneomai, profess, promise, 19,14; 39,9; 88,3; 98,19
hupnos, sleep, 15,20.24
hupobeblêmenos, subjected, 56,10
hupodedesthai, be shod, 20,6; 25,2

hupodeigma, example, 41,10; 51,13; 72,14
hupodiaireô, subdivide, 32,11
hupodiairesis, subdivision, 9,27; 13,8.9
hupographê, description, 54,6.7.8.20.23; 55,1.13; 56,6.12.15.18; 57,8.14; 58,16; 61,19; 63,8; 64,11; 68,22; 69,5.10; 70,21.23; 71,4; 76,13.21.25; 77,10.14; 78,16; 101,8; 106,9; 110,15; 114,10.15.24
hupographô, describe, 57,9; 80,15
hupokateimi, descend, 31,4
hupokatô, below, 89,15; 97,13
hupokeimai, underlie, serve as substrate, 2,11; 44,14; 45,14; 52,22; 56,16.19; 70,26; 88,11.13.16; 106,23; 107,2; 113,27; be given, 115, 20
hupokeimenon, subject, 27,3.4.5.9.20; 33, 9.24; 60,16; 70,25; 71,2.7; 76,13.15; 92,26; 96,18.20; 97,1; 101,10.20; 103,28; 106,15; 109,7; 110,18.26; 111,2.3.10.22.25.26; 112,5.6.10.12.15.19.21.25.26; 113,15.20.21.23.26; 114,22; 115,2; substrate, 1,18.19; 2,1.3.5.20; 3,6; 43,18.24; 44,24; 45,14; 88,9.10.23; 92,12.16
hupokeimenos, underlying, 54,9; 103,25.27; 107,6
hupokeisthô, let it be supposed, 84,2.5; 85,21
hupolambanô, assume, suppose, 21,20; 81,8; 122,23
hupoleipô, be left behind, 59,16; 62,5
hupolêpsis, notion, 46,17
hupomnêsis, reminding, 38,11
hupopiptô, fall beneath, 63,15
huposkhesis, promise (n.), 43,2
hupostasis, subsistence, (extra-mental) existence, 10,25; 11,26.27; 27,26.28; 28,3.7.29; 29,14; 112,7
hupostatikos, bringing into existence, 103,15.16
hupostornumi, be spread out, 106,21
hupostrephô, return (v.), 22,20
hupothêmosunê, prompting, 9,15
hupotithêmi, suppose, 42,16; 103,11
huptia, from below, 52,5
hustatos, last, 110,10
husterogenês, last-born, 41,20; 42,13; 69,1

husteros, posterior, 52,1.10; 72,22; 74,21.22; 75,10.12.13.14.24.25; 78,5.16; 82,6.13

iama, cure (n.), 7,8
iaomai, cure (v.), 112,2
iatreuô, practise medicine, 109,14
iatrikê, medicine, 2,6; 6,11; 7,31; 52,23
iatros, doctor, 105,2
idea, idea, 10,21; 44,3
idiai, individually, 117,12
idiaitata, in the most proper sense, 92,22.24.26; 93,5.10.14; 95,16.17.24; 108,4; 114,5
idiopoieô, claim for oneself, 25,24
idios, proper, 23,15; 35,17; 112,5.6.12; 119,11.15; 124,14
idiotês, property, 90,6.9.12.15.17
idiôs, properly, in the proper sense, 64,3; 67,7; 92,19.23; 93,3.9.11; 94,13.19; 95,16.17.24; 108,2
idiôtês, layman, 13,13; 35,9
idou, indeed, 121,9
ikhnos, trace, 13,21
isodunameô, be equivalent, 28,24
isopleuros, equilateral, 51,4
isos, equal, 12,16; 29,16; 51,2; 121,6
isoskeles, isosceles, 51,5
isôs, perhaps, 76,2
isteon, it should be known, 90,9; 91,14; 99,10; 103,9; 104,32; 110,12; 113,27; 115,20

kainos, novel, 50,19
kaiô, burn, 44,7
kairos, time, moment, 16,4; 22,2
kakia, vice, 102,17
kakos, bad, 104,4
kakunomai, be ruined, 67,16; 68,23
kaleô, call (v.), 19,16; 31,20; 34,11; 43,12; 44,4; 46,15.16; 56,10; 69,1; 70,19; 78,5; 83,8.15; 93,19
kalôs, well (adv.), 91,13; 97,21; 105,9; 114,3; 120,4
kamêlos, camel, 30,4
kampulos, curved, 111,5
kanôn, rule, 48,18; 69,20; 92,1; 118,7; 120,15.20; 123,14
karpos, fruit, 49,1; 71,2

kata: *kata bathos*, vertical, 97,10.12.22; *kata deuteron logon*, in the second instance, 116,17.22; *kata meros*, particular, 17,3.6.10.14.18.28; 18,6.12; 19,20; 21,3; 28,17; 42,10; 59,18; 78,4.14; 86,1.21.22; 87,18; 90,7.14; 116,24; *kata platos*, horizontal, 97,9.21.22; *kata to lepton*, in detail, 43,6; *kat' epinoian*, conceptually, 94,15; *kat' exokhên*, par excellence, 23,5.6; *kath' h(e)auto*, by itself, 14,6.13; 40,16; 92,11.26; 94,11; 96,3.5; 112,9; *kath' hekaston*, singular, 42,8; 44,10.11; 59,3; 63,16; 85,9; 107,23; *kath' hen*, one by one, 117,12; *kath' huperbolên einai*, exceed, 86,3
kataballô, deposit, 105,2
katabasis, descent, 70,25.26.27.28; 76,15.16.20
katadeês, inferior, 3,13; 11,15
katadeô, chain, 5,4
kataginomai, be concerned with, 1,19; 2,17; 6,2.12; 8,23; 13,31; 14,3.7.10.16.20.23; 42,25; 88,7.17
katakhraomai, use in a loose sense, 109,25
katakhrêstikos, in a loose sense, 72,15
katalambanô, apprehend, 97,6; seize, 112, 15.16
katalêpsis, understanding, 31,2
kataltmpunô, leave, 62,9; 68,3
katantes, downhill, 37,9
katapauô, conclude, 124,15
katapheromai, descend, 8,29
kataphroneô, neglect (v.), 15,10
katarithmeomai, list (v.), 69,23
kateimi, descend, 87,15
katêgoreô, predicate, 27,2.4.5.6.7.10.21.24; 29,1.14.16; 43,17.19.23.24; 44,15.19; 45,1.14.15; 57,10.11.13; 59,3.7.11; 60,114; 61,2.3.4.6.11.21.24; 62,10.15.17.20; 64,10.17.18.20.21.23; 65,1; 66,7.10.16; 67,8; 70,2.4.22; 71,28; 72,11.22; 74,7; 76,14; 78,12; 88,10.14.15.18.20.21.22; 89,4.5.6.7.16; 107,20; 116,17.19; 117,15.17.18.23–25; 118,2.3.5; 119,13.14; 120,5.10.11; 124,19; 125,4
katêgoria, category, predication, 20,13.15.21; 26,4.10.12.13; 27,19; 29,18; 34,7; 57,2.7; 70,8.12; 77,3.5; 78,20; 81,11.13.15.16; 82,3.11.20.22.24; 83,7.20; 84,19.20.22; 103,8; 113,6; 118,1
katharos, pure, 96,21
kathetos, plumb line, 8,26
kathexês, coming after, 82,14
kathexis, possession, 112,18
kathezesthai, to, sitting, 62,18; 93,4; 108,3
kathezomai, sit, 93,8
kathêmai, sit, be sitting, 20,4; 62,24; 92,6.7; 93,12.23
kathêsthai, to, sitting, 33,2; 111,1
kathizô, sit down, 94,20
kathodos, way down, 71,1
katholikos, universal, 7,14; 28,21.22; 31,17; 32,17.18; 33,19; 34,9; 55,9.16; 104,32; 105,1.3
katholou, universal, general, 17,6.10.22.23; 18,4; 32,3; 49,9; 51,23; 63,14.17; 64,4; 66,6; 79,2; 85,10; 89,19; 106,6; 116,23.24; 117,1; 125,10.11
kathôthen, from below, 87,19
katorthoomai, be achieved, 16,8.16
katô, below, 71,1
katôkara, with head down, 52,5
katôthen, from below, 76,16
kauma, heat, 12,18; 48,25
keimai, be present, be in force, 8,10; 15,14
keisthai, being-in-a-position (category), 20,5.12; 84,23
keleuô, order (v.), 13,26
kenodoxia, vanity, 15,9
kentron, centre, 8,28
kephalaion, chapter, 21,9
kephalaiôdês, summary, 38,10
kephalaiôdôs, in summary form, 60,5
kephalê, head, 29,6; 36,5; 81,22; 113,28
kerannumi, mix (v.), 112,2.13.27; 126,9
kêdemôn, protector, 103,18.19
kêrion, piece of wax, wax tablet, 41,14.18; 42,12
kêros, wax, piece of wax, 10,26; 11,2; 12,4; 41,15
khalkeos, (made of) bronze, 12,3; 107,2.13
khalkos, bronze, 10,27; 106,19.20.23
kharaktêrizomai, be characterized, 108,19
kharin, for the sake of, 72,15; 80,20
kheir, hand, 29,6; 36,5; 81,22
khersaios, terrestrial, 49,3; 82,1; 84,10
khiôn, snow, 19,21; 44,6

khliaros, lukewarm, 102,16
khordê, string, 13,19; 98,4; 111,21
khôra, place, 76,26
khôreô, traverse, 110,25
khôriôn, land, real estate, 1,8.9; 67,16; 112,17.18; passage, 34,25
khôristos, separable, 11,25; 12,6.7.9.11.13.22.23; 13,7; 33,12; 42,7.14.19.24; 92,4.8.10; 94,12.13.20; 95,15.20.21.22; 96,2; 110,25; 111,9
khôrizô, separate (v.), 12,6; 30,11; 33,12; 41,9; 50,4.16; 63,8; 64,12; 92,5.18; 94,14; 95,14; 107,26; 108,3; 109,6.7; 111,5.13; 114,4
khraomai, use (v.), 26,5.8; 31,2; 35,21; 36,7; 42,25; 48,4; 51,3; 59,9; 62,3; 69,20; 74,9.26; 76,26; 77,16; 92,1; 93,18; 103,6.12; 115,22
khremetistikos, capable of neighing, 17,17.24; 101,3; 109,21; 110,6
khremetizô, neigh, 109,23; 110,6
khrêizô, require, 35,11.16; 37,3; 101,17
khrêma, thing, 25,7
khrêsimeuô, be useful, 26,3; 31,6; 93,1.15; 99,7; 103,8
khrêsimos, useful, 21,8.16.17.20; 22,5; 23,18; 25,1.21; 26,3; 30,1.3; 36,11; 43,2; 46,19; 47,1; 61,19; 88,6; 89,3; 93,14
khrêsis, usage, 91,16
khrêstos, good, 16,3
khroia, colour, 110,23
khronos, time, 8,23; 20,4; 29,20; 41,2; 47,14.16.24; 69,19; 90,22; 97,7; 101,20.25; 102,4; 121,14
khrôma, colour, 19,23; 65,18; 117,27
khthes, yesterday, 20,2
khumos, humour, 8,3; 36,22
kineô, move, 67,23; inspire, 81,7
kinêsis, motion, 52,19; 60,5; 105,6; 113,6.12
kinêtos, mobile, 14,4
klêtikos, vocative, 43,5
klimax, ladder, 10,22; 13,5; 70,27
knax, example of a meaningless word, 59,1; 60,7
koimizô, calm, 13,20
koinoneô, share, have in common, 11,1; 13,6; 19,17; 33,23; 84,8.10.17.20; 109,3.6; 115,12.19; 117,6.7.13; 118,11; 120,1; 121,13; 122,9

koinos, common, 18,23; 19,2; 23,14.15.17; 44,10; 56,6; 63,5.19; 68,16; 70,6; 76,27; 81,14; 84,12.13; 107,1.3.16; 109,26; 112,17; 115,17; 119,11.12.13; 120,2.10; 124,14
koinotês, commonality, 17,15.28; 18,7.16; 19,11.19; 20,11.26; 21,1.2
koinônia, commonality, 28,7; 84,18; 115,7; 122,3.12.14.15
koinôs, in the common sense, 29,19; 64,3; 72,11.22; 92,8.23.24; 93,3.9.11; 94,12.19; 95,15.17.23; 108,2; 117,20
kolazô, punish, 15,14; 100,19
komêtês, with hair on one's head, 94,14
komizô, introduce, 8,21
korax, crow, 101,1; 111,4.12.14.15.16; 114,3
kosmeô, set in order, 2,1; 4,12.13; 11,19; 15,4.7; 106,17
kosmos, order, 16,6.13; world, 17,11.13
kôluô, prevent, 23,6; 73,2
kôlutikos, preventing, 12,18
krasis, temperament, 113,21
krateô, dominate, 5,13; 15,19
kreittôn, superior, more powerful, 97,13; 104,25; 108,5
krisis, judgement, 32,14
krustallos, ice, 102,24
ktaomai, acquire, 122,12
kubernêtês, pilot, 9,11
kuklos, circle, 11,31; 12,2.3.13; 73,13.16
kuknos, swan, 19,21; 101,2
kuôn, dog, 17,25.29; 27,27; 28,3; 30,3; 32,10; 48,25; 49,1.3; 50,18; 53,17; 62,14; 68,11; 78,18; 81,18; 82,1.10; 84,10; 85,17; 90,14; 94,7; 107,15; 109,21
kurios, proper, 49,11
kuriôs, properly, 49,10; 71,26; 72,13; 75,17.22; 106,14.16.18.20; 107,9; 109,4.24; *kuriôtata*, in the most proper sense, 97,2

lambanô, assume, take on, 7,25; 12,4; 48,24; 49,19; take, 22,8; 50,7; 55,8; 57,14.18; 58,17; 69,6.7; 70,13; 71,24; 74,19.21; 75,3.4.10.11.12.14; 76,22; 78,9.22; 85,8; 87,1; 99,4; 101,1; 106,9; 109,27; 116,2.5.11; 117,6.11; 118,15.16.17; 120,4.7; 123,2

lebês, cauldron, 107,3.5
legô, say, speak, state, 16,5.18; 20,14; 21,17; 22,3; 72,20; 74,14.21; 76,16.26; 78,4; 80,4.5.11; 81,3; 82,1.21.24; 83,14; 84,16.18; 86,14.15; 88,11.13.15.25; 90,12; 91,5.7.9.11.12.25; 92,1.2.3.26; 93,8.9.16-20; 95,9; 96,14; 97,1.21; 100,17; 101,2; 102,6.7.10.13.23; 103,10; 104,29; 105,5; 106,20.22; 109,22; 110,3; 112,3.26; 115,1.6.14; 117,25; 118,11; 119,2.8.15.22; 121,13; 122,20.27; 124,20; 125,5; 126,4.10
leipetai, it remains, 78,15; 82,3; 83,21
leipomai, be less than, 7,18; 72,12
leukainomai, whiten, 20,9; 114,4
leukansis, whitening, 113,11
leukos, white, 19,20.27; 33,1; 65,15.16.17; 89,20; 96,19.20.21; 98,14.15; 101,2; 104,2; 111,12.17; 117,27; 122,19.20; 126,8; 128,3
leukotês, whiteness, 19,6.20.27; 40,16.18; 62,17; 63,23.24; 65,18; 127,8
lexis, terminology, 38,16; 39,1.10; text, 105,13
lêgô, stop (v.), 71,15
lêmmation, assumption, 85,20
lithinos, (made of) stone, 12,3
lithos, stone, 12, 18; 18, 11.13.18; 19, 11; 99, 27; 101, 17.18
logikê, logic, 22,24.25; 23,23.24; 88,4.6
logikos, logical, rational, 8,24; 10,2.13; 17,12.24; 23,3; 32,11.16.22; 33,6; 35,5.14; 42,3; 43,4; 44,12(adv.); 53,2; 54,14.18; 58,8.11; 61,8; 62,15; 68,7.12.8; 69,9.23; 70,16; 78,2.24; 79,12.13; 85,4; 88,4.6.7.17; 89 3; 90,8.15; 92,21.22; 93,5.7; 94,6.16.18; 95,3.8.10; 96,3.4.14.15.16.23; 97,10.14.15.24; 98,11; 99,2.5.11-13.21; 100,7.9.12.13.14; 101,10.26; 103,11.13.16.17.18.20.22; 105,8.17; 107,16.26; 114,6; 116,19; 119,17; 120,13; 125,5.9.15; 126,2-5.8
logikôteron, in a more logical way, 45,2.12; 88,3; 98,19
logismos, rational argumentation, 41,12
logon poieisthai, discuss, 110,11
logos, reason, statement, phrase, account, rational formula, ratio, speech, argument, definition, discussion, doctrine, 7,1; 13,16; 15,22; 21,3; 29,13; 32,13; 36,2; 43,4.19; 44,5.7; 45,13; 54,12.13.14; 55,11.15; 60,13; 63,13; 69,14.21; 70,7; 71,2; 78,4; 92,1; 96,11; 101,8; 102,12.18; 103,12; 104,1.3.4.5.27.30; 105,7; 109,9; 110,11.14; 112,5; 116,17; 118,4
loipon, for the rest, 90,15; 105,13; 113,22; 115,18
loipos, rest, remaining, 31,8.9; 70,23; 72,8.9.10; 82,8.10.22; 86,2.11.16; 95,22.23; 96,6; 99,15.25; 102,21; 113,11; 114,16.18; 115,1.7.9; 117,7.11.26; 123,7.10.13
lumainomai, damage (v.), 33,13; 110,21.26; 111,3
luô, solve, 5,9; dissolve, 111,22
lusis, release (n.), 5,11; solution, 30,6; 103,6

mageiros, butcher, 35,8
makhaira, dagger, 65,10
makhomai, conflict, 112,6.10.16.19
malista, most of all, 97,3
mallon, more, 96,13.14.17.19.22; 97,4.8.10.13.14.16.17.20.21.23; 98,3; 126,2.3
manthanô, learn, 12,24; 20,19; 31,21; 56,2; 58,16.17; 77,15; 115,20; 123,14
matên, in vain, 31,15; 49,11
mathematikê, mathematics, 14,1
mathêma/mathêmata, mathematics, 12,23.26; 13,5; 126,5; studies, lessons, 16,5; 22,14
mathêmatikos, mathematical, 10,22; 11,22; 11,31; 12,9.11.20; 13,10; 14,2
mathêtês, student, 47,19; 50,12
mega, large, 19,16
megethos, magnitude, 7,16; 13,18
meionektês, excessively humble person, 67,20
meionexia, excessive humility, 67,20
meioô, diminish, 87,26; 110,20
meiôn, lesser, 99,20; 100,18
meiôsis, diminution, 113,10
meizôn, greater, 86,8.9.10.21; 87,5; 121,5
melania, blackness, 19,6; 62,18; 63,23; 111,4; 127,8
melansis, blackening, 113,11

melas, black, 19,22; 33,1.13; 96,5.6.7.8.20.21; 98,14.15; 101,1; 104,3; 111,10.14; 114,3; 117,27; 118,21.23; 122,20; 126,2.8; 128,3
meletaô, train, 5,18
meletê, training, 4,16
mellô, intend, be about to, 1,2; 23,9.10; 24,15; 46,17; 48,19; 50,19; 92,2
melos, song, 13,20
memphô, blame (v.), 74,8; 76,2
menô, remain, 40,14; 111,6
merikos, particular, 2,13; 8,14; 17,20; 28,21; 31,17; 32,15.20; 33,20; 53,17; 59,18; 60,1.12; 63,11.13.23; 64,4; 89,19; 104,32; 105,1; 106,6; 125,12
meristos, divisible, 18,22; 103,28
merizô, divide (v.), 115,24
meros, part, 11,19; 16,17; 21,5.24; 29,4.6; 43,4; 71,19; 73,6; 78,22; 81,19.21; 82,2.24; 83,2.4.5.7.11.12.17; 90,25; 91,1.4.9–15; 108,12.13
mesos, middle, intermediate, 10,19; 11,30; 57,26; 60,3; 70,18; 77,21; 78,6; 79,18; 80,3; 97,18.20; 100,8; 121,16
metaballô, change (v.), 7,5; 11,3; 94,22; 102,22; 103,3.4; 106,24; 107,1.2.4
metabatikos, concerning motion, 77,21
metabolê, change, 113,6.8.9.12.13.15.16.23.25
metaikhmion, border-land, 109,3; 121,9
metalambanô, take in the sense of, 67,16
metaphora, metaphor, 98,4
metaxu, between, 102,1
meteimi, pursue, take part, move on, 9,9; 124,14
metekhô, participate, 18,11; 19,26; 24,4; 33,5; 79,5.6.8; 82,12.15; 84,9; 97,20; 103,28; 105,7.8.17; 122,18; 125,3; 127,7
methistêmi, shift (v.), 9,16
methodos, method, 35,1; 98,21; 99,7; 115,21; 122,25
metokhê, participation, 82,7
metrios, moderate, 113,18
metron, measure (n.), 24,5; 87,3
mêkos, length, 7,19; 26,7; 38,15; 39,2
mêlon, apple, 110,23
mênis, wrath, 108,10
mênuô, announce, 24,10
mignumi, mix (v.), 96,18.20

mikros, small, 19,16; 96,15
miktos, mixed, 6,11.16.18; 73,16.18.22
mimêma, imitation, 55,3
mimêsis, imitation, 53,14
mimnêskô, mention (v.), 20,16; 22,11; 48,11.15; 74,5.7; 76,5.9
mnêmoneuô, make mention, 36,11; 37,5; 69,18; 76,4
mokhtheô, labour (v.), 37,15
monakhôs, in one way, 49,13.16
monas, monad, unit, one, 60,22.23; 115,22.25; 116,3; 123,1.4
monos, only, alone, 75,17.22; 78,25; 79,1.19; 80,22; 109,10.11.12.13.20.24
monôs, only (adv.), 78,18; 81,4; 90,25; 100,2.3.4.6.8
morion, part, 14,11.23; 16,9.10; 36,22
morphê, shape, 31,19; 69,25; 71,9
mousikê, music, 8,23.24; 13,11.22.28; 14,16.21.22
murios, countless, 85,23
murmêx, ant, 122,8
muthopoiia, mythology, 81,10
muthos, word, 49,14

nautillomai, navigate, 108,17.18.19
neos, young, 12,26; 13,25; 38,14
neuron, sinew, 36,6; 83,5
nêkhomai, swim, 108,16
nikaô, overcome, 15,9
noeô, think, understand, 12,20.25; 25,14; 28,1; 69,16; 76,6; 94,17; 111,6.13
noêma, notion, 38,16
noêsis, comprehension, 25,12.20; thought, 42,17
noêtos, intelligible, 10,16; 42,18; 44,3
nomizô, consider, 74,9; 100,20
nomos, law, 5,7; 15,12.14.22
nomotheteô, legislate, 15,15
nomothetikos, legislative, 15,11
noseô, be ill, 62,24; 66,17
nous, intellect, 11,17; 54,15; 95,10; 97,14; 108,4.12; 119,18; meaning, 34,25

oida, know, 41,24.25; 42,4; 76,10; 87,3; 110,16
oikeios, appropriate, proper, 35,10; 36,13; 54,10

oiketês, slave, 15,16
oikodomos, house-builder, 8,25
oikonomikos, economical, 15,3.6.17; 16,4
oikos, house, household, 12,17; 13,3; 15,5.8; 29,7; 101,18
oikothen, in itself, 101,13
oiomai, think, 41,5
okneô, hesitate, 21,13
oknêros, reluctant, 38,14
olethrios, fatal, 7,10
oligos, scant, 122,3
oligostos, minimal, 122, 10.12.14
ombros, rain, 12,18
on, onta, being, beings, 17,1; 19,13; 20,25; 22,4; 26,21; 28,6.15; 81,10.12.14.15.16; 82,2.10.12.15.19.23; 83,6.8.15.17.18.20; 84,15.18.22; 85,12; 106,14; 113,9.10.13.14.24; 115,6
onoma, name, noun, 19,3; 21,1; 27,7.8; 36,3; 46,5; 48,20.21; 50,16.20; 54,12; 56,3.14.19; 70,5; 83,3.9.13.16.17.19; 84,8.9.10.11.12.13.17.18.19.20; 93,17.18.19; 98,4
onomasia, nomenclature, 53,22
onomatothetês, name-imposer, 53,12.19.22
onomazô, name (v.), 9,23; 19,26; 83,3.11
onos, ass, 102,4; 125,11.12.17
ontôs, truly, 35,23; 44,3
opheilô, one should, 51,10; 115,22
ophthalmos, eye, 83,13.14; 104,2
opsa, food, 35,8
oregomai, desire, 24,6; 43,9
orektikos, appetitive, 11,18; 43,8
organon, instrument, 23,19.24; 46,8; 50,20; 96,16
orgê, anger, 108,11
orthios, straight, 8,26
orthogônios, right-angled, 72,3
orthoperipatêtikos, walking upright, 54,20
orthos, right, 8,29; nominative, 91,5
ostoun, bone, 11,28; 36,6; 52,3.7; 81,20
ostreon, oyster, 77,23; 78,7
oudepote, never, 88,22
oukoun, thus, 87,6; 89,8
oulê, scar, 63,24
ouranios, heavenly, 97,15
ouranos, sky, 14,9
ousiôdês, substantial, essential, 33,4.10.17.18; 54,17(adv.); 59,3; 60,14.15.17; 61,12(adv.); 64,20; 85,3.4; 101,3.4; 109,2.4; 113,13; 119,12
ôps, face, 57,17

paidion, child, 102,9; 104,17
pais, child, 96,15
palaios, ancient, 9,8; 10,15; 22,22; 40,11; 46,20; 93,18
palin, again, 85,2; 87,7
pantôs, of necessity, 19,7; 20,27; 65,21.22.26; 66,3; 99,21.28.29
para meros, alternatively, 102,25; 103,4
parabainô, transgress, 15,16; 16,1
paraballô, compare, 115,18; 116,3.7; 117,5.7.11.12; 119,22; 120,1; 121,4; 122,24; 123,7.10–13.23–29; 124,1–4.7.8.12
parabolê, comparison, 116,5.10; 122,23.26
paradeigma, example, 8,5; 31,21; 64,8; 71,23; 80,20; model, 41,21
paradidômi, impart, 12,26; 39,7; 46,18; 99,3; 102,12; 122,25
paradosis, treatment, 38,10
paraiteô, decline, 42,22
parakeimai, be adjacent, flank, 41,14; 67,19.20.22; 68,4
parakeleuomai, exhort, 4,28; 10,29
parakoloutheô, understand, 22,16.19; 92,2; be a constant attribute of, 115,17
paralambanô, accept, take up, include, 2,16; 12,14; 48,4; 58,18; 66,11; 67,6; 75,4; 80,20; 99,2; 100,24; 108,7; 118,20
paraleipô, omit, 39,13; 78,22; 100,16
paraplêsios, similar, 18,11; 96,5; 111,24; 113,2
paratêrêsis, observation, 16,7.14
paratrepô, infringe, 15,13
pareimi, be present, 21,10; 82,6; 102,15; 103,1
parekhô, provide, 48,5; 84,18; 107,19
parepomai, be concomitant, 35,25
paristêmi, present (v.), 39,12; 55,6
parônumos, paronymous, 19,26
paskhein, being affected (category), 20,10.12; 84,23
paskhô, experience, suffer, 21,14; 112,22; 125,14
patêr, father, 47,11; 50,14; 80,22; 91,6
pathos, passion, 12,20

patris, fatherland, 50,9
pauô, cease, 13,27; 40,1
pentagônon, pentagon, 72,8
pente, five, 123,22.23
pephuke, tend, be suited by nature, 64,21; 92,4.18; 102,22; 108,6; 110,2.4; 126,10
perainô, limit (v.), 86,11; 87,1;
  peperasmenos, limited, finite, 17,4.7.26; 85,12.15.18.19; 86,18.25–27; 87,2
peratoô, limit (v.), 7,17.18; 86,9.11
periekhô, contain, 12,15; 18,6.16; 32,3.19; 41,2; 43,11; 68,19; 80,11
periektikos, containing, including, 17,16.28; 19,19; 32,2.4.23; 47,8; 57,3; 70,21; 71,9; 76,18; 78,15; 87,18; 110,22
periepô, cultivate, 5,22
perigraphô, circumscribe, 63,19
perikardios, around the heart, 57,19
perikleiô, enclose, 54,9
perilambanô, comprehend, include, encompass, 1,8.9; 17,5; 19,13; 31,19; 67,15; 123,9
periorizô, circumscribe, 63,21; 68,2
peripateô, walk, 93,23
peripatêtikôs, in a Peripatetic way, 102,3
periphereia, circumference, 12,16; arc, 73,15.22
peripoieô, procure, 67,21
peripoiêtikos, producing, 2,7.9; 6,3.14
perissartios, odd-times-even, 14,15
perisseuô, exceed, 101,9
peristera, pigeon, 122,7
perithesis, placing round, 20,7
peritteuô, be excessive, 16,10; 67,17; 68,5.7.10.11.20–3
perittos, odd, 13,17; superfluous, 21,11
perusin, last year, 20,3
peteinos, winged, 109,17
petra, rock, 77,24
phainomai, appear, be apparent, clearly do, clearly be something, 29,25; 32,12; 49,8
phaios, grey, 19,22; 126,9
phalakra, baldness, 113,26.27
phalakros, bald, 58,3; 66,18; 90,17.20.21; 94,14
phaneros, evident, 75,1
phantasia, imagination, 11,17
phantasma, apparition, 5,23
phaskô, say, 74,7; 120,20

phatta, dove, 122,7
phere eipein, let us say, 81,9
pherô, wear, 20,6; bring, 102,8; *pheromai*, circulate, be transported, 13,24; 93,18; 108,16; be applied, 68,15
phêmi, say, 76,2; 82,15; 84,7.15; 102,19; 111,4
philaitios, censorious, 2,18
philanthrôpôs, out of love for mankind, 20,18
philia, love, 9,22; 112,3
philos, friend, 50,13; 91,7
philosopheô, practise philosophy, 109,14
philosophia, philosophy, 9,24; 11,21; 15,1; 17,1; 21,5; 22,6; 23,6.8; 34,24
philosophos, philosopher, 11,18; 15,12; 20,25; 21,7.11; 34,26; 36,4; 39,4; 43,2; 46,17; 52,13; 53,14.21; 58,3; 59,17; 60,13; 63,12; 67,18; 71,9.10; 74,10; 75,25; 78,4; 81,3; 90,17.20.21; 98,5; 101,8; 109,9; 110,14.17; philosophical, 1,2(adj.)
philosophôs, philosophically, 49,5
philosômatos, body-loving, 5,21
philotês, sex, 15,20
philotimia, ostentation, 2,18
phlebotomeô, bleed, 24,13
phleps, vein, 81,20; 83,6
phobeomai, fear (v.), 15,21; 103,11
phora, translation, 113,12
phônê, word, 20,16.19.28.29; 22,24; 23,13; 28,3.4.9.16; 30,10; 31,6; 50,16; 58,18; 59,9; 60,2.7; 61,17; 62,2–6.8.9; 63,2.4; 64.15-21; 77,7; 81,23; 82,3; 83,5.21; 84,22; 88,3.9.10; 110,13; 114,16.19
phôteinos, bright, 13,4
phôtizô, illuminate, 13,2
phrasis, phraseology, 22,10
phronêsis, intelligence, 3,27
phroura, prison, 5,1.4
phthanô, do something in advance, 57,18; 76,2; 81,7; 124,18; arrive at, 87,22
phthartikos, destructive, 103,15.29; 112,10
phthartos, perishable, 17,3
phtheirô, destroy, perish (pass.), 30,3; 31,18; 63,19; 103,14; 111,2.14.15.20.22.25; 112,7.8.12.15.21–5; 113,1.4.15.19.20.21.26.28; 125,19
phthora, corruption, destruction, 3,5; 33,24; 111,20; 113,8.9.14.16

phulattô, maintain, 125,14.18
phulax, guardian, 103,19
phusikoi, hoi, natural philosophers, 105,9
phusikos, natural, physical, 5,11; 9,19; 11,28.29; 12,21; 42,25; 44,4; 45,6(adv.); 52,23; 69,17; 99,28.29; 106,15.18; 107,8; 119,8
phusiologeô, talk about nature, 106,5
phusiologikos, pertaining to the science of nature, 10,15; 11,23; 12,9.10; 13,8
phusis, nature, 11,29; 28,16; 31,19; 35,24; 40,4; 42,1; 44,5.7.24; 48,3; 50,13.17; 51,18.21; 52,1.2.9; 73,18.20; 74,2; 77,1.2; 85,13.18; 87,7.8.10; 96,11; 104,1.32; 118,7; 120,15.16.19.22.30; 121,14; 125,18
phuton, plant, 18,6; 35,14; 70,15; 77,18; 78,6; 79,10; 99,26; 118,24
pikros, bitter, 19,23
piptô, fall (v.), 32,22.23; 70,1.22
pistoomai, confirm, 8,14.15
pithanos, persuasive, 1,14; 35,18
plagios, oblique, 91,5
planaô, wander, 10,7
planê, error, 48,23; 49,2
platanos, plane tree, 18,3.5
platos, 7,20, width
platônikos, Platonist, 105,11; 106,4
platukos, detailed, 60,6; 62,1
platuônukhos, having flat nails, 54,21
pleiôn, more, several, many, 90,10.13
pleista, a great many, 86,1
pleiston, most, 122,2.5
pleistos, maximal, 122,11
plekô, weave, 70,13
pleonasmos, superabundance, 16,8.14
pleonazô, be in excess, 112,14
pleonektês, greedy person, 67,21
pleonexia, greed, 67,20
pleô, travel by water, 108,16.17
pleura, side, 11,4; 51,2; 73,7.11.21
plêmmelêma, offence, 5,4
plêroô, complete, 69,14
plêsiazô, come near to, approach, 87,24; 121,10; 122,11
plêsios, close, 33,9.21
plêthos, plurality, multitude, 49,19; 51,16.22; 85,21; 86,26; 87,20.21.24; 115,9
plêthunô, multiply, 87,25
plêthuntikos, plural, 91,15
pneumôn, lung, 25,6
poiein, to, acting (category), 20,8.12; 84,23
poieomai, carry out, cause, 64,6.15; 73,19; 76,9; 93,6; 114,24
poieô, do, make, carry out, produce, 32,11; 36,14; 42,1.19; 44,7.8; 48,6; 51,19; 74,11; 75,3.5.24.25; 88,17; 89,19; 94,6.8; 95,3.16; 101,17; 104,8.14; 107,16.17; 110,15; 113,8; 116,10; 119,17; 120,8.14; 123,6; 125,9
poiêtês, poet, 23,5; 94,21
poion, qualified, 19,25; 20,11; 34,6; 56,21; 57,5; 65,16; 77,4; 83,18; 84,23; 113,7.10
poiotês, quality, 65,18; 112,4.6.10.11.13.24.25; 113,11.19
polemeô, fight (v.), 112,17
polioomai, turn grey, 109,18.19
polis, city, 15,5.9.13
politikos, public, political, 1,15; 15,3.6.8; 16,4
pollaplasiasmos, multiplication, 116,4
pollaplasiazô, multiply, 116,8; 123,1.3
pollaplasios, many times as many, 86,3.4.7.13.21.23
polloi, many: *en tois pollois*, in the many, 41,19; 68,25; 69,3; 104,31; 105,8; 117,1; 119,8; *epi tois pollois*, after the many, 41,19; 69,1; 69,4; 117,1; *pro tôn pollôn*, before the many, 41,18; 68,25; 69,3; 104,29
pollôi mallon, a fortiori, 99,28
polumerês, having many parts, 54,13
poluplasiazô, multiply, 115,23; 116,4
polustikhos, lengthy, 38,18
poluthrullêtos, well-known, 8,1
porizomai, obtain, 17,9
porrô, far, distant, 33,11; 52,6; 87,25; 122,9
poson, quantified, quantum, 14,2.6.8.10.12.18.21; 19,17; 20,11; 34,6; 56,21; 57,4; 77,4; 81,12; 83,10.18; 84,23; 113,7.10
posos, how many, 17,11
pote, when, 20,3.11; 84,23; sometimes, 28,15
pou, where, 20,2.11; 84,23; 113,7
pous, foot, 36,5; 81,23

pôs ekhein, relative disposition, 93,25; 94,1.2
pragma, reality, thing, 1,5; 10,5; 19,3.19; 23,4; 27,26; 28,5.18.29; 29,2; 31,17; 32,7; 35,2; 36,5; 39,4; 50,17; 51,7; 54,9.11; 55,1.5.12; 56,3.20; 59,21; 63,3.4; 67,14; 68,3.6.9.14; 70,9; 77,1.2.6.7; 83,9.16; 84,9.11; 87,20; 96,11; 98,6; 106,15; 107,8; 117,21
pragmateia, treatise, study, discipline, 26,17; 45,2.13; 53,2; 69,24; 84,3; 88,4.6.17; 89,3; 105,11
pragmateuomai, deal with, 8,17
praktikos, practical, 10,13; 11,6.20.21; 15,2.8.10
prattô, do, 15,3; 43,10
prepontôs, appropriately, 44,13; 53,2; 88,4
prepô, be suitable, 26,6; 44,13
presbeuô, maintain, 106,6
presbus, ancient, taking precedence, 25,22; 47,10.15.16.18; 48,2; 58,6.11.12
pro oligou, shortly before, 58,7
proagô, bring, 26,26; 102,7; 104,19
proairesis, choice, 50,13
proairetikos, voluntary, 5,12
proanakrouomai, introduce by way of a prelude, 23,17
proaulion, prelude, 43,3
probainô, proceed, 101,21
proballomai, project, 104,2.9
prodêlos, obvious, 97,19
proeimi, proceed, 32,6; 36,24; 48,5; 70,7
proektitêmi, set forth beforehand, 122,25
proepiluô, solve beforehand, 56,22
proepinoeô, presuppose, 86,19
proerkhomai, proceed, 33,17; 37,10; 45,7; 97,7
proêgomai, precede, 20,22
proêgoumenôs, primarily, 116,16.22
progastôr, pot-bellied, 58,3; 90,18.22
prohuparkhô, pre-exist, 47,14; 48,7; 101,23
prohuphistamai, bring into existence beforehand, 105,1
prohupokeimai, pre-subsist, 72,23; 120,12
prokataballô, state beforehand, 105,12
prokeimai, be at hand, be present, be under discussion, have as one's task, 4,16; 23,20.25; 37,6; 45,18; 52,20; 53,1; 61,18; 69,2.22; 71,14.22; 88,3; 98,19; 110,10; 115,10.23; 122,26; 123,3.18.19
prokheirizomai, examine, 52,12; 70,7
prokheiros, at hand, 51,14.15.17
prokoptô, advance, 97,7; 106,7
prolambanô, assume beforehand, 85,21; 101,12
prolegô, say beforehand, 21,7.11; 22,1.2; 77,10; 101,21; 115,11
pronoeomai, exercise providence, 3,13; 11,15
pronoêtikos, providential, 3,13; 11,12
pronoia, providence, 3,18; 5,6
prooimion, prologue, 23,17; 26,1
pros: *pros allêla*, mutual, 14,19; *pros heteron*, to something else, 14,19; *pros ti*, relative, 14,6.13; 19,29; 20,11; 47,9–14.23; 48,2.13.15.16; 69,15; 76,5; 84,23; 91,4
prosagoreuô, call, address, 6,24; 9,20; 21,7; 43,9.10.13; 83,4.5.8.13.17.19
prosagô, apply, 7,11
prosdekhomai, admit, 15,24
prosdiorismos, quantification, 28,18.19.20.24
prosdiorizomai, add an additional specification, 69,21
proseimi, approach, 77,25; 79,9
prosekhês, proximate, recent, 8,2; 11,30(adv.); 32,2; 37,18; 45,17; 51,12(adv.); 52,5; 79,17.19(adv.)
prosekhô, pay attention, 5,8
prosepinoeô, think up in addition, 21,11
proserkhomai, be added, 107,26; mount, 125,12
prosêgoria, appellation, 9,16; 83,8.11
prosêmainô, indicate beforehand, 52,20
proskeimai, be added, 3,20; 4,5; 27,6
proslambanô, receive, take on, 12,5; 94,5; 120,1
prosonta, attributes, 22,6
prosôpon, face, 83,12.14
prosphôneô, address, call by name, 22,12.13; 43,10
prosphuô, grow upon, 77,24
prospiptô, come up, 105,14
prostaktikos, imperative, 43,5
prostatês, champion, 41,6

prostithêmi, add, 12,19; 68,19; 87,4; 88,5; 89,19; 93,17; 100,23; 110,19.20; 114,22; 117,20; 123,15.16.18.20.21

prosupakousteon, one must supply, 105,16

protasis, premise, 35,18; 36,8; 74,23.24.25; 75,1.4; 88,8.9.14.16

protassô, place before, 31,9; 33,17; 37,22; 48,3; 69,16; 120,10

protekhnologeô, provide technical treatment beforehand, 21,7

protereuô, precede, 31,10

proteros, prior, previous, 52,10; 70,21; 75,10–14; 78,25; 82,13; 91,24; 118,7; 120,15.16.19.20.23; 121,14; 127,4

prothesis, purpose, 26,2

prothumos, eager, 21,12.16

protithêmi, propose, 2,23; 17,10; 31,11; 35,4; 37,7; 39,6; 105,10; set forth, 123,1.14

protrepô, urge, encourage, 24,7; 38,17

prouphistêmi, pre-subsist, 47,14.24

proupostrônnumi, act as a prior subject, 120,13

prôteuô, come first, 44,17

prôtos, first, primary, 57,26; 71,27; 72,7.20.22; 73,17.19.23; 74,11.12.21.22; 75,24.25; 78,5; 82,6.11.13; 92,26; 97,2.19(adv.)

psammos, sand, 87,1.3

psektos, blameworthy, 75,18

pseudomai, be false, lie, 43,12.14.15; 44,21

pseudos, falsehood, 43,11

psilos, mere, 28,4.9.29; 41,4; 56,3.14

psimmuthion, white lead, 19,8.21; 40,18

psophos, sound, 98,5

psukhê, soul, 11,16.19; 13,20.24.30; 18,11; 19,1.10; 35,20; 43,8.14.21; 46,7; 74,14.15.16.19; 88,13.14; 97,14; 99,28; 100,19; 104,3.9; 126,6

psukhoô, ensoul, 48,5; 105,5

psukhô, cool (v.), 20,8; 44,6; 111,1

psukhros, cold, 19,24; 102,10.13.14.16.21.24; 104,4.15; 111,27; 112,19

psukhrotês, coldness, 107,7

psuksis, cooling, 102,25; 111,23.26; 113,18; chill, 113,1

ptaiô, be fallible, 7,7

pteron, wing, 111,16

ptôsis, case, 29,3; 91,5

pur, fire, 22,15; 44,7; 102,24; 104,16; 107,6.8; 113,3

puretos, fever, 111,20; 112,11.23.26; 113,1.3.4.15.23

pusmatikos, interrogative, 43,5

rezô, do, 16,1

rhadion, easy, 122,3.8

rhêma, verb, word, 21,2.22; 27,7.8; 36,3

rhêtor, rhetorician, 35,18; 39,5; 49,9; 59,17

rhêtorikê, rhetoric, 1,13.14; 9,18

rhêtorikos, rhetorical, 23,3

rhis, nose, 83,12.14; 111,6

rhizoomai, be rooted, 79,10

salpinx, war-trumpet, 13,22.23

saphêneia, clarity, 80,20

saphênizô, clarify, 51,1; 70,7; 75,1; 105,14

saphês, clear, 22,10; 26,5; 39,10; 41,10; 52,10.13; 74,13.25; 75,3.10–25; 102,5; 105,13

sarkion, piece of flesh, 105,2

sarx, flesh, 11,28; 36,6; 52,3.8; 83,6

seira, series, 70,13; 81,9

sêmainomenon, meaning, 25,9.13; 49,18; 51,11.20.22; 52,16.17; 53,7; 54,3; 69,20.22; 70,5; 71,8.15.17.22.23; 81,23; 82,4; 83,22; 92,2; 101,8; 109,8.13.27; 110,14.16

sêmainô, signify, 23,4; 28,22; 29,2.3.5; 45,18; 48,20.21.22; 49,6; 51,6; 54,11; 55,12; 56,4.14.16; 83,10; 84,9.11; 93,17; 101,7; 108,9; 126,4

sêmantikos, significant, 20,2.3; 21,3; 50,16; 59,1.10; 62,7.8; 64,17.19.20.21; 106,10

sêmeion, point, 7,15; 9,4

sidêros, iron, 113,3

simos, snub-nosed, 66,18; 90,20.22; 92,15.17.19; 93,4.9.13; 94,17; 95,1; 108,3

simotês, snubness, 92,14; 111,2

siôpaô, keep silent, 13,10

skalênos, scalene, 51,5

skepasma, shelter, 12,18

skepê, shelter, 12,20

skeuos, object, 107,2.13

skênê, tent, 12,19

skhesis, relation, 13,15; 14,15.21; 19,29; 34,4; 37,10; 48,9; 49,18; 50,1.7.11; 51,16; 53,7.8.11; 56,9; 57,2.7; 70,24.25.27; 71,3.6; 76,14-19; 79,21; 80,2.4.5.9.10; 109,28; 117,22; 118,2.5; 122,22.23.26; 123,3.6.8.9.14.16-24.27.29; 124,2.5.10
skhetikôs, relationally, 117,25
skhêma, figure, 11,2; 12,14; 13,19; 40,16.19; 71,25-7; 72,8.11.15.19-21; 73,14.16.22; 74,3; 106,22; 107,11.13
skiagrapheô, sketch roughly, 64,7
skiagraphia, rough sketch, 55,2
skindapsos, example of a meaningless word, 59,1; 60,7
skioeidês, shadowy, 5,23
skopeô, investigate, consider, 3,1.14; 14,17; 34,3
skopêteon, one must consider, 6,5
skopos, goal, 20,21; 21,8.13.23.25; 22,3; 23,17; 47,2
skoteinos, dark, 13,2
sophia, wisdom, 9,7.17
sophos, wise, 9,9
sôma, body, 7,26; 11,29; 18,17.21; 40,12.13; 41,5.11; 42,14; 52,23; 57,3; 70,14; 77,16.17; 78,9.10.21; 79,2.4; 81,22; 88,28; 89,9-11; 97,15; 100,6; 103,25.27.28; 105,3.4; 110,18-22.25.27; 112,4.5.11.14.24.25.27; 113,1.3; 122,19
sômatikôs, corporeally, 104,7
sôphrosunê, temperance, 67,22
sôtêr, saviour, 103,18
sôzô, preserve, 111,25; 112,15
sperma, seed, sperm, 48,4; 71,1; 105,2
speudô, hasten, strive, 5,5; 112,17
sphodros, intense, 98,5.6
sphragis, seal, 41,17
sphragizô, stamp, 41,14
spongos, sponge, 77,24; 79,8
sporadên, scattered, 25,22
spoudaios, good, 1,4
spoudazô, strive, 112,15
stasis, standstill, 17,8; rest, 52,19; 59,21
stathmê, line, 9,2
stenoomai, contract, 68,14; 87,20.24
sterêsis, privation, 16,7
stikhos, line, 39,2
stoikheion, element, 7,31; 8,1; 36,6.23; 52,2.8; 72,16.19; 73,5; letter, 36,4

stokhazomai, aim at, 1,19; 39,2; 47,5
strephô, turn, 13,26
strongulon, sphere, 104,7.11
sukê, fig tree, 18,3.4
sullabê, syllable, 36,3
sullegô, collect, 22,21
sullogismos, syllogism, 8,5; 36,7; 88,8.17
sumbainô, happen, occur accidentally, 4,26; 22,17; 34,8; 54,17; 56,9.17; 57,1.2.7; 58,4; 70,12; 82,17.18.19; 87,14; 104,5; 109,13; 111,22.24; 112,14; follow, 73,16; 86,20; 116,9; 123,9
sumballomai, contribute, 25,2.12; 33,9; 34,27; 35,1; 59,16; 98,20; 105,11
sumbebêkos, accident, 7,11; 14,16; 19,5; 20,17; 22,5; 29,18.21.26; 31,12; 45,5; 55,2; 56,8.16; 57,15; 66,6; 70,2; 82,15.16.18; 92,4.10.12.16.20.24.25; 93,25; 94,1.2.12; 95,24; 100,24; 109,6.16; 113,16.19.22.24
summetaballô, change along with, 11,4.5
summetria, proportion, 67,18; 111,24; 112,21; 113,19.21
summetrôs, moderately, 39,1
sumperainô, conclude, 74,20.22
sumperasma, conclusion, 74,23.24.25; 75,2.5
sumperilambanô, encompass, 6,19
sumpherô, be expedient, 8,19
sumphônia, harmony, 13,19
sumphtheirô, destroy together, 112,8.9; 113,4
sumphutos, innate, connatural, 7,30; 11,2
sumplekô, combine, 23,14; 88,16; 99,4.24; 109,28; 119,16.17.18; 126,8
sumplektikos, copulative, 31,2
sumplêroô, complete (v.), 54,19; 60,16; 99,6; 119,17.19
sumplêrôtikos, completive, 33,2.4.17; 50,2; 60,15; 92,11.16.20.25; 94,5; 98,10.11; 118,13.18; 121,2
sumplokê, combination, 115,21.24; 116,2
sunagô, collect, 20,29; 25,22
sunanaireô, co-eliminate, 29,28; 30,3.4; 48,8; 73,3; 82,14; 120,17.18.19
sunaptikos, unitive, 36,26
sunaptô, contact, 14,12
sundesmos, binding, 5,10; 25,9; conjunction, 31,2

sundromê, concourse, 56,16; 57,15
sunduazomai, be coupled, 68,18
suneimi, come together, 125,13.14.17
suneispherô, entail, 118,8; 120,21–5
sunekhês, continuous, 14,3.7.10.11; 19,16.17; 57,4
sunengizô, be near, 122,5
sunephelkomai, entail, 14,24
sunethismos, habituation, 12,26
sunêtheia, customary usage, 20,17; 51,14; 53,19; 70,7
sungeneia, kinship, 121,9
sungenês, akin, 33,22
sungignôskô, be familiar, 97,6
sungramma, writing, work, 20,23; 21,10; 23,12; 25,17; 26,7; 34,26; 38,15; 105,10
sunistêmi, sunistamai, constitute, exist, 58,7; 70,11; 95,20.22; 96,18; 97,1; 99,6.11.12.16; 109,29
sunkeimai, consist in, be made up of, 36,2.24; 52,7.8; 55,18; 60,21; 72,18; 73,16.23; 74,2; 86,25.26; 88,9; 91,11
sunkheô, confuse, obliterate, 60,22; 104,8
sunkhôreô, agree, 97,8
sunkrima, compound, 63,20
sunkrinô, combine, 115,25
sunkrisis, aggregation, 116,2; comparison, 120,8
sunousia, conversation, 46,6
sunônumon, synonym, 84,11.17
sunônumôs, synonymously, 29,24; 84,16; 119,13.14
sunteleô, contribute, 22,1; 23,21; 92,13
sunthesis, composition, 37,7; 38,38; 73,1
sunthetos, compound, 5,9; 23,22; 36,2.25; 37,13–17.24; 40,3; 68,14; 111,27
suntithêmi, combine, compose, 7,26; 37,20.21; 68,17; 94,7; 99,10; 125,9.10
suntomos, concise, 1,7; 25,23; 38,10; 39,9
suntrekhô, coincide, 109,20
sunuphistêmi, subsist simultaneously, 48,8; 76,5
sustasis, constitution, 22,7.8; 45,7; 106,15
sustatikos, constitutive, 35,12; 36,15; 47,12.17.25.26; 55,8.19.20.22; 58,5.6.7.9.11; 96,12; 98,22; 99,1.5.8; 100,4.6.9.13.14; 108,4; 118,13.15
sustellô, contract (v.), 78,1.9
suzeugnumi, be coupled, 27,7

suzugia, combination, 95,19.21; 96,2; 99,10.15.24

talaipôreô, toil, 37,14
tassô, place (v.), 33,18
tattomai, range (v.), 21,22
tauton, identical, 65,5–8.10.11
tautotês, identity, 52,19; sameness, 115,4.6.10.12
taxis, order, position, rank, 10,4.19; 11,24; 21,9.21; 23,1; 31,14; 33,17; 35,2.26; 44,16; 47,7; 48,4; 57,24; 69,14.17; 75,2.3; 99,20; 100,18; 109,2; 110,10
tekhnê, art, 6,26.27; 9,5.6.9; 21,12; 23,8; 50,11.19; 52,22
tekhnêtos, artificial, 106,19; 107,10
tekhnitês, craftsman, 46,8; 106,21
teknon, child, 50,1
tektonikê, carpentry, 2,14; 52,22
tektôn, carpenter, 2,3; 9,1; 101,17
teleioô, perfect (v.), 24,4; 102,12
teleios, perfect, complete, 76,21; 84,4; 95,13; 104,22.23.25; 106,9
teleiotês, perfection, 3,24; 16,7.14
teleiôsis, perfection, 11,19
teleô, accomplish, end up, 16,1; 20,13; 60,4; 61,17
teleutaô, end up, 36,21; 37,13
teleutê, death, 46,10
telos, end (n.), 1,18; 22,9; 24,11–13
temnô, section (v.), 28,10; 34,2.10; 35,8; 47,25.26; 63,17
terpomai, be glad, 3,16
tetragônon, square, 72,1–10.17.23; 73,1–6.10.12.19.21.23; 104,7.11
tetrapous, four-footed, 17,17.23
tettares, four, 72,1; 73,2
thalassa, sea, 87,3
thalattios, marine, 49,4; 82,1
thanataô, wish to die, 5,7
thaumastos, surprising, 17,27
thaumazô, be surprised, 57,7
theaomai, observe, 12,2; 17,25; 20,9; 40,3; 41,15; 42,10
theios, divine, 11,26; 12,21.25; 13,6.12.28; 16,17; 35,7; 46,5; uncle, 49,21; 50,1
thelô, wish (v.), 80,19; 115,20
theologia, theology, 13,1.5

theologikos, theological, 10,14; 11,22; 12,8.10; 13,8; 43,25; 45,2.10(adv.)
theos, god, 11,11.16; 15,21; 19,2; 40,15; 44,1; 78,2; 99,13; 103,17; 108,5
theô, run, 3,28
theôreô, observe, consider, 8,19; 10,22; 11,24; 13,14; 14,24; 22,4; 27,27; 28,1; 34,12; 44,11; 54,12; 70,11; 77,3; 82,6; 93,25; 97,12; 103,23; 105,9; 106,18; 115,4; 118,13
theôrêma, theorem, 13,13; 22,11; 25,20; 26,7; 99,3; 103,10; 115,15
theôrêtikos, theoretical, 6,11; 10,12; 11,6.13.14.20-22; 12,8; 14,25
theôria, consideration, 6,14; 9,19; 25,15.19.23; 38,6; 43,4; 44,13; 88,6
thermainô, heat (v.), 20,8; 102,13.24; 111,1
thermansis, heating, 113,11
thermasia, heating, 113,18
thermê, heat, 111,26
thermos, hot, 19,23; 102,10.13-16.22; 104,4.15.16; 111,27; 112,19
thermotês, heat (n.), 7,12; 107,7; 111,23; 113,2
thesis, position, 14,7.8; 20,5
thnêtos, mortal, 17,12.24; 32,17; 33,6; 35,6; 43,15; 54,14.18; 58,9; 62,16; 68,8.10.12.18; 69,9; 79,12.13; 90,8.15; 92,21; 94,6.17.19; 95,9.10; 96,14.15; 97,24; 99,2.5.12.14.21; 100,7.9.11.14.15.20; 101,10.25; 103,12-17.20; 105,17; 107,16.17.27; 119,18; 120,14; 125,5.15
threptikos, nutritive, 77,19
thrix, hair, 113,27
thumikos, angry, 13,22
thumos, ardour, 11,18; 103,22
ti estin, essence, 108,11
tiktô, give birth, 75,6-13
timaô, honour (v.), 15,22
tithêmi, place, posit, promulgate, lay down, coin, 8,9.21; 15,12.15.18; 93,17.19; 120,4.24
tmêma, section (n.), 41,6; 47,26
toikhos, wall, 8,26
toinun, therefore, 72,12
toionde, of such-and-such a kind, 107,19
toiôsde, in a certain way, 112,27
tomê, cut, section, 7,25; 9,29

tonos, tone, pitch, 8,23; 14,19
topos, place (n.), 20,2; 41,1; 46,16; 77,21.23; 85,19; 110,22; 113,12
tragelaphos, goat-stag, 39,15; 40,6; 114,21
tragos, goat, 40,4
tranês, clear, 97,13
trekhô, run, rush, 9,19
trephô, nourish, bring up, 18,9; 50,10; 79,5; 105,5
triaina, three-pronged spear, 9,11
trigônon, triangle, 11,2; 11,31; 51,2; 71,24-8; 72,3.6-10.15-21; 73,2-6; 74,1.3; 104,7.11
trikhêi diastatos, three-dimensional, 18,18.21; 112,5
trikhôs, in three senses, 91,21; 93,9
trittos, threefold, 65,5.11; 68,25; 104,28
trophos, nurse, 64,1
tropos, mode, way, 26,5; 47,3; 67,17; 72,7; 101,22; 109,9; 113,6; 123,6
tukhê, chance, 50,12; 58,17
tukhon, to, just anything, 44,23; 108,2; 113,2
tunkhanô, receive, 33,23; 84,21; 105,6; happen to be, 1,4; 80,19; *ei tukhoi*, for instance, as the case may be, 57,11; 61,5; 80,22; 90,22; 93,22; 118,21
tuphlôttô, go blind, 13,1
tupoô, stamp (v.), 106,23
tupos, impression, 41,17; 42,6; 104,8; type, 109,8
tuptô, strike, 20,8.9; 91,7.8

xenoprepês, extraordinary, 50,19
xêros, dry, 112,1
xêrotês, dryness, 107,7
xiphos, sword, 65,10
xulinos, wooden, 12,2
xulon, wood, 2,14; 11,28; 12,19; 18,11.18; 52,22; 83,4; 101,15.16; 107,10

zesis, boiling, 57,19
zêlon, emulation, 26,14
zêteô, seek, inquire, 11,7; 17,1; 18,23; 31,14; 34,1; 41,5; 44,1.9.13; 45,5.7.9; 48,11; 99,14; 126,5
zêtêma, question, 38,20; 39,10; 47,4
zêtêsis, question, 21,22; 59,22
zô, live, 25,6

zôê, life, 103,22
zôion, animal, 10,2; 17,17.28; 32,5.9; 33,4.5; 35,5.14; 44,9; 48,6; 54,14.18; 58,10; 61,5; 62,13.16; 63,15.19; 65,8.15.17.25; 68,7.10.12.17.18; 69,9; 70,15.16; 77,18.20; 78,1.9–12.17; 79,4.7.11.13.18; 81,18; 82,7.9; 84,13.14; 85,3; 88,19–23.29; 89,7.8.11; 90,12.14.15; 92,21; 93,7.12; 94,5; 95,8.10; 97,11.16.18; 98,11; 99,3; 100,8.11.12.16; 101,2.11; 103,23; 105,6.7.17; 107,14.16; 111,12.13.24.26; 112,4; 113,1.3.19; 116,16.18; 117,15–17.22–6; 118,1.21.23; 119,16; 120,13.14.18.19.22; 121,6; 122,18.19; 124,20; 125,1.5; 127,2
zôophuton, zoophyte, 70,16; 77,18.21
zôopoieô, animate (v.), 5,12; 48,5
zôtikos, vital, 11,18.21

Subject Index

Note: Numbers in **bold** refer to the paragraph of Greek text indicated in the margin of the English translation, while numbers in regular type refer to the pages of the Introduction. Numbers followed by 'n.' refer to notes.

abstraction (as a psychological process) **12,2f.**
accidents **19,5ff.**; **110,10ff.**
   belongs to/predicated of several species **61,17**; **62,17**; **64,23f.**
   concourse of **56,16f.**; **57,15f.**
   as existing in substance or substrate **29,25f.**; **115,1ff.**
   has lesser extension than genus **118,20ff.**
   as incorporeals **110,18ff.**
   predicated relatively **62,22**; **64,22**; **66,15f.**; **67,5**
   separable from substance without destroying it **33,1f.**; **110,17ff.**; **111,9ff.**
   separable from subject in thought **109,7f.**; **111,5f.**; **114,4f.**
   separable vs. inseparable **111,2f.**
   as what can belong or not belong to the same thing **114,9f.**
Achilles **41,14**
actuality
   as perfect **104,22f.**
   vs. potentiality **102,6ff.**; **105,1ff.**; **110,2ff.**
   what is potential produced by what is actual **104,14ff.**
Adrastus 130 n.68
Alexander of Aphrodisias 130 n.71; 134 n.137
Alexandria 1
al-Fārābī 5
alteration **113,17f.**
Ammonius, commentary of
   authorship of 6f.
   as collection of scholia 7; 131 n.88; 138 n.213
   /text of 7ff.
   compromises by 9 nn.9, 12
   In Cat. 135 n.159; 135–6 nn.169–70; 139 n.244
   In Int. 135 n.170
   lectures on Plato 8 n.3
   life of 1
   not first commentator on the *Isagogê* 5f.; 10 n.30; 130 n.61
   philosophy of 2f.
analysis **36,2ff.**
   contrary to division **36,20**
   opposed to definition **36,25**
   opposed to demonstration **37,5**
angel(s) 2; 134 n.54; **32,15f.**; **40,15**; **62,16**; **70,17**; **97,15**; 138 n.212; **100,15**; 138 n.219; **114,8f.**
   as protectors of mortals **103,19**
Antisthenes **40,7ff.**; **41,5**
Apollonius of Rhodes **16,13**
apple **110,24f.**
Arabic 127 n.8
Archilochus 128 n.22
Archytas **26,17**; 130 n.69; **30,6**
Aristotle 1–4; **49,11**; **108,10**
   Analytics **36,9**
   Categories **30,11ff.**; **43,4ff.**; **46,21f.**; **56,3**; **84,4**; **97,2**; 10; 136 n.182; 137 nn.209–10
   concerns himself with things *qua* physical **43,1**
   disagrees with Plato **42,23ff.**; **44,2ff.**
   On Interpretation **38,17**
   On the Soul 134 n.142
   Physics **53,1**; 134 n.130
   Posterior Analytics **38,17**; 137 n.194
   succeeds Plato **46,10ff.**
   Topics **34,20**; 134 n.136; 135 n.154; 138 nn.222,.225

arithmetic 1; 2; **13,10**; **14,17**
ascent from the sensible to the intelligible 6
Asclepius 2; 11 n.30
astronomy 1; **2,9f.**; **13,10.32**; **14,9f.**
authenticity **21,17ff.**; **22,10f.**
axioms
    etymology of **101,14**
    that contraries cannot coexist in same
        substrate at same time **101,19f.**
    that nothing comes into being out of
        nothing **101,14f.**

baldness **113,25f.**
Baltes, Matthias 130 n.59
Barnes, Jonathan 137 n.204
being (s)
    division of **82,4ff.**
    imaginary **39,15ff.**
    as homonymous **28,17**; **83,24f.**; **84,22ff.**
    as mere word **28,7f.**
    necessary vs. contingent **26,20f.**
    not a genus 6; **28,15f.**; **29,16f.**; **81,16ff.**;
        85,12
    as principle of the categories **81,12f.**
Blank, David 134 n.145
Bobzien, Suzanne 130 n.71
body
    as made up of contraries **111,26f.**
    as mutually impenetrable **110,25**
    qualityless **112,5f.**
Boethius 4
Busse, A. 7–8

Callimachus 127 n.9
Cardullo, R. Loredana 10. n.19
case
    nominative **29,3f.**
    genitive **29,5f.**
categories
    Archytas and **31,5ff.**
    Aristotle's treatise on **30,11ff.**; **43,2f.**
    Chrysaorius and **22,14f.**
    considered *per se* and in relation
        34,3ff.
    differ in name and reality **83,9**
    generation of **19,14ff.**
    go back to one principle **81,11f.**
    as parts of being **83,7f.**
    Stoic 135 n.157
    as ten in number **84,5ff.**
    various authors of treatises on **26,14f.**
celestial bodies 2; **97,15f.**; 128 n.28
centaur **40,2ff.**
change, four types of **113,6ff.**
character **16,7ff.**
Christians, and pagans 1ff.
Chrysaorius **22,13f.**; **38,6**
Chrysippus 127 n.1
circle **12,14f.**
co-elimination **29,27f.**; **48,9**; **72,5ff.**; **82,8f.**;
    121,15ff.
    indicates natural priority **118,7f.**;
        120,16ff.
combinations **16,9f.**
    number of **99,10ff.**; **109,26ff.**; **115,20ff.**;
        122,22ff.
coming into being **113,13f.**
commonality, and difference **122,2ff.**;
    124,10ff.
concepts **39,15ff.**
continuity **14,10f.**
continuous vs. discrete **57,5**
contraries
    can exist potentially in same substrate
        102,4ff.
    cannot exist in same substrate actually
        106,2
    conflict between **112,15ff.**
    as constitutive of bodies **111,26ff.**
    knowledge of, as one **104,5**
    as mutually destructive **101,21f.**;
        103,14ff.
    as susceptible of more and less **96,16f.**
convertibility, and coextensiveness **88,24f.**

Damascius 1; 7
David 1; 4; 8
Death, as twofold **5,15f.**
definition (*see also* description) **1,5f.**;
    35,9f.; **37,5f.**; **64,15f.**
    derive from genus and constitutive
        differences **35,12f.**; **55,18f.**; **57,2f.**;
        96,12ff.
    etymology of **67,15f.**
    excess and deficiency in **67,18ff.**
    from form **57,20f.**
    indicate nature of a reality **35,24**
    from matter **57,19f.**

method of **98,22ff.**
prior to division **37,23**
requires division **36,17**
not susceptible or more or less **98,10ff.**
signifies the essence **54,18**; **108,10f.**
vices of **67,17f.**
De Libera, Alain 132 n.102; 135 n.152
Demiurge 9 n.16
    contains models of things **40,22ff.**; **45,10f.**
    contains universals 4; **63,15**
    creates by looking at archetypes **42,18f.**
    as highest principle 2
demons **99,19f.**; **100,19f.**
demonstration **22,8ff.**; **35,16f.**
    requires definition and division **36,17f.**
    starts of from premises that are clear and agreed-upon **74,25f.**
    as syllogism **88,8**
description
    from accidents **54,20f.**; **57,18ff.**
    vs. definition 6; **54,6ff.**
    by elimination of alternatives **114,16f.**
    from etymology **57,16f.**
    used for individuals **58,2ff.**
    like a sketch **55,3ff.**
    used for species **76,26f.**
Dexippus 134 n.140; 136 n.176
diagrams 139 n.234
dialectic, Platonic vs. Aristotelian 6; **34,17ff.**
difference
    accidental **92,10ff.**; **93,25f.**
    as analogous to form **107,12**; **119,9f.**
    between genus and difference **61,9f.**
    between property and accident **61,14f.**
    completive **92,20ff.**; **98,9f.**; **119,17ff.**; **121,1.**
    constitutive vs. divisive 6; **55,18f.**; **58,4ff.**; **98,20ff.**; **100,2ff.**; **108,4f.**; **118,12ff.**
    contrary **100,10f.**
    divided into those that make the substrate of a different sort, and those that make it something else **93,1ff.**; **94,10ff.**; **95,16f.**
    horizontal vs. vertical **97,22ff.**
    in most proper sense, inseparable even in thought **114,5f.**

kinds of **65,1ff.**; **92,2ff.**
more particular than genera, but more universal than species **32,21f.**
as otherness **92,3f.**
precedes species **31,10f.**; **91,24**
predicated of species: things that differ in species **64,19f.**; **116,15**
predicated qualitatively **61,9f.**; **62,23**; **64,18**; **66,8**; **67,5**; **106,13**; **107,20**; **124,19**
predicated relatively **66,15f.**
predicated synonymously **119,13f.**
as present in genus potentially **119,2f.**
as present in genus in actuality **103,10ff.**
separable vs. inseparable **92,4ff.**; **94,12f.**; **95,14ff.**
specific **94,5f.**; **95,3f.**; **96,14f.**; **100,2ff.**
subordinate **100,13f.**
as substantial **119,11f.**
as that by which one thing differs from another **32,7**
as that by which the species exceeds the genus **109,9f.**
dimensions **7,17ff.**
Dionysius of Halicarnassus 127 n.2
Dionysius Thrax 127 n.1.
divisibility **7,25f.**
division **9,27f.**; **35,4ff.**
    into chapters **22,13f.**
    and definitions **93,14**; **98,19ff.**
    divides genera into species **36,13f.**
    types of **81,17f.**
dog **122,7**
    homonymy of **49,1ff.**; **82,1ff.**; **84,10–11**

economics **15,2**
elements, four **8,1ff.**
Elias 1; 4; 8
embryology 133 n.119
entailment **118,7f.**; **120,20f.**
ethics **15,2**
Epictetus 3
Etna, Porphyry's interest in **22,15f.**
Euclid 5; **73,3**; 128 nn.21, 34; 129 n.42
Euripides **49,14**; 133 n.125; 136 n.174
Excess, vs. deficiency **16,8ff.**; **67,15ff.**

fever **112,23ff.**; **113,15ff.**
  definition of **113,2f.**
figure, as genus of the triangle **71,25ff.**
five words 3
  choice of, necessary rather than random **58,16ff.**
  order of **31,21f.**; **33,17f.**; **44,16ff.**
  substantial vs. adventitious **33,3ff.**
forms, intelligible
  Aristotle vs. Plato on 4; **42,22ff.**; **44,1ff.**
  not equivalent to thoughts of the Demiurge **42,16f.**
Fortier, S. 132 nn.107–8

Galen **38,16**; 132 n.99
Gauricus, Pomponius 8
genealogy **80,20f.**
generation, order of **48,3ff.**
genus **47,6ff.**
  analogous to matter **102,19**; **107,8 ff.**; **119,9f.**
  conceptual, as subject of *Isagoge* **69,5f.**
  contains species **32,4f.**; **47,7**; **87,18**
  divisive differences of **98,20ff.**
  does not allow prior and posterior **29,19f.**; **71,27ff.**
  everything predicated of the genus also predicated of species and individuals **117,15ff.**
  existence of 3; **40,11ff.**
  has wider extension that difference **118,12ff.**
  as homonymous **56,2f.**
  horizontal vs. vertical **97,10ff.**
  as incorporeal **103,26f.**
  Intermediate **70,19ff.**
  meanings of **49,6ff.**
  most generic (= categories) **55,9**; **80,16f.**; **85,15ff.**; **89,16f.**
  not predicated of species or individuals **117,16ff.**
  not things **77,2f.**
  of being **52,20**
  predicated essentially **61,5f.**; **62,22**; **66,8**; **74,7**; **106,11ff.**; **107,19f.**
  predicated relationally **117,25f.**
  predicated of many **57,10f.**; **62,11f.**; **119,20f.**
  predicated of species **88,18ff.**; **116,15ff.**
  predicated of what differs in species **61,2**; **64,13f.**; **74,7**
  predicated synonymously **119,13f.**
  as prior **47,9**; **120,15**
  as relations **77,2ff.**; **117,22f.**
  prior to species **47,9f.**
  as relative **48,12f.**
  signified by a description **55,8ff.**
  as substantial **119,11f.**
  threefold division of **41,21ff.**; **69,1ff.**; **104,29f.**
  as whole **90,24f.**
geometry 5f.; **7,5f.**; 14f.; **9,2f.**; **13,10**; **14,7f.**; 129 nn.31; 40
  projection of geometrical figures **104,10ff.**
goal (*skopos*) **21,9f.**; **22,4f.**; **23,18**; **26,2ff.**
goat-stag **40,1ff.**; 132 n.103; **114,21**; 139 n.239
God; *see also* Demiurge
  assimilation to 3,8; **4,7–15**; **6,10**; **11,12**
  activities/powers of **3,10f.**; **4,8f.**
  brings mortal and irrational things into existence **103,17f.**
  providence of **3,14f.**
  as superior to knowledge **108,5**
  as wise **9,11**
ghosts **5,22**
Golden verses 3
good
  divided into end and means **24,10ff.**
  as principle of being and object of desire **24,3f.**
grammar **1,11**; **8,24**
grammarians **20,25ff.**
Greek Anthology 133 n.122

Hadot, Ilsetraut 2; 10 nn.18, 20
Hadot, Pierre 134 n.140
harmonics **14,20f.**
harmonization 4; 10 n.18
harmony
  in strings **111,21f.**
  in animal bodies **111,23f.**; **112,14ff.**
heavenly bodies, rationality of **97,15**
Heracles **47,1ff.**; **49,20**; **50,8f.**; **51,21**; **53,17**
Hermias 1
Herodotus 137 n.195
Hippocrates **112,2**; 128 n.14; 139 n.237

Subject Index

Homer **23,5**; 127 nn.6–8; 128 nn.23–4; 129 n.52; 135 n.158; 136 n.191; 137 n.206; 138 n.215
homoeomeries **53,2**; 133 n.127
homonyms 5; **28,3f.**; **84,9ff.**; 131 n.73
   description of **56,15ff.**
   disambiguation of **71,14ff.**
   division of **48,19f.**; **81,24f.**
   have no definition **56,3ff.**
   as mere names **56,4**; **15**
Horapollo 1
horse **17,20ff.**
   mates with ass to produce a mule **125,10ff.**
Huh, Min-Juh 8
human being
   definition of **54,15**; **95,10f.**; **108,13**; **119,19–20**
   as most specific species **78,15f.**; **79,1ff.**
   no human being more human than another 6; **97,10f.**; **128,1f.**
   universal **116,24f.**; **125,10f.**
   as receptive of intellect and knowledge **108,4ff.**
humanism 6
humours **8,2f.**

Iamblichus 2; 3
ideas, *see* forms
identical, meanings of **65,5ff.**
Illus 1
implication of existence **27,2**; 131 n.71
incorporeals **18,22f.**; **40,11ff.**; **104,1ff.**
   can contain contraries in actuality **104,13f.**
   division of **40,14ff.**
individuals **78,14f.**
   etymology of **63,17f.**
   as finite **86,26**
   as infinite **85,2ff.**; **86,28f.**
   lack genus and constitutive differences **58,2**
   as parts **90,25f.**
   and predication **62,10f.**; **63,10f.**
   said of one thing **61,23**
   uniquely identified by concourse of properties **90,17ff.**
induction **8,12f.**

infinity
   and individuals **86,12ff.**
   and most specific species **85,21ff.**
   no multitude greater than **86,7ff.**
   intensification, and remission **98,2ff.**; **14f.**; **126,2ff.**
Isagogê 3ff.
   Arabic tradition of 4–5; 10 n.28
   goal of **20,17f.**
   manuscripts of 4; 11 n.37
   posterity of 4ff.
   title of **20,21f.**
Isocrates 3; **15,22**

Legislation, vs. judging **15,12ff.**
lemma, repetition of 134 n.134, 139 n.240
logic **22,25f.**; **23,20f.**; **88,4ff.**
   chiasmic 137 n.207
   as instrument of philosophy **23,24**
   logical theory **44,13ff.**
   vs. physics and theology **45,5ff.**

Marius Victorinus 4
mathematics
   divisions of **13,10f.**; **14,1ff.**
   as ladder **10,23**; **12,20ff.**; **13,5f.**
   objects of **12,1ff.**
   as part of philosophy **11,23**
matter **11,25f.**; **12,12f.**
   vs. form **106,13ff.**
   as potentially all contraries **102,18ff.**
   underlies all things **107,1ff.**
mechanical arts **8,25f.**
medicine **2,1–8**; **6,1f.**; **7,8ff.**; **8,1ff.**
Middle Platonism 6
Militello, C. 132 n.109; 135 n.169
Milk, as sign that a woman has given birth **75,5ff.**
Miskawayh 128 n.15
monads **60,22ff.**
more and less, *see* intensification
motion, four varieties of **113,6ff.**
music **8,24f.**; **13,11**; **21f.**; **14,22f.**

names
   imposition of **50,20f.**; **53,13f.**; 133 n.126
   as separative **50,16f.**

nature
    as creator 9 n.16; **11,30**; **42,2ff.**; **44,5ff.**
    invents genera and species **31,18f.**
    journeys from universal to particular **105,1f.**
    order followed by **48,3ff.**
    priority by **118,6ff.**; **120,15ff.**
    produces contraries **104,1ff.**
    science of **10,16f.**
    things prior by nature are posterior to us **51,17ff.**
navigation **108,15f.**
necessary, meanings of **24,22f.**
Nemesius 134 n.142
numbers **13,12ff.**; 129 nn.37, 42
    discrete vs. continuous **14,13f.**
    infinity of **86,27f.**

obscurity **38,17**
Odysseus **64,1**; **94,22**
order of reading **21,21f.**; **22,24f.**
otherness, types of **65,11f.**

painting **55,3ff.**; 134 n.138
participation, mediate vs. direct **97,16ff.**
particulars **62,22ff.**
    ascent from, to universals **17,9f.**
    as infinite **59,19f.**
parts
    similar vs. dissimilar **81,19f.**; **83,1ff.**
    subject to demonstrative reference **63,11ff.**
    and wholes, as relatives **91,4f.**
perfection **3,24f.**
Peripatetics **46,2ff.**; **101,13**; **102,4**; **103,8**; **104,28**; **105,12**; **106,6**; **119,2**
    origin of name of **46,5f.**
Peter Mongus 1; 9 n.10
Philoponus 6–7; 11 n.31; 134 n.143; 139 nn.238, 241
philosophy
    as art of arts and sciences of sciences: **9,5**; **23,9**
    definitions of 6; **1,2ff.**; **2,16ff.**; 11 n.32
    divisions of **10,14ff.**; **11,5ff.**; **15,1f.**
    divisibility of **9,25ff.**
    generality of **2,15f.**
    as knowledge of beings qua beings **17,1f.**
    as love of wisdom **9,7**
    nature of 3
    parts of **22,1**
    superiority of **6,25f.**
    as training for death **4,15ff.**
phrase
    declaratory, as either true or false **43,11f.**
    parts of **43,4ff.**
Pindar **50,11**; 134 n.132
plants **18,2ff.**
    as animate but not animals **79,7ff.**
    faculties of **77,20f.**
Plato 1; 3; 4; **22,22**; **32,1**; **33,8**; **34,18f.**; **42,17**; **46,6**; **19**; **50,10**; **59,2**; **60,11**; **62,11**; **23**; **65,9**; **20**; **78,4**; **80,11**; 127 n.8; 129 nn.48, 51
    Cratylus **59,20**; 134 n.141
    on Ideas **44,2ff.**
    Parmenides **45,12**
    Phaedrus **35,7**; **20**
    Sophist **85,8**; 133 n.128; 136 n.193
    Timaeus **72,19**
Platonists **103,10**; **104,29**
Plotinus 128 n.36; 134 n.140
politics **15,2f.**
polyonyms 135 n.159
Porphyry 2–4; 10 n.18; 128 nn.13, 15
    Ad Gaurum 133 n.119
    on Council of Sages 9 n.16; 133 n.126
    In Cat. 133 n.126
    In Cat. (to Gedalius) 134 n.140
potentiality, *see* actuality
predicate
    extension of 5; **27,17f.**; **88,22f.**
    vs. subject **27,5f.**; **43,17ff.**; **44,22ff.**; **88,9f.**
Prime mover 2
principle
    first principle of all things **67,16**; **87,24**; **115,7**
    ten principles, categories as **84,1ff.**
priority and posteriority 6
Proclus 1–2; 9 n.16; 10 n.24; 11 n.30; 127 n.8; 136 n.181
proof
    circular 5; **74,10ff.**
    genuine, as proving what is unclear from what is clear **75,18f.**

Subject Index 199

property
   belongs to/predicated of only one species **32,24ff.**; **61,16f.**; **64,22**
   as between substantial and adventitious things **109,1f.**; **121,9f.**
   concourse of, predicated of only one individual **90,10ff.**
   fourfold division of **109,10ff.**
   of human beings **108,16ff.**
   potential vs. actual **109,22f.**
   predicated non-substantially **64,20**; **101,3f.**
   predicated of what differs in number **62,19**
   predicated primarily of individuals **116,18f.**
   properly so called, belongs to its subject alone, to all of it, and always **109,4ff.**; **25f.**
   reciprocates with definition **27,3f.**
   separable from subject in thought **109,7f.**
proportion **67,18ff.**
providence **11,13f.**
Publius Hordeonius Lollianus 127 n.2
purpose, *see* goal
Pythagoras **9,7ff.**; **13,25ff.**; 129 n.38
   Carmen aureum **15,19**; 129 n.43

Quality, generation of **19,2ff.**
Quantification, four types of **28,18f.**
quantity **14,2f.**
   change in **113,10f.**
   generation of **19,15f.**
questions, preliminary 5
   to each book **21,7ff.**
   to the *Isagogē* **22,2f.**

rational, vs. irrational **32,10ff.**
reciprocation of existence **27,1f.**
recollection **10,20ff.**
reading order 3; 10 n.20
relations **80,1ff.**
   calculation of number of **123,14ff.**
   kinds of **50,11f.**; **53,7f.**
relatives **47,9ff.**; **49,18ff.**
   and cases **91,5ff.**
   generation of **19,27f.**
   genus and species as **48,12**

   kinds of **50,11f.**
   priority among **47,9ff.**
   as simultaneous **76,6f.**
   wholes and parts as **91,45**
reluctance, of youth, to read ancient works **38,14ff.**
rhetoric **1,14**; **8,5f.**; 17f.
   adduces proofs from generally admitted premises **35,18f.**
   characterized by aiming **39,5ff.**
ring, simile of **12,5ff.**; **41,12ff.**

sameness
   as characteristic of all things **115,4ff.**
   and otherness, of the five words **115,10ff.**
science
   vs. art **7,2ff.**
   etymology of **17,7**
Scylla **99,17**
separability **11,25ff.**
simple, meanings of **49,9f.**
Simplicius 130 nn.57 68; 133 n.123; 136 n.176; 139 n.241
Singulars, knowledge of, as impossible **85,9f.**
Sirius 133 n.121
Socrates **32,1**; **33,6**; **58,3**; **59,2**; **60,11**; **62,11**; **65,20**; **66,17**; **78,3.14**; **80,11**; **88,12**; **89,9.11**; **90,18.24**; **92,17–18**; **94,13**; **97,17–18**; **116,16–30**; **117,19**; **125,2**; **127,6f.**; 140 n.254; **128,1**
Sorabji, Richard 8 nn.1–3; 9 nn.9, 11–12, 16; 10 nn.22, 24–5; 11 n.33; 132 n.102; 134 n.140; 135 nn.157, 169
soul
   bonds of **5,10ff.**
   immortality of **35,20f.**; **43,14ff.**; **74,14ff.**
   powers/faculties of **4,9ff.**; **11,17ff.**
   as self-moving **88,13f.**
species
   and definitions **76,25f.**
   do not co-eliminate one another **30,1ff.**
   as compared to individuals **87,10f.**
   contain particulars **32,2ff.**; **87,18.**
   horizontal vs. vertical **97,10**; 137 n.211

meanings of **69,20ff.**
most specific **70,18**; **77,15ff.**; **80,9f.**; **17f.**; **85,17f.**; **87,11**.
participate equally in the genus **82,6f.**
predicated essentially **64,19**; **70,4f.**; **124,19f.**
predicated of individuals **89,17**
predicated of many **119,20f.**
predicated of what differs in number **61,2**; **62,19**; **64,15–20**; **70,4f.**; **76,24ff.**
predication of, entails predication of genus **89,4ff.**
as relative **69,15**
as simultaneous **29,20**
subordinate **120,5f.**
as what falls beneath the genus **70,1ff.**; **74,8ff.**
speech, parts of **21,1ff.**
Speusippus 135 n.166
square **73,7ff.**
Stoics 137 n.204; 139 n.235
subdivision **10,6f.**
subject, *see* predicate
subordinate genera **78,6ff.**; **80,19f.**
substance **19,1f.**
change in **113,7f.**; **15f.**
defined **19,9f.**
degrees of **97,3ff.**
division of **70,13ff.**; **77,17ff.**
as existence **115,6ff.**
gives being to accidents **82,16**
has no contrary **96,23f.**
intelligible **10,24f.**
as most generic genus **70,9ff.**; **75,8ff.**; **78,25f.**; **91,20**
as primary **97,5f.**
as prior **82,14**
as self-subsistent **70,9ff.**
substrate, things that are the same in substrate but different in relation **70,25ff.**; **76,15ff.**
suicide **4,27f.**
syllogism **8,6ff.**; **88,17f.**
analysis and **36,7ff.**

synonyms 5
defined **84,11f.**
synthesis, and analysis **37,8ff.**; **38,4**
Syrianus 2

Tarán, L. 135 n.166
Taurus **22,22**; 130 n.59
teaching, mode of **26,5f.**
starts out from what is most clear to us **52,12f.**
ten **60,22f.**
Themistius 2
theology **10,14ff.**; **11,22f.**; **12,10**; **13,1**
theurgy 1
time **41,2**
title **21,23**; **23,2f.**
triads, divine 127 n.8
triangles **11,2f.**; **12,1f.**; **71,25f.**
Euclid on **73,2ff.**
figure as genus of **71,24ff**
names of **51,1ff.**
Plato on **72,19ff.**

universals 4; **17,20f.**; **117,2f.**
vs. particulars **17,3ff.**; **31,16ff.**
universe, as beginningless 2; **87,9**; 137 n.197
usefulness (*khreia*) **21,16f.**; **22,5f.**; **25,21ff.**; **26,4ff.**

virtues, and vices **67,20f.**

Wakelnig, Elvira 11 n.32; 127 n.8
Wilberding, James 133 n.119
wisdom **9,6ff.**
words (voices/terms)
five **20,16f.**; **115,10ff.**
meaningful vs. meaningless **59,1ff.**; **60,8ff.**; **106,10f.**; 135 n.156
substantial vs. adventitious **109,3f.**

Xenocrates **46,10f.**

Zeus, as father of men and gods **80,11**
Zonta, Mauro 10 n.29

www.ingramcontent.com/pod-product-compliance
Lightning Source LLC
Chambersburg PA
CBHW052043300426
44117CB00012B/1954